TEN
MEN

TEN MEN

YOU MEET IN THE HUDDLE

LESSONS FROM A FOOTBALL LIFE

BILL CURRY

FOR CAROLYN,

the wonder and light of my life

CONTENTS

Up until I was 16 years old, my goal in life
was to pitch for the New York Yankees.
But a funny thing happened on my
way to Yankee Stadium ...

GET ME TO THE CHURCH ON TIME

The very first day of my very first training camp with the Green Bay Packers, and I was going to be late.

Vince Lombardi and Bart Starr and 50 or so other guys in gold helmets were already there. Not me. I was going to be *late*. My first day in the NFL was going to be my last, I was sure of it, because *I ... was ... going ... to ... be ... late.*

How could this be happening to me? I had been in Chicago for the 1965 College All-Star Game. Now I was in the Milwaukee Airport. The Packers were at our—their—training camp in some place called De Pere, just outside of Green Bay, about 125 miles away. Short hop. Piece of cake. Except that an agent from North Central Airlines had just regretfully informed me that I had been bumped from my flight to Green Bay and ...

What?!

Panic has many levels, many manifestations, but the sensation that best sums up the feeling that swept over me was an overwhelming sense of certain doom. No guillotine ever traumatized a soon-to-be headless victim more than the bit of news I'd just received.

1

At age 22, I faced the prospect of returning home to College Park, Georgia, an NFL reject, forever banned from realizing my five-year-old dream because I had showed up *late, tardy, not on time* for a Vince Lombardi training camp.

Take a deep breath, Bill. Pull yourself together. Through the years, I have been cocky, even arrogant, about my ability to stay calm and function normally under extreme duress—that is, to stop panic in its tracks. I can truthfully say that at no time in my life—not before, not since—was that ability ever put to a sterner test.

My only salvation, as things would turn out, lay in the viral obsession with the *Lombardi Mystique* in Wisconsin that would soon spread across the United States. But I didn't know this at the time. All I could do was hope.

In a firm voice that belied my inner terror, I called for the branch manager of North Central Airlines, who dutifully presented himself, listened a moment, then promptly rolled into his best Pacify the Jerk persona. Gazing over my right shoulder as if checking out something more important, he said in a polite but dismissive tone that I was confirmed on the next flight, scheduled to depart the following morning.

The following morning?

In desperation, I ostentatiously jotted down the manager's name, rank, and serial number ... loudly announced that I was now going to be late to Vince Lombardi's training camp on my very first day ... and that The Coach would be the first to learn tomorrow that North Central Airlines was responsible.

Obviously taken aback, the hitherto blasé functionary stiffened briefly, then broke out his best smile and stepped around the counter. He grabbed my hand and shook it as if it were a pump handle. He expressed a keen interest in my future, and then started barking orders to his underlings. In short order, he had my luggage pulled and placed in a chartered single-engine plane that whisked me off to Manitowoc, where North Central had a van waiting to deliver me to the Packers camp in De Pere.

I made it with plenty of time to spare.

SINCE CHILDHOOD—AND I was born in 1942, so that was a while ago—I have been enthralled by stories of real people who lived out dreams and beat the odds, overcame adversity, and made the world a better place. As a kid, I devoured biographies like they were chocolate kisses, wondering if I could someday lead like Abraham Lincoln or inspire like Jackie Robinson.

Once television entered our lives as an alternative to reading, the first thing to catch my eye was baseball. Every Saturday from April through September, I would get up early so that my chores would be done by the time "Game of the Day" flickered into black-and-white life on our 12" Philco.

Every day during the summer, my best friend, Ronnie Jackson, and I would scour the sports page of the *Atlanta Constitution*, reading every AP and UPI game summary from both leagues and poring over the box scores as if they contained the secrets of the universe.

And every day during the first two weeks of October, I'd run home from school in College Park, a suburb of Atlanta, to immerse myself in the World Series. The New York Yankees were always there, as if by entitlement, and Berra, Ford, Mantle, Howard, Rizzuto, & Co. became the objects of my adoration. I was transported.

My mind was made up, my destiny made clear: when I grew up, I would become a New York Yankee.

Back then, the team of choice in my hometown was the vaunted Atlanta Crackers, whose heroics we could catch in person at Ponce de Leon Park in downtown Atlanta. Ronnie and I would go to the clinics they put on for Atlanta kids. But they were merely the best *minor* league team in the country, and while I can still recite starting lineups from that era, my aspirations were much higher.

I wanted to be one of those demigods in pinstripes.

In high school, I "showed up" for football and basketball, just to have something to do until baseball began. Classes bore little interest for me; they served mainly as cover for the next biography I could lay my hands on.

It was only when I took the mound each spring that I felt at home, in love with my sport and my heroes.

As a junior, I was the starting pitcher in the 1959 state AA finals against Rossville (Georgia). We got beat that day 4-1; I didn't have great stuff. Perhaps I should have interpreted this as a sign that I might not be wearing pinstripes some day after all. I didn't. I continued pitching in American Legion and Connie Mack ball beyond high school. If someone started a team today, and if there were no age restriction, I'd try out for it in a second. That's how much I *still* love baseball.

Half a century later, I still dream about it. I can feel the texture of a baseball in my hand. I distinctly remember climbing chain-link fences to get into locked ballparks, leaving my shirts in tatters, just for a chance to stand on a mound to fire balls past an imaginary Duke Snider or Hank Aaron.

I mimicked no one. While I liked Carl Erskine's mannerisms and consistency and I was awed by Juan Marichal's high kick, I wanted to be my own man. I didn't want to be *like* those guys; I longed to *be* one of them.

At dusk, I'd stand in the street in front of our house and throw rocks at telephone poles—okay, the occasional street light, too, but that would be down the block somewhere. I'd be guided by my own personal vision of Yogi, hunkered down behind the plate, famous ears sticking out on either side of his mask, target just behind the outside corner, ready for my four-seamer, down and away.

Dear God, how the hours flew by.

MUCH LATER IN life, I encountered the following quotation from Goethe: "Whatever you can do or dream you can, begin it. Boldness has genius, power, and magic in it."

Needless to say, even if I'd heard Goethe's words as a teenager, I'd never have fully understood his famous admonition. But even back then, I had witnessed the *genius*, I had felt the *power*, and I had been possessed by the *magic* of baseball.

I had begun my own adventure, and in so doing had unwittingly conferred upon sports all the trappings of religion. I could never have guessed that the graceful, cerebral allure of baseball would merely be the acorn for what would grow next in my imagination: football.

Football, with its raw violence and less refined talent requirements, would only slowly make its way onto my radar screen. And yet it did. I would have scoffed at the idea in my early teens, but I believe now that even if I had possessed the talent to stand in pinstripes on that mound in Yankee Stadium—and I didn't—I would have some day, some how gravitated to the aggression and confrontation of the gridiron.

As a kid, I believed my destiny was to be out there on a diamond with its inviting spaces and its focus on the individual. Early on, I had been captivated by the geometry and the elegant choreography of baseball. I loved the wonderful panoply of color and life its artists brought into my small world.

Inevitably, though, recognition of the gap between what I brought to the game and the talents and skills required to reach my goal began to sink in. And so I moved slowly, and by no means surely, from the diamond toward the huddle.

FOOTBALL MEANT NEXT to nothing to me when I was growing up. True, I played center for the College Park Rams for four years, but a lot of that was going through the motions. The games themselves were genuine fun, but the weekly grind—practice, practice, practice, practice, and only then a game—was just that: a grind. And preseason workouts? All grind, no game, and thus no fun at all.

Many of my fellow Rams couldn't wait for the bell signaling the end of the school day on fall afternoons so they could go suit up and spend a couple of hours banging each other around. On that score, I was definitely not one of the guys.

For me, football was a strictly a means to an end. Where I grew up, *when* I grew up, football players got their pick of the prettiest girls. Wasn't that motivation enough?

But somewhere along the line, without any conscious awareness, my soul drifted toward the orchestrated violence, the *mano á mano* confrontations, and the close harmony of 11 brothers acting as one. In my heart of hearts, the idea began to grow that I might belong to a gritty, gutsy warrior unit.

I still loved baseball, but without my even knowing it, I had become ripe for conversion.

That conversion took place when, on December 28, 1958, I sat down with my father to watch a football game between the Baltimore Colts and the New York Giants. I was 16 years old. I had never before watched an NFL game in its entirety.

All this one did was completely redirect my life.

Now the consensus pick among devotees of professional football as The Greatest Game Ever Played, the 1958 Colts-Giants NFL championship game was a highlights tape from first whistle to last.

> • The upstart Colts and the established Giants played to a 17-17 tie at the end of regulation, the first in NFL Championship history.
> • There was a sudden death overtime period, the first in NFL Championship history.

7

- The photo of Alan Ameche's winning touchdown burst to give the Colts a 23-17 victory would become an icon for the ages.
- "Unitas to Berry" joined "Tinker to Evers to Chance" among the most famous sports combinations ever.
- Johnny Unitas became the standard-bearer for the sport of football, and the performer against whom all quarterbacks, and to some extent, all players would be measured. (As this is being written, if I go to NFL.com on the web and click on "History," I can see, in the upper left-hand corner, a picture of a familiar face: John Unitas, No. 19.)
- The National Football League impressed itself upon the American consciousness in a way that abides to this day, making football, not baseball, America's Game.

I was one of the early, eager, utterly smitten converts to America's Game, rising from the back row as surely as the repentant sinner in a Billy Graham Crusade. With every head bowed and every eye closed, I quietly raised my hand, went forward, and fell to my knees in adoration of the new state religion of the United States of America.

Pro football.

TO JOIN THAT congregation, of course, meant abandoning my pinstripe dreams and making my bones in college football.

Step one along that path would be to get myself accepted into a high-profile program where I could demonstrate my worthiness to move up in class after four years. Given my unimpressive high school football résumé, that was by no means automatic.

A lightly recruited high school kid, I made exactly two official out-of-town visits, one to Auburn and one to Clemson.

On the first, I was paired with another kid from my high school, Jimmy Tumlin, a top-rated basketball player. We spent most of the weekend hanging out with basketball players, which told me that I'd been brought along to make Jimmy feel more at home, not to be groomed to become Auburn's next All-American center-linebacker.

On the second, the legendary Frank Howard took one look at my 190-pound frame, learned that I was a center-linebacker, not a halfback, and terminated our interview on the spot. A few weeks later he did offer me a scholarship, but by then, for admittedly non-football reasons, I had my sights set on Georgia Tech.

More precisely, I had my sights set on Miss Carolyn Newton, a graduating senior from College Park High School who planned to enroll at Agnes Scott College in the fall of 1960. The Agnes Scott campus and the Georgia Tech campus are just eight miles apart, so my decision was a no-brainer: I would be a Yellow Jacket.

Good call on my part. A few years later, Miss Newton would become Mrs. Carolyn Newton Curry. Forty-five wedding anniversaries later, I think she's decided to keep me in her huddle, and there's no other place I can even conceive of being. But I know better than to become complacent in these matters.

ANOTHER DEEPLY MOVED convert on that momentous afternoon in 1958, a frustrated quarterback on a terrible football team, watched Johnny Unitas perform miracles and rededicated his life that day.

The other new believer's name: Bart Starr.

Like me, Bart watched The Greatest Game Ever Played. Like me, he says, his understanding of the sport was transformed. And later, he would become my escort through the looking glass of the Green Bay Packers into the National Football League.

Our coach in Green Bay had been a participant in The Greatest Game Ever Played: Vince Lombardi was then the obscure offensive coordinator for the Giants. (The Giants' equally obscure defensive coordinator would be a factor in all our futures. His name: Tom Landry.)

And while Bart Starr and Vince Lombardi escorted me into the National Football League in 1965, three years later I would join up with no less than No. 19 himself, when I moved on to the Colts and began snapping the ball to Johnny Unitas.

Those riveting figures, along with other larger-than-life characters you will hear about in these pages, have been my spiritual guides on a magical excursion that's lasted half a century—and counting. In the beginning, I was standing on the outside when, one by one, they noticed me, beckoned to me, took my hand, and brought me into their huddle.

The story of that long and eventful trip, with all its twists and turns, is one I have long wanted to tell.

On two ...

Break!

Coach Badgett was big, imposing, and —when he challenged us to a 60-yard dash—the fastest man on the College Park (Georgia) Rams football team.

1

BILL BADGETT
BUILDER

My road to the National Football League began in day camp.

Most little Caucasian boys in College Park, Georgia, back in the early 1950s went to day camp in the summers. Or so it seemed. I know I'd gone to summer day camp since I was seven. But now I was 12 going on 13, and the summer of 1955 was going to be my last as a camper. That fall I would enter eighth grade, which back then in our part of the world was the first year of high school.

Much as I liked the idea of growing up, I knew I was going to miss summer camp.

Even today, I can close my eyes and feel the stifling heat of the gym, relieved only by the huge window fans, the swimming pool, and the occasional breeze wafting through Mr. Dukes' candy stand bearing promises of Sun Drop soft drinks and Baby Ruth candy bars.

We played games like Capture the Flag and Bring Home the Bacon. We caught June bugs and tied fine thread to their little legs so we could control their flight, clueless to the cruelty involved. Fortunately, we were caught by our counselors, who threatened to tie *our* legs if we didn't stop the little-boy brutality. We played softball, made lanyards, and even learned to play chess on rainy days.

You know, day camp things.

So there we were at the side door of the College Park Gym at 8 a.m. on an already sweltering morning, ready to register for another annual installment, when ... "Look! There he is!"

"He" was Bill Badgett, head football coach at College Park High School. Thinning brown hair topped a 6' 3", 270-pound body clothed in beige shorts and a coaching shirt. A whistle hung from his sturdy, sun-burnished neck. A graduate of the University of Georgia in my father's class (1939), Badgett had been at College Park for six years. He commanded the respect and awe reserved for the top few male standard-bearers in a southern town back then. He was the *coach*.

Coach Badgett glanced at my name as I walked up to the desk, looked into my eyes, and phrased a command in the form of a question: "Bill Curry, you coming out for football this fall?"

As a white male of good size for his age in the South about to enter high school, I was naturally expected to take part in the only Rite of Passage in those parts that would signal my emergence into manhood. I was *expected* to play football.

And so I offered up the only answer that I could muster under that scrutiny, the only answer that was acceptable in that day at my age:

"Oh, uh ... yes, sir."

DAY CAMP? OVER in a flash, faster that summer than ever before. Before I knew it, mid-August had arrived and, like it or not, I was getting ready to play football.

We had an unusual grade system in our part of the world. High school was grades 8 through 12, with all of us packed into one building every day. The good thing about that setup was that we were thrown in with the big boys at age 12 or 13. And the bad thing? We were thrown in with the big boys at age 12 or 13.

The first order of business before preseason practice could begin was physical exams at the College Park Health Center. That meant stripping to my skivvies and lining up along with all the other guys. I looked around me, wide-eyed. Roy Betsill had muscles all over his body. Cowboy Freeman was like a rock, striations running across his tanned abdomen, where I was soft and white. What a neck on Larry Lancaster! My plump, 5'3" body didn't come close to measuring up.

My size (or lack thereof) was brought home to me a few years back when Carolyn and I went to visit my first high school flame, Sue Lunceford, who had also been Carolyn's best friend. Sue was in a hospice, dying of melanoma, and it was a sad, sad reunion for us. But she was in a rare spell of lucidity and we were trading banter back and forth when I asked her, "Sue, why did you dump me back in the eight grade?"

She laughed and answered in the bat of an eye, "Because you were so short! I was embarrassed to dance with you because I was so much taller."

By the end of my sophomore year, I was pushing 6'0", and when Carolyn and I had our first date in my senior year (on her 17ᵗʰ birthday, as a matter of fact), I was 6'2". I told Sue she shouldn't have given up on me so soon.

She laughed again. She reminded us that she had predicted after that first date that Carolyn and I were going to get married. And when we did, Sue was in our wedding. The three of us remained buddies through all the years.

Sue died, at age 59, soon after our last visit.

LIKE MOST HIGH school coaches of his day, Coach Badgett was required to be a jack of all trades—and master of all. He taught Health & Hygiene; classroom teaching, grading, and counseling took up the first six hours of his day. Then his real job began—coaching.

As head coach, he was assigned one assistant coach, one student manager, and high expectations. He was, as the situation required, trainer, equipment man, field maintenance staff of one, offensive coordinator, defensive coordinator, special teams coordinator, recruiter, disciplinarian, and motivator. He told us once that he had calculated his hourly pay and that he had earned 37 cents an hour the previous year.

On this August morning in 1955, my first day of "real" football, he was the equipment man. As each of us moved to the front of the line at the little window, he fixed us with a near smile, a balanced mixture of humor, patience, and seriousness that froze us on the spot. He delivered a brief soliloquy on the care of the sacred tools of our game to each player: "Take care of your pads and they will take care of you. Learn how to wear things the right way. If you have questions, ask one of the older boys or me. Do not take *anything* out of here except to wash it. *Never* wear the jersey except to practice football."

This was very serious business.

OF ALL SPORTS, football pays the most attention to its paraphernalia.

You must have the correct stuff at all times, and it must look exactly right and feel exactly right. And it must bespeak power. Like the shields and helmets of ancient Spartans, football gear must project the great warrior spirit. We would come to expect it to keep us from harm's way, and to allow us to run and smash with reckless abandon.

We would, of course, expect too much.

Coach Badgett's equipment assistant was a sophomore named Jack Martin. While Coach manned the window to the storage room, Jack was his feeder system. Jack was a small, wiry kid who incessantly jabbered about going to downtown Atlanta, where there were hookers on every street corner. I asked him what a hooker was, and was pleased rather than embarrassed when all the guys laughed.

My first day, and I was the locker room comedian!

Jack threw a pile of plastic, leather, cloth, and canvas at me, and I toted it all to the green steel locker I had been assigned. The dank surroundings reeked of ammonia and the temperature was somewhere north of 85 and climbing. No air conditioning, of course, and the heat of the day hadn't kicked in, so this was as comfortable as it was going to get.

Welcome to pre-AC Atlanta in August.

At my locker, I started sorting my stash. Some of the items were mysterious; others evoked mild panic. There was a *big* jock. "How will it stay on?" I wondered. "Why doesn't it have a cup, like my Little League jock?"

The big question in my mind—and I'm dead serious about this—was how I was going to get all this equipment on my chubby body without taking all my clothes off?

Coach Badgett noticed Tommy Fields and me hesitating, still fully dressed in front of our lockers. He walked over and lied to us for the only time in our experience with him. He said sternly, "Go on, boys—take your clothes off and get your gear fitted. Nobody's going to look at your peanut."

The upper classmen were already undressed, strutting back and forth to the toilets buck naked, with their manly appendages swinging between hairy legs. Some were hirsute but not particularly well-endowed; they passed muster because of the hair and weren't ridiculed. Some weren't hairy but were all man. A lucky few were both. It was the first time I'd ever heard the phrase "well-hung."

Nobody teased those guys.

But woe, woe aplenty, to the hairless ones with tiny peanuts! That tag fitted most of us eighth-graders, but each was too focused on his own lack of manly endowments to notice that he was a member of a large club. We heard the catcalls through flushed earlobes, slipped our drawers down with trembling hands, and tried mightily to keep tears from forming in the corners of our eyes.

The Rite of Passage had begun in earnest. Insecurities blossomed like dandelions as we neophytes stood, ashen faced, in varying stages of undress, trying with brave profanity to sound like part of that mysterious, magical entity known simply as ...

... the team.

THE HEADGEAR IN use at our school for the first time that year was strictly new-tech, the latest thing. It featured a plastic, see-through face bar, about an inch and a half wide, that formed an elliptical protective radius about tooth level, attaching at the ears on the outside of the helmet.

I soon found out that it served as a sort of prism, scattering bits of refracted light like a low-power magnifying glass. When you got into a football stance, the thing made little guys look big and big guys look bigger. Unfortunately, the face bar had a disturbing propensity to shatter if a fierce enough blow were struck, often producing tooth dislodgings, facial lacerations, and deviated septums. But it *was* state of the art.

The Riddell suspension helmet, so-named for its interior, had a network of canvas straps covered by leather and stapled to the shell. Their function was to form webbing that prevented the head from contacting the hard walls of the helmet. They were designed to fit very tight, and ears were often worn raw just from the process of getting in and out of them.

We linemen quickly established permanent scabs on our foreheads from the friction of the leather coating attached to the straps. Blood and ooze were constants, since the scabs were torn off each practice. Infections laden with pus meant swollen foreheads and missed practices, so stinging Merthiolate became the orange war paint of our tribe.

The right earpiece on my helmet was broken and frequently cut the skin behind my ear, even though Coach tried to tape it up. I insisted on wearing it, because the only alternative was the leather variety, the kind that Jim Thorpe or Red Grange once sported. I had missed the leather helmets by one scant year.

This prevented much future embarrassment, since my son and my players over the years often asked if I had ever worn one of those things. No, thank God, but late arrivals and transfers did—evoking Knute Rockne speeches and jokes about "winning one for the Gipper," even though none of the jokers had a clue who the Gipper was.

None of the pads fit the way they were supposed to. There was one particularly uncomfortable thing that buckled in the back and had a long plastic piece that hung down to cover one's privates. "Oh," I thought, "this will make up for the absence of the cup." One problem: I couldn't get into my football pants because of the long piece in front. I wasn't alone; the scene resembled a ballet recital for six-year-olds, with much sidewise glancing and stumbling.

At that moment of helpless disarray, Tommy leaned over and said, "Those are hip pads, you dope. The long thing goes over your butt, not your crotch. Turn it around before Freddie or Don sees you!"

As ruthless as seniors Freddie Starrett and Don Griswold could be with eighth graders, my first inclination was to risk their abuse rather than accept guidance from Tommy Fields. He was a great pitcher, and he'd struck me out innumerable times in our Little League games. I'd been on the wrong side of unpleasant encounters with him too often. But after struggling with those unwieldy, unfamiliar, cushioned pads for a few more minutes, I gave in and rotated them 180 degrees.

At that moment, Tommy became one of my best friends.

Next came the canvas pants characteristic of 1950s football. Huge by necessity, because they had to accommodate knee and thigh pads while covering the hip pads, they had all the elasticity of your basic pup tent.

The shoulder pads were the final (and simplest) piece to the pad puzzle, and they worked well enough, unless the curvature was too extreme, in which case the wearer had to endure a sort of hunchback effect. Not a good look.

Once assembled under the loose-fitting pants and jersey, the pad combo created a staccato *clack-flop-clack* when you walked, and a fortissimo *clackety-whack-clackety-whack!* when you ran.

The shoes were invariability too large since limited supply precluded close sizing and too big was better than too small. They were high-tops, of course, with long aluminum cleats that clattered and skidded on the concrete, often causing lightning-quick backward spills. The metal cleats turned into weapons when they wore down, producing sharp, serrated edges. And when they fell off, which they did with dreary frequency, the exposed posts ripped jagged lacerations into the flesh of opponents and wearer alike during pileups.

Once the big clunkers got wet from the morning dew, they weighed almost as much as VW Beetles, privately imported editions of which were just beginning to grace American roadways. The few exceptions were the Kangaroo shoes, lightweights made with thin leather and reserved for the team stars.

The socks we received (and were required to wear) were thick wool with no elastic, so they slid down, got gobbled up by our over-roomy shoes, and formed stinking masses behind the heel on each foot.

Blisters were facts of life. Coach Badgett told us to paint our heels with Tufskin before being taped. The caustic, sticky goop smelled of resin and was impossible to remove from one's fingers. And it didn't do much to prevent blisters.

Our jerseys were thick, hot, and long—great for showing off when we were away from the football field. We quickly learned that Badgett was serious about unauthorized use of the sacred garments, though. If he spotted you on the street wearing your jersey, he'd stop you and say, "Take my shirt off, son. *Now.*"

If you were walking with your girl to the drugstore on a Sunday afternoon, looking like a stud in your uni shirt, and you encountered Coach Badgett, it meant making the return walk home shirtless, your mind diverted from romance by contemplation of the extra wind sprints that would be forthcoming the next day.

Often such a defrocking would trigger a repeat performance of his infamous feminine hygiene lecture at the next practice: "You shouldn't even be *thinking* about girls. They don't care what your shirt looks like. They are *dangerous.* You're better off kissing your dog. Canines have enzymes that purify their mouths. Human females do not. But whatever you decide, I'd better not catch you with my uniform shirt on away from this field."

Any dream I might have harbored of strutting down Main Street, resplendent in my College Park Rams jersey with a starry-eyed Carolyn Newton on my arm, remained just that: a dream.

BUTTERFLIES IN MY stomach began to flutter as I pedaled my bike down the dark silent streets of my hometown toward

---

TAKE A HIKE

Early on in my first training camp, assistant coach Jesse Shaddix called all the newcomers together. He'd watched us run sprints, do push-ups and side-straddle hops, throw and kick the ball—and then look around to figure out what came next.

His task, based on that info, was to assign positions to members of the B-team—that is, the eighth graders and any ninth graders who were coming out for football the first time.

"Tommy, you have a good arm, so you're a quarterback," he said authoritatively. "Richard, you're big and tough-looking, so I want you at fullback. Ronald? You've got some speed and look like you have good hands—you're a halfback."

And so it went, him barking directives, my new teammates grinning and jogging to their assigned positions. It was clear from the outset that he was matching up the most obvious skills with the most desirable positions. I can guarantee you that none of the 12-year-olds assembled had ever dreamed at night of playing center. But that was the position left for one short, chubby kid when all the other slots had been filled.

"Well, Bill," Coach Shaddix said, "I guess you're going to be our center."

(I thought, "No shit, Shaddix.")

[continued on following page]

He looked at me sternly, and I feared for a moment that he could read my mind. Instead, he wisely observed that I needed to "learn to hike the ball to the quarterback."

(I thought, "No shit, Shaddix.")

Maybe all smartass little kids who are just biding their time in football until they can go off and pitch for the Yankees ought to be required to play offensive center.

Anyway, that's what I did for the next 20 years—hike the ball.

Between August 1955 and August 1975, I would hike the ball to, among others, Zeke Bratkowski, Len Dawson, Lynn Dickey, Marty Domres, Stan Gann, Bob Griese, Tommy Fields, John Hadl, James Harris, John Huarte, Ron Jaworski, Daryl Lamonica, Billy Lothridge, Earl Morrall, Craig Morton, Joe Namath, Dan Pastorini, Bart Starr, Roger Staubach, Richard Stephens, Francis Tarkenton, Bob Timberlake, Johnny Unitas, Bill Wade ... and George Plimpton.

That estimable list of hikees earned the following honors:

• Seven NFL Hall of Famers (Dawson, Griese, Namath, Tarkenton, Starr, Staubach, Unitas)

• 14 NFL Pro-Bowlers (Dawson, Dickey, Griese, Hadl, Lamonica, Lothridge, Morrall, Morton, Namath, Pastorini, Tarkenton, Starr, Staubach, Unitas)

• Two Heisman Trophy winners (Huarte, Staubach)

• 14 collegiate All-Americans (Bratkowski, Dawson, Griese, Lamonica, Lothridge, Hadl, Huarte, Morrall, Morton, Namath, Pastorini, Staubach, Tarkenton, Timberlake)

• The most famous PSJ (Participative Sports Journalist) of all time (Plimpton)

> Learning to hike a football set the course for the rest of my life. How so? Just this: in all of sport, offensive center was the only position at which I would have ever had a chance to compete at the professional level.
>
> Hut-one! Hut-two!

the high school that late summer of 1955. Heat lightning might flicker on the horizon, with its false promise of rain. Preseason practices began at 6 a.m. sharp, occasionally later only if bad weather (tropical storms, tornadoes, hurricanes) was forecast. Being late was unthinkable.

Every morning, the scraping sounds of kickstands from our Schwinns and Rollfasts on the pavement outside the gym were the rim-shot drumbeats accompanying our death march. When I approached the locker room, my olfactory senses would go on red alert. The stench oozed fog-like out of the locker room as we silently pulled up from every corner of our little town.

Inside, assorted pieces of uniforms were draped over pipes and locker doors, piled in corners and on the floor. Jocks, jerseys, pants, and the cloth that lined the pads were in varying stages of decay from the filth and perspiration. The ammonia content of the air caused your head to swim, and the organism population would have kept scientists at the Centers for Disease Control office in Atlanta busy for months. There were times we couldn't wear Bermuda shorts after practice because our jock itch extended below the hem on our inner thighs.

We competed to see who could practice the longest without washing his uniform. The only uniform washers were our mothers, and we thought it somehow noble to spare them the trouble. Try to imagine what it felt like to slip on a cold, wet jock at 5:30 a.m., cover the rest of your body with dank, stinking gear, and tug soggy socks onto blister-torn feet. Got it? Now you're beginning to understand what playing football in the South in the 1950s was like.

Next came the ordeal of getting your wet jersey on. Not by yourself, though; that couldn't be done. You needed a buddy to stand behind you and pull the salty thing over your pads while you squirmed and struggled and tried to avoid suffocation. You hoped it wouldn't rip, because the unleashed shoulder pads would spend the rest of the afternoon flopping in counterpoint to their lower relatives in the britches. An exposed pad could fly up just before contact, exposing a shoulder.

(That's why in today's game a torn jersey means the player must leave the game.)

Understand, many of the guys loved this whole smelly ritual because it was part and parcel of a game they adored. I hated every minute of it, and would have quit in an instant if I thought my father would have permitted me to do so.

"What the hell?" I would snarl to Fields. "Hey, how about a pull?"

GETTING TO THE practice field from the locker room required a hike down a steep bank, through double wire gates, to a scruffy, hard-baked expanse that abutted the lush green field where we played our games. As you negotiated the short walk, your body recorded rises in the temperature and humidity as the sun made its way up over the eastern horizon. At the end of the two-minute walk your pungent uniform reeked anew as it sought to absorb the new perspiration, already freely flowing.

Once you passed through the practice field gates, you were expected to jog or run wherever you went. You never "walked" on Bill Badgett's football field. A brisk, two-lap "warm-up" around the cinder track set the tone for the misery that would follow. In short order, the dew conspired with the sweat running down your legs to convert the long, tall shoes, sordid socks, and blistered feet into a sodden set of heavy lumps, obviously conjured up by the football gods to strengthen young limbs during the four-hour marathon practices to come.

Oddly enough, in an evocation of the religious motif of all this, the first thing we did after the warm-up laps got our juices flowing—literally—was to gather together, take a knee, and recite the Lord's Prayer in unison.

Amen.

Calisthenics came next, with the team lined across the field. Not the gradual, muscle-relaxing stretches of today, but side-straddle hops, chase the rabbit, and the dreaded leg lifts. For those we lay on our backs, lifted our leaden feet straight-legged, then held them while spreading and closing to toughen the abs. The agony of calisthenics mercifully ended with everybody leaping up to sprint eight or ten 40-yard dashes.

Then practice began.

What followed was an amalgam of collisions, pain, fatigue, blood, screams, whistles, and dehydration that I could scarcely take in. The three dominant realities of those first days: the horror of what we were doing to each other, the blind staggers, and the urge to quit. Whenever one of us began to go weak at the knees, to wobble as he tried to run, or to lose partial vision, someone would yell out, "Look at Curry! Man, he's got the blind staggers!" There would be a roar of laughter as Curry struggled to regain his faculties, composure, and dignity.

SPRING PRACTICE? The very idea of spring *football* practice seemed sacrilegious to me.

Why use springtime for anything other than the most important thing in life—baseball? Goodness, what if I hurt my arm and couldn't pitch that year? That would slow down my progress toward Yankee Stadium, where I was destined to be a star right hander for the Yankees.

How could I be certain of getting to New York on schedule if I wasted my time on football? Really, the game made no sense to me when I first started playing it. Why on earth run into another person at full speed when I could stand 60 feet, six inches away and throw something at him?

Yet there I was, in the second half of my eighth-grade year, putting on shoulder pads instead of breaking in a new glove.

How I hated football, especially in the spring.

COACH BILL BADGETT was, to us, a giant of Biblical proportions. He was maybe 6' 3", 270 pounds, with a huge, protruding belly that belied his amazing athletic ability. He had been a starting tackle at the University of Georgia on a team that produced one of the Bulldogs' most famous triumphs, a 7–7 tie in 1936 in New York's Polo Grounds against mighty Fordham and its Seven Blocks of Granite.

(Much later on, I would become acquainted with one of these Blocks, a smallish guard named Vince Lombardi.)

Coach knew how to use his powerful presence on us. He was quiet, almost silent, while moving about the halls at school, but on the practice field he spoke directly and earnestly to us, and we hung on every word. He never screamed or shouted. He had that most remarkable ability in a leader, the capacity to be simultaneously feared and loved.

One of his tactics was to call us together now and then at an unusual time during practice. Everybody took a knee in a tight semi-circle in front of him. I loved those impromptu gatherings because they allowed me to catch my breath.

Sometimes his whistle and "Huddle up!" meant someone was about to get a chewing out, maybe a whole unit, maybe all of us. Sometimes it was to loosen us up by telling a joke. Occasionally it would be to challenge us to race him the length of the football field. (No one ever beat him; the man could *fly*.)

We never knew exactly what he was up to, and that was his goal.

So when he called us together one cold, windy, mucky day in March, we listened.

I know this is hard, men. This is the drudgery of football, but it is absolutely necessary. Everybody out here is cold, wet, and dirty. I know that. I know this red clay is sticking in your cleats and making it hard to run. I know everybody here is hurting one way or another. But I also know that football is life marked off in 100-yard segments. You will learn lessons out here that you will not learn anywhere else. You are learning about adversity, and how to fight through it. It will make you a better man.

At the time, for a teenager to hear that what he was doing would make him a better man was pretty heady stuff.

"Today"—Coach Badgett wasn't quite finished—"we're going to have a surprise scrimmage. It'll be different from our normal ones because I'm going to keep the first string intact and you young kids are going to go against the big boys in a full-speed game situation for the first time."

The big guys began to dance and cheer, anxious to play 11 on 11 against the little guys. Think tigers at the zoo and the smell of fresh meat.

Yet everybody was into it, including us sacrificial lambs. After all, scrimmaging is playing football, which is a whole lot more fun than any drill ever invented. All of Coach Badgett's teams loved to scrimmage. I wouldn't learn until many years later how difficult that desire was to maintain.

For my first shot at taking on the first string, I wasn't afraid. Honest. I didn't know enough to be afraid. Had I known what was coming, I might have wet my little jockstrap, but I was fearless going in. We little kids took hard shots at the big guys and were rewarded with cheers from the rest of the team, even as we were being overpowered.

Then something happened that will always be frozen in my memory.

Our All-State senior fullback, Roy Betsill, 205 pounds of power and speed, broke a run off tackle. I slid over, ducked my head, turned it ever so slightly—and it ricocheted off his huge thighs like a possum challenging a pickup. Roy rumbled on into the end zone, the stragglers cheered, and I got up. I wasn't embarrassed because Roy did that to everybody; that's how he got to be All-State. I just got off the ground, fixed my shoulder pads, and got back into formation. Nothing unusual about that.

Then came the silence. It took me a second or two, but at length I noticed that no one was moving. We were frozen in place like a squadron of penguins because Coach Badgett had stepped from behind the offensive huddle and was looking intently at me. Then he spoke, deliberately and just loud enough for everyone to hear:

"Run that play again. Don't block Curry. Bill, you tackle Roy Betsill."

Me? Tackle Roy Betsill? I might as well try to tackle the Nancy Hanks II, the starship of the Central of Georgia railroad that had been whistling through our town since 1947. (Train buffs will know that the Nancy Hanks I began her runs in 1892.)

The varsity team broke the huddle and lined up in a two-tight-end, full house formation. The linemen were in three-point stances, the three backs erect, hands on thighs, in a T formation behind the quarterback. I was the left inside linebacker. Sure enough, when the ball was snapped, I was left alone by the blockers as the backs broke to my left with Betsill carrying the ball. Again I slid over into position, again I ducked my head, but this time I forced myself directly into his path. He trampled me, up the front and down the back, and powered into the end zone again. I got up, checked for broken bones, and jumped back into our huddle.

Coach Badgett didn't move a muscle.

"Run it again," he said. "Bill, keep your head up and tackle Roy."

We performed the futile exercise again, like puppets on strings.

Same result.

"Run it again," came the soft but insistent voice.

Same result.

And so we did it again. And again.

Teammates watched with rapt attention. By this time I had a bloody nose, my face a mask of tears, snot, and utter humiliation. But there was no place to hide. When I looked at my buddies for moral support, they averted their eyes.

After the sixth or eighth train wreck, I heard a small voice from deep within: "Badgett is going to keep you here forever. You have a choice in this matter."

At the next snap I again slid over into Roy's path, again squared my feet and shoulders. This time, though, I kept my head up and square to the target. Rather than receiving the blow, this time I delivered it. I drove my shoulder pad into Betsill's gut, knocked him up and back, then over onto the ground.

Roy grinned and patted my helmet, my teammates cheered and hugged me.

Coach Badgett almost smiled.

I had joined the team.

IF I'M TELLING this story to coaches, they smile and nod. If I'm speaking to a group of parents, I see a lot of frowns.

Coaches see the potential for bringing out the best in a kid, for helping him tap an inner strength he didn't know he had. Parents see the potential for a hideous injury to a kid—not so much to his body as to his psyche

They're both right.

Look, anybody can beat up a kid on an athletic field and kill her or his spirit. Anybody. It happens every day in youth leagues all across the country.

A special gift is required to know when extreme pressure of the sort I experienced—to an outsider, brutality—can help a kid find his way to success. Coach Badgett had that gift.

Had he done the same thing four months earlier, I might have been irreparably damaged. But he sensed correctly the exact time, place, and instrument—Roy Betsill—to kick-start me into growing up. In today's world he would have been required to do it differently, but in those days, this was SOP.

Penn State's Joe Paterno tells the story of an analogous situation at a spring practice in State College, Pennsylvania, during the same era, but one with quite a different result.

To test the mettle of a fine young prospect, Paterno and his coaches lined him up against future All-American and All-Pro Dave Robinson. Time after time, snap after snap, Dave destroyed the kid.

"We were going to 'make a man' out of him," Joe recalls. "We failed. We destroyed his will. He vanished at the end of practice and went home. We never saw him again. To this day, I am ashamed."

What underscored the failure, and made Paterno's regret so long-lasting, is that when the Penn State coaches studied the Nittany Lions roster the next day, they realized Robbie would have done the same thing to *every player on the team*.

"You must set your players up for success," emphasizes Joe. "You push them harder than they've ever been pushed, but you must set them up for success. *You must!*"

Coach Badgett set me up for success.

PRACTICE BECAME BEARABLE. Scrimmages became fun. And the games that fall? Ecstasy.

A great mentor had studied me and decided on a time and place to make a football player out of me. I would love to say that after that day I became a great player. I didn't.

But here is what I did do: I recognized that it's not enough to wear the jersey, go through the motions, and think of yourself as a part of the team. On that day, I received my first inkling of the essence of the greatest team sport ever devised. And I learned that there is a price, a dear price, if one wishes to *belong* in the huddle.

Left to my own devices, I would have continued to choose the path of least resistance, letting myself be run over by the Betsills of this world. I would never have understood the huddle.

I would never have won the respect of Roy, Coach Badgett, my teammates, or myself.

I would own no Super Bowl rings.

And I just might be sitting in some bar bragging that I could have pitched for the Yankees if I had ever just gotten a break or two.

Thanks, Coach.

*A legendary figure in college football history
and my role model when I became a coach,
he always put first things first. If you
didn't go to class, you didn't play for
Bobby Dodd. Period.*

BOBBY DODD
PHILOSOPHER

Everybody who played football for him referred to Robert E. Lee Dodd—behind his back, of course—as The Whistle.

The obvious origin of the moniker was that infernal device that hung around his neck. With it, Coach Dodd controlled every move of every minute of every football session at Rose Bowl Field, where we practiced.

Beyond that, there was the collective feeling among Yellow Jackets who played for him that The Whistle seemed to be everywhere, seemed to know everything, and seemed to control every detail of his players' lives, seven days a week, off the field as well as on.

But it was on the turf of Rose Bowl Field that The Whistle made itself—*him*self—heard the loudest.

Rose Bowl Field, by the way, got its name because it was purchased with funds generated by Georgia Tech's appearance in the 1929 Rose Bowl. That glorious year, the Golden Tornado (the team nickname back then) capped a perfect 10-0 season and won the national championship by beating the California Golden Bears in the Rose Bowl. California center Roy Riegels was the surprise star—for Georgia Tech.

WRONG WAY! WRONG WAY!

There's no such thing as the Greatest College Football Story of All Time because everyone has his or her favorite. (Win one for the Gipper, anybody?) But this one from the 1929 Rose Bowl has to rank in the Top 5.

Late in the first, half Cal center Roy Riegels caught a fumble by Georgia Tech back Stumpy Thomason in mid-air, got bumped and spun around, and started racing toward the goal line 64 yards away.

His own.

You know how "fast" your typical center is, right? Well, Riegels was an exception. He outran everybody on his own team—some Tech players were coasting along in disbelief, hoping he wouldn't come to his senses—until finally, at the Cal 3-yard line, a teammate caught him and informed him of the error of his ways.

Too late. Tech tacklers overwhelmed Riegels and knocked him down at the 1.

Hoping to dig out of the hole, the Golden Bears lined up to punt. Riegels snapped the ball but the Golden Tornado blocked the kick. The ball rolled out of the end zone for a safety.

That safety was the eventual margin of victory in Georgia Tech's 8-7 triumph.

It also gave Roy Riegels a nickname that will live until the end of time: henceforth and forever more, he was known as Wrong Way Riegels.

And, of course, to Yellow Jackets fans, as a Georgia Tech hero.

A charter member of the SEC in 1932, Tech left the conference before the 1964 season and played as an independent for the next 15 years. Since 1980, the Yellow Jackets have been members of the ACC. Over the years, Tech has gone 22-13 in bowl games, but the greatest victory was in that very first one.

Every year for the last couple of decades, players from Dodd's Georgia Tech teams of the 1960s have held a reunion. Engineers, corporate CEOs, bank presidents, teachers, entrepreneurs, airline pilots, ministers, military officers, and even a couple of old football coaches turn up at the joyous occasion.

What brings us back every year is not just that once upon a time we all wore the White and Gold. (Officially, the Tech colors are White and Old Gold, but I've never cared for the implied association with a cigarette brand.) The bond that unites us, along with thousands of other ex-Yellow Jackets across the country, is that we all negotiated the transition from boy to man under The Whistle.

We heard The Whistle and we grew up in a hurry.

THE LIFE OF a college freshman football player is a jarring mixture of excitement and fear. That's true of any step up in class—say, from junior high to high school, from sophomore to junior to senior. But for an athlete, going from high school to college is a real jolt.

Bigger? Stronger? Faster?

Way more than you could possibly have guessed during your senior season of high school glory.

At Georgia Tech, the process was especially daunting because it involved two distinct and competing disciplines that collided in rapid succession with immature psyches. One, of course, was football at a level that was a quantum leap forward from high school. The other was a core academic curriculum that included calculus, physics, chemistry, and statistics—even for football players.

We arrived on campus well in advance of the start of fall classes in 1960, not only for preseason workouts but also—just as important, if you hoped to stay eligible—mandatory tutoring sessions.

My first tutoring session was held in the chemistry building in a small classroom. There were eight or ten of us in desk chairs, all facing a large blackboard covered with equations. As the small, mousy tutor began his lesson, I was preoccupied with the cast on sophomore quarterback Ben Ferguson's broken wrist. It provided an excellent palette for graffiti, which I was happily providing.

Suddenly there was silence. Heads turned my way, following the tutor's fixed glare.

"What's your name, young man?" he asked.

"Me?"

"Yes, you," he said quietly.

"Uh, my name is Bill Curry, sir," I said, speaking a bit too loud.

"You are excused, Mr. Curry," he said.

"I am?" I couldn't believe it. "I mean, I'm *excused*?"

"Yes, Mr. Curry," the tutor said firmly. "Get out of my room, and do *not* come back."

The next morning there was a notice in all caps on the bulletin board in the locker room:

BILL CURRY:
SEE COACH GRIFFIN IMMEDIATELY.
COACH DODD

When I walked into offensive coordinator Jack Griffin's office, I was not asked to sit down. Coach Griffin looked at a small piece of paper and said, "You've been dropped from chemistry tutoring, Bill. The tutor doesn't want you back. Coach Dodd is not happy about this."

Coach Dodd knows.

I flashed back to the year before, when my high school counselor, Mrs. Ruby Crowe, called me in for a special meeting.

"I understand you're considering Georgia Tech," she said.

Offering her a bright smile, I confirmed that I was. She looked at me and then, in a voice that couldn't have been more emphatic, she said one word: "Don't."

"Don't what?" I asked, a little stunned. And then I figured it out. She didn't think I had the smarts to go to Georgia Tech.

"Look Bill," she said in a quiet but firm voice, "you're not stupid, but you've frolicked all the way through high school and you have *no chance* of surviving the academics at Tech. You simply aren't prepared."

I thanked her, excused myself, and went straight to the library, where I picked up a dictionary and looked up the word "frolic."

Six months later, there I was fulfilling her prediction, and classes hadn't even started.

CHEMISTRY 101: DR. A. C. TOPP
LECTURE M-TH 8 A.M., LAB TH 1-4 P.M.

Dr. Topp was a distinguished gentleman who always wore a perfectly pressed dark suit. He had a smartly trimmed mustache, wavy brown hair, and walked with a cane. He looked like he'd escaped from the House of Lords. He spoke in a clear, strong voice, but for the life of me I could *not* understand a word he said. There were more than a hundred students in the lecture portion of the class, so I was sure no one would notice if I slept in. And so, in the second week of classes, still drained from the previous fortnight of two-a-days, that's exactly what I did.

The next morning there was another notice on the bulletin board in front of the locker room. It read:

BILL CURRY:
REPORT TO GRANT FIELD
WEDNESDAY, 6:00 A.M.
RUNNING SHOES AND SHORTS
COACH DODD

When I arrived at Grant Field the next day, the sun was just coming up. Standing in the shadows along the West Stands was a lone figure. He gestured for me to approach him. It was Coach Dick Inman, the varsity defensive line coach. He did *not* look happy. He had me stretch a few minutes and then pointed to the stands.

"We're going to run the stadium steps this morning."

"We" was a misnomer; he meant me.

By my 50th trip up and down the steps, I was gagging,

retching, practically sobbing, and thinking how wonderful Chemistry 101 was at 8 a.m. At the end of the ordeal, all Coach Inman did was ask what I thought about class attendance. When I responded that I thought it was a good idea, he cut me loose to get ready to go pay close attention to Dr. Topp.

The Whistle, with his presence, his values, his system, and his consistency had refused to let me self-destruct my first week on campus.

It worked.

I never missed another class in my four and a half years at Georgia Tech. I learned that if I went to class, paid attention, and worked hard, I could make up for not having been prepared to be at Georgia Tech in the first place.

I graduated from the Georgia Institute of Technology with a 2.8 GPA in Industrial Management. Not great, but way better than my high school counselor would have predicted.

So did most of my teammates. Bobby Dodd's graduation rate, at a school where every student is required to take the dreaded calculus, was over 90 percent during his 22-year career as head coach at Georgia Tech.

We had heard The Whistle.

MAYBE ONE REASON Coach Dodd was so fanatic about class attendance and graduation was that he hadn't earned his degree from the University of Tennessee.

He had fallen in love with football as a child, and it was his abiding passion for the rest of his life. He is one of only three men to be elected to the National Football

Foundation Hall of Fame as a player *and* a coach. But at Tech he was just as obsessed with the notion that his players should get an education—not just "stay eligible," but get an education—as he was with teaching them how to play football.

His brilliance as a builder of men was matched by his genius in preparation and as a game-day strategist. Bear Bryant once said that he would rather look across the field and see *anyone* other than Bobby Dodd. And yet here's a paradox: other coaches of the era and savvy sportswriters who covered college football in our neck of the woods for decades were united in their puzzlement that anyone could have coached with as light a hand as did Bobby Dodd and still have won so many games.

We players bristled at the suggestion that we were not as tough as our football brethren at other SEC schools— we didn't leave the conference until 1964—who signed 60 freshmen every year and ran off half of them before the first game with grueling drills and distance running.

Coach Dodd secretly loved the criticism. He knew that his Books First rep caused moms and dads—mine included—to favor Georgia Tech over his competition.

He set forth his basic philosophy on Day One:

> Men, you are here because I want you here. *I did not bring you here to kill you at practice.*
>
> If you turn out not to be a very good football player, that's not *your* fault. That's *my* fault. I invited you here. I will love you,

discipline you, keep you here, and encourage you. I will make sure that if you work hard enough, you will get your degree.

I want every single one of you to graduate.

And then he walked us through his basic rules. He didn't have many, he told us, but there were three that would get us in big trouble if we broke them:

1. *Go to church.* (Or, in the case of the half dozen Jewish players on the team, *Go to Temple.*) He offered up North Avenue Presbyterian, First Methodist, and First Baptist as nearby options. (Maybe we were a little paranoid, since his assistants attended those churches, putting them in a position to check on us. But most of us fell into one of those three denominations, so we took our chances.)

2. *Go to class.* Coach Dodd was adamant on this one. "I don't care how smart you are, you cannot survive at Georgia Tech unless you go to every single class. I will be *real hard* on you if you cut class. And *do not cheat in school.* That will get you kicked out of here immediately." (The captain of the football team had been expelled for cheating the spring before our arrival.)

3. *Do not drink, carouse, or break curfew.* He had a public record of dismissing some of his best football players for violating Rule No. 3. "Don't test me," he said. And in the five years I was at Tech—I red-shirted the 1961 season—no one did.

Practice under Coach Dodd was tough, really tough, but always with the *clear* intent of improving us, strengthening us, and never crossing the invisible line into brutalization.

45

For instance, we never scrimmaged full speed during the season—never. Many coaches I heard of, and one I played under, used full-speed, in-season scrimmages as a form of punishment for bad play.

Coach Dodd knew exactly what he wanted, and he had a precise plan for getting it. Tech was, after all, a school built around engineering and the sciences, so creating and following a carefully articulated plan wasn't exactly uncommon.

Most days during the season, he spent practices underneath his coaching tower with sportswriters, dictating their columns to them for the next day. (No head coach before or since has understood public relations the way Dodd did.) But he never missed a thing on the field. And The Whistle always had his whistle at the ready.

Our freshman coach in 1960 was Jim Carlen. (He would go on to head coaching jobs at West Virginia, Texas Tech, and South Carolina.) Jim was demanding and physical in his approach. We freshmen, who were ineligible for varsity competition in those days, practiced on a baseball field adjoining Rose Bowl Field, where the varsity team worked out. We could hear the shouts, whistles, and collisions from the adjacent field, but lived pretty much in our own little world.

On one occasion during that first summer, Carlen was driving us particularly hard in conditioning drills when a familiar whistle blew from the hill leading to the Rose Bowl Field gate. The varsity team had just gone in. Carlen froze, turned, and looked at The Whistle towering over us from his vantage point next to the gate.

"Send 'em in Jimmy!"

Carlen shouted back, "Yeah, Coach. Just a couple more!"

There was a short pause.

"Send 'em in Jimmy!"

Carlen took one more shot: "Coach, I've got a few..."

"Send them in, Jimmy!"

There was distinct edge to The Whistle's voice.

"Right now!"

UNDER BOBBY DODD, we learned routine, system, moral compass, and unselfish teamwork. We learned to *think under duress*. We learned the fundamentals of winning football with the same diligence required in the physics lab. We learned to respect tough faculty, tough opponents, and tough situations without fearing them.

Coach Dodd's lesson plan for us had an immense impact on the world of college football.

At an Atlanta function in 1980, where Ohio State legend Woody Hayes was a guest speaker, he surprised everyone when he said this about Coach Dodd: "If Bobby hadn't been so generous in teaching us his belly series in the mid-50s, I wouldn't have been nearly as successful as a football coach."

Hayes wasn't alone in his appreciation of The Whistle's contribution to the game. Ask Joe Paterno today who his early role models were, and Coach Dodd will be among the first he mentions. When current Buckeyes coach Jim Tressel was awarded the Bobby Dodd Coach of the Year Award in 2002, he said that *Bobby Dodd on Football*, published in

1954, had been one of his primary guides since the beginning of his career.

I can see Coach Dodd now, walking crisply into our cramped meeting room beneath the east stands of Grant Field before a game. Dressed in a custom tailored gray suit that fit his tall, lean frame perfectly and a crisply starched white shirt with a gold tie, he would slip off his brown fedora, exposing his trademark shock of gray hair. His wingtip shoes sparkled. Every detail of his appearance bespoke preparation for the moment.

On game days, we used a backup nickname: The Whistle became The Gray Fox.

Bear in mind that, unique among college coaches, Coach Dodd had to motivate us to get our game faces on while our heads were still in the grip of Saturday morning classes. That's right, most of us had classes on Saturday mornings. People today don't believe me when I tell them. But we had to hustle from the classroom buildings to the locker room to get ready.

We were often still focused on our studies—at Georgia Tech, you *were* a student-athlete, or else—while going through the rituals of getting taped, getting our gear on, dressing, and getting our minds ready for the day's business before sitting down for our pre-game meeting with him.

Coach Dodd could have simply stood and eyeballed us and not said a word, and I do believe we would have been ready to play. But he came armed with a rare combination of charisma, calm, and control. He exuded mastery of the situation. His psychology was the opposite of the public's notion of pre-game speeches, and I am convinced he is the only person who could have taken this approach with such stunning success.

Like a presidential candidate, he had his basic stump speech, whose core message he delivered from game to game with little deviation in substance. We especially liked the version he delivered before the big game with the University of Georgia, our number one rival, because he steadfastly refused to pronounce the University's name correctly. While he had no trouble saying *Georgia* Tech he always said "Georgie" when referring to our cross-state rival Bulldogs, both in our locker room and at press conferences. (See "Georgia Tech vs. Georgie," page 50.)

Bulldog Nation was not amused; we ate it up.

MORE OFTEN THAN any football "expert" could have predicted, he was right on the mark. Most weeks we played teams that were physically superior to us. They would run up big numbers, 400 yards of offense and 20 first downs to our 200 and 10. And yet the score would somehow end up something like 7-6, Tech.

The experts called it "Dodd luck."

But it wasn't luck, unless one's definition of luck begins with a deep understanding of motivational psychology, football strategy, and innovative game-planning. I am convinced the "Dodd luck" derived from a genius who understood his people, understood his game, and understood his opponents better than any other coach in the history of the game.

And yeah, okay, there may have been a little ordinary luck in there somewhere, as well.

GEORGIA TECH VS. GEORGIE

Men, Georgie's a fine football team, a very fine football team. Georgie's bigger and faster than we are. Probably a little tougher than we are, too.

That's okay, because we're smarter than they are.

Now, let me tell you what's going to happen today. That Georgie team's going to come running out of the tunnel screaming and foaming at the mouth and smashing one another upside the head just to get warmed up. A couple of them will throw up on our sidelines for good measure.

We will not do *any* of that. While they waste their energy, we'll conserve ours and direct it into constructive action. I've told you that they're bigger, faster, and tougher than you. That's true. But we do have that one big advantage.

We … are … *smarter* … than they are.

Now, when the game starts, they'll come out and knock us around for a while. They'll probably pull ahead. But because we're smarter, and because you'll play the way I've taught you, they won't get very far ahead.

Think now about what I teach you. Play field position. Play great defense. Make no mistakes on offense. Be great in the kicking game. Do that and we'll keep it close.

As the game goes on, they'll start to get tired because they wasted so much energy in the beginning. Because we're smart, we'll have plenty of energy, and at some point in the fourth quarter they'll make a mistake.

When they do make that mistake, we'll get the football. And when that happens, I'll think of something and we'll win!

I DIDN'T MAKE my first start until the fourth game of my fourth year at Georgia Tech. I was a junior. (Since I had been red-shirted, I received a fifth year of eligibility.) Many coaches would have tried to run me off, something that was commonplace in that era. But I was first encouraged, then driven to succeed by the magic of Dodd confidence.

I owe a great deal to the combination of Georgia Tech and Bobby Dodd.

Like most of my teammates, I needed both to succeed. From the grueling pace of the classroom I learned how to work and how to think. From Coach Dodd I learned that perseverance and grit would lead me to personal victory. Those lessons, combined, turned out to be perfect preparation for what was right around the corner for me.

Bobby Dodd was a man of many parts: self-described "football bum" in high school ... Hall of Fame college player ... Hall of Fame college coach ... inspirational leader, Presbyterian elder, educator, humanitarian, mentor ... dedicated husband and father ... addicted gambler (only on checkers and doubles tennis, with his buddies) ... raconteur ... rabid bass fisherman ... youth camp co-director (with me, when I coached at Tech) ... and football genius.

Those of us who loved him don't claim sainthood for him, but we steadfastly believe that he continues to represent all that is good about college football.

The Whistle still pierces my consciousness every day—and as the years pass, its clarity only increases.

Why is this man smiling? Probably because he's in the middle of a two-year run (26–5–1) that included wins in the last NFL title game (1965) and the first Super Bowl (1966). Unfortunately, what I remember most about those years is a snarling, belligerent, angry scowl.

3

VINCE LOMBARDI
GENERAL

The call came early on a Sunday morning after my junior season at Georgia Tech. Carolyn and I were in our first year of marriage, living in Norcross, about 15 miles out of Atlanta. The caller was her brother, Ronnie Newton.

"Good morning, Green Bay Packer!" he practically yelled in my ear after I'd managed a sleepy hello. Sure that he was messing with me, I hung up on him. He called back immediately and said, "Take a look at the morning paper!"

Still not convinced he was doing anything but pulling my chain, I stumbled out of bed, grabbed the *Atlanta Constitution* from my front porch, and plucked out the sports section. Sure enough, there it was in black and white: I had been drafted by the Green Bay Packers of the National Football League.

Drafted?

I hadn't even known the NFL was having a draft.

See, I was a 212-pound offensive center with another year of eligibility remaining, not exactly a prime candidate for the NFL. But in those days one could be drafted as a "future," complete one's eligibility the next year, and then become a professional.

I was thrilled. This was the beginning of the next stage of my life. This was step one in beginning to realize a potential in myself I had never touched. I was about to learn what was required to join The Huddle at the highest level.

The NFL draft had 20 rounds. The rival American Football League had 26 rounds. I had been drafted in the 20th by Green Bay and in the 23rd by the Oakland Raiders. In the NFL, I was the 279th of 280 players selected. I did somewhat better in the AFL, but the Oakland Raiders never had a chance against the Packers in getting my signature on a contract.

Pat Peppler, the Packers' director of player personnel, later told me that he'd been with Vince Lombardi as the 1964 draft drew to its conclusion. At around 2:00 a.m., Lombardi turned to him and said, "I'm exhausted and I'm going to bed. Have some fun with the 20th pick."

Peppler followed instructions, and that's how I became a Green Bay Packer.

(A little late, perhaps, but I'd like to tip my hat to Richard A. Niglio, a halfback from Yale. He was the last pick in the 1964 NFL draft, thus sparing me from earning—retroactively—the nickname Mr. Irrelevant, the sobriquet hung since 1976 on the last selection in the draft. A business executive for nearly four decades—Kentucky Fried Chicken, Mister Donut, Children's Discovery Centers of America—Niglio is currently the CEO of an online software marketing firm. And I bet he has two working knees.)

I had only perfunctory contact with Green Bay and Oakland for the next seven months. But when I walked off the field in Athens, Georgia, on November 28, 1964, after the last game of my Georgia Tech career, Green Bay assistant coach Red Cochran was waiting on the sideline. He asked if Carolyn and I would like to ride back to Atlanta with him, have dinner, and then fly to Dallas to catch a Packers-Cowboys game the next day and meet Coach Lombardi. We accepted on the spot, and less than 24 hours later we were sitting in the stands at the Cotton Bowl next to Marie Lombardi.

At the beginning of the fourth quarter, Peppler came and got me. We made our way down the stadium steps to field level, through a guarded gate, and out onto the sideline. There, up close, in their distinctive gold headgears with the green G on the side were Bart Starr, Paul Hornung, Jimmy Taylor, Jerry Kramer, Fuzzy Thurston, and the rest of the team that dominated pro football in the 1960s.

And there also was the already legendary Vince Lombardi, standing with pursed lips and a slight smile playing about his features, his eyes still fiercely focused on the field as yet another victory was about to go into the books.

When the game concluded—a 45-21 Packers rout—Peppler led me onto the field and introduced me to the man himself. There I stood at the 30-yard line of the Cotton Bowl, face to face with the dominant sports figure of our day.

I was dumbstruck, and the next few minutes were a blur. But I do recall that Coach Lombardi was cordial, that he shook my hand, and that as he continued to walk toward the locker room, he asked me to accompany him.

When we got to the entrance to the visitors' locker room, he turned and looked me squarely in the eye. "Well, son, would you like to become part of the Green Bay Packers?"

"Yes, sir," I mumbled without hesitation, certainly without thinking about the Oakland Raiders or contract terms or anything but saying "Yes, sir" before he had a chance to change his mind. He smiled, nodded, turned on his heels, and went into the locker room.

Peppler and I remained outside for about 10 minutes while Coach conducted his customary post-game talk with his team.

Once we were allowed to enter, I was puzzled to find that the players' faces ranged from stoic to borderline downcast. What was wrong with this picture? They'd just pushed the other guys all over the field, winning by 24 points. Shouldn't they be laughing and celebrating?

Only later did Peppler confide in me that Coach had probably torn into them pretty good. *What*? Why? "We were stopped on the goal line there near the end," Peppler said, "and Coach tends to focus on something like that after an easy win to keep the guys from getting complacent and too full of themselves."

One exception stood out amidst the glum faces in the room. Jimmy Taylor sat at his locker with a look of bemused detachment, smoking a cigar, confident that he'd done his job and utterly unperturbed by his coach's ritual harangue.

Taking the whole scene in during those few minutes was enough to seal my future.

FOLLOWING THE GAME, we were taken to dinner with former Packers linebacker Bill Forester and his wife, who charmed us with tales of the Packers Tradition. When we returned to the hotel, Peppler and another Packers executive, Tom Miller, took me to a separate room while Carolyn returned to ours. Tom said that he and Pat had been instructed to offer me a contract with the Green Bay Packers. I sat stupefied, trying to comprehend all that was occurring. At that moment, Carolyn called and asked that I come back to our room, that she had news.

I was glad for the excuse to get up and walk, so I headed back to our room, where she greeted me breathlessly with the fact that the Oakland Raiders guy was in the hotel. He told Carolyn that the Raiders wanted in on the bidding for my services.

She asked me, "Do you have any idea what first-year players make?"

"Not really," I said, "but Jim Minter told me that anyone who negotiates a $12,000 salary and a $12,000 bonus would make more than any first-year lineman ever from our area."

Jim is a friend who at that time was a sportswriter in Atlanta. No one had agents in those days, so a beat reporter was usually a pretty good source for information like that.

She said, "Do you think we could get something like that?"

"I don't know," I responded. "It seems like an awful lot."

We'd both been raised in modest circumstances. No one on either side of our families had ever made much money, and no one I knew other than Jim had been able to give us any perspective. Carolyn and I had to be among the least prepared couples in the history of pro sports negotiations. Here we were, being recruited by two different teams in two different leagues, and we had no clue how to use that fact.

By now we were giddy, but at Carolyn's behest we sat down and planned our strategy. I would go back and "play it cool," make them commit to a number first, bide my time, get a feel for the situation, and then spring my own big proposal on them.

Maybe we could get close to 12 and 12 from the Packers, especially with the rival league in the building. In our hearts we both knew by now we would have paid the Packers to let me sign, but maybe we could be coy by using the Raiders threat to up the ante.

With that plan in my head, I went back to my sitdown with Peppler and Miller. They told football stories, made jokes, and talked about just about everything besides a contract. Every now and then they asked if I would like to suggest a basis for making a deal, to which I politely said no, that I would wait for them. My growing fear was that at some point they would tire of my intransigence and simply decide to send us back to Atlanta with no contract.

After an hour or so of small talk, Miller left the room. A few minutes later returned and announced, "I just talked with Coach Lombardi. He said to me, 'Tom, get that guy signed! Stop messing around and do what it takes to get him signed!' That's what he said."

Miller smiled and looked at me. It was my turn. I've thought of that moment hundreds of times since then. It was my signal to get aggressive and go for the 12 and 12. But I hesitated. The silence in the room seemed to grow. The insecure kid could no longer breathe.

"Twelve and 12," I finally croaked, honestly not knowing whether they would laugh at me, throw me out, or offer something like $8,000 and $8,000 to commence the negotiations.

There was another long pause as they glanced at each other. Then Tom said evenly, "Bill, how about this: we'll sign you to a contract right now for a $12,500 bonus and a $12,500 salary for the 1965 season."

I don't remember the next few minutes because my brain went blank. All I know for sure is that I somehow managed to hold a pen steady in my hand, sign a standard NFL player contract for the awesome amount of $25,000 total for one year, and float back to our room.

Back in that little Ramada room with Carolyn, lucid thought returned. Two unspoiled kids sobbed with joy in each other's arms. We were going to the NFL! We were set for life!

The next couple of weeks brought a little reality back into play.

Big money was being thrown around as the NFL and the AFL slugged it out. My Georgia Tech teammate, Dave Simmons, got exactly twice what I signed for—$25K bonus, $25K salary—*plus* a Pontiac Bonneville from the St. Louis Cardinals. True, he was drafted in the second round (vs. 20th for me). Yes, he was the 26th pick overall, while I was next to last at 279. And he played a glamour position, linebacker, while I was an offensive center.

But still.

I did pick up the phone once to call Tom Miller to ask if he thought I was maybe worth something a little closer to what my teammate Dave received. But I came to my senses and hung up on the second ring.

After all, I had my 12 and 12, and then some.

I started training.

I was going to join the Packers huddle.

THE GREAT MAN looked as if he'd been standing, fidgeting, and scowling since before dawn.

It was 4:15 p.m. on August 7, 1965, less than 24 hours after the 1965 College All-Star Game. I reported for duty as instructed to the first floor of Sensenbrenner Dormitory on the campus of St. Norbert College in De Pere, Wisconsin.

I was 15 minutes early.

As I approached Vince Lombardi, the famous smile with the even more famous teeth flashed in greeting. He stuck out his right hand, which I took, only to be surprised at the lack of firmness in the grip. I was soon to learn that his gentle grasp was the only aspect of the man that lacked power.

The former member—at 5'8", 185 pounds—of Fordham's legendary Seven Blocks of Granite in the mid-1930s was now, at 52 years of age, a living, breathing force field who exuded tangible, visceral energy. I wonder now if he intentionally lowered the squeeze factor of his handshake to put people at ease.

(Five years later, I would find his left hand more compelling as I timidly held it in mine in his hospital room at Georgetown Hospital.)

Coach eyeballed me and asked, "Are you ready to go to work?" I nodded yes, tried to speak, came up dry, and finally croaked "Yes, sir. Uh, yes. I'm really ready."

Good thing I had rehearsed.

Coach said that we'd be having our annual intrasquad scrimmage in front of Green Bay fans that night, and that I'd dress out but probably wouldn't play.

"Probably" wouldn't play?

"Probably" left open the possibility that I *might*, but how could I *possibly* play? The entire population of Green Bay was going to be there to see the fabled Packers for free, and this guy *might* stick me out there in front of them, when I had just played every snap against the World Champs 20 hours earlier? And I don't know the snap count? And I don't know how to get in the huddle? And I not only don't know the plays, but I haven't even been issued a playbook? Or equipment? Or *anything?*

Probably wouldn't play? My communication gap with Vince Lombardi had begun in earnest, and I had only just met the guy.

The night before, I had sustained a slight concussion in the College All-Star Game and I had experienced for the first time the speed and velocity of NFL collisions. I'd spent my few sleepless hours in bed trying to process all *that.*

(My wife, Carolyn, calls those vivid recollections "the reruns," referring to my lifelong tendency toward sleepless nights after any defeat, during which I replay every down over and over. Hey, some people count sheep.)

And now I was hearing that I "probably wouldn't play?"

My mind reeling, I was directed to a sparsely furnished classroom, where starting center Ken Bowman patiently began to teach me the rudiments of the Packer system. I was immediately captured by Ken's intelligence and wit, which

I soon discovered were common characteristics among this particular pack of Packer players. A natural teacher, Ken made the terminology and signal system come alive.

Ken looked and talked like Lee Marvin, the tough guy movie star (*The Man Who Shot Liberty Valance, The Dirty Dozen*, and many more). He was cordial and clever, and before I knew it he had me laughing, which I genuinely appreciated, considering that I was there to take his job. While he had nothing to fear, and realized it, I remember hoping I could respond as well if faced with similar circumstances.

Finally, Ken looked at his watch and said that would be enough for now. I looked at mine and realized I hadn't eaten since the night before. He went back to his room and I started for the dining hall.

THIS WOULD BE my first pre-game meal with the Green Bay Packers, the most famous football team in the world, and I was tormented.

Where would I sit? I didn't even know the other rookies yet. What if I sat at a veterans' table and was ordered to leave? Would Lombardi be there monitoring table manners? Would rookies be forced to sing their school songs?

Dear God, how could things be happening so fast? My fatigue and the hangover from my concussion the night before in Chicago made me queasy. And my head was overloaded with information, vibrations, questions, and foreboding. What if I threw up?

Suddenly, I sensed a presence at my left side. Someone called my name, his voice seeming to come from an adjacent room, a closed door between us. I think he had to repeat himself a couple of times. He was talking plenty loud enough, it's just that my mind was racing too fast for me to hear.

"Bill, do you remember me?" asked Bart Starr as we walked in step across the grass.

"Yes, uh, why of course. How are you Mr. Starr?"

"Bart," he said. "None of this Mr. Starr stuff."

"Okay," I smiled. Maybe I was in the right place after all.

I had no reason to expect that the famous quarterback would speak to me until the first center-quarterback exchange drill. We had met in passing a couple of years earlier at my father's sporting goods department in an Atlanta store, but I had been told that no veteran would talk to any rookie unless it was to give an order, issue a challenge, or deliver an insult. That was an NFL rule.

After a little back and forth, Mr. Starr—*Bart*—said, "Bill, I don't know what your religious affiliation is, but we have a fine minister at the First Methodist Church in Green Bay, and Cherry and I would like to invite you to go with us to Sunday services tomorrow."

"You're, uh, asking me to go to church with you and your wife?" I stammered. My first day in camp and Bart Starr was inviting me to go to church? And me being a Methodist on top of it? Even though I would have gladly skipped church for a bit of catch-up rest, I said "Yes, sure. Thanks, Bart. I think I have a clean dress shirt."

We hadn't gotten around to the Packers' snap count, Bart's preferences for the center-quarterback exchange, or the team's audible system. We hadn't talked practice procedure, Vince Lombardi, or the Packers Tradition. We had begun a relationship by striking an unspoken chord, and the tenor of our friendship would remain anchored in that resonance. In the space of two minutes, Bart Starr had entered my life.

Less than 24 hours earlier, I had been running onto Soldier Field in Chicago as the starting center for a bunch of NFL wannabes against the World Champion Cleveland Browns. Now I was making plans to go to church with the great Bart Starr.

BUT FIRST, I had to put on a Green Bay Packers uniform and play a football game. (Well, probably not, but I had to be ready.)

In the most surreal night of my life, I boarded the team bus with the Packers veterans and the few remaining rookies (four would make the 40-man roster) for the seven-mile drive to Lambeau Field in Green Bay. There I drew my equipment, got taped, dressed in the Green and Gold, and ran onto the hallowed grounds of Lambeau as a *Green Bay Packer*. While it was just a scrimmage, it would nonetheless pit arguably the best offense in football against the uncontested best defense.

And I had never practiced so much as a down with either unit.

Coach Lombardi stood in front of the assembled team in the locker room. It was pouring outside, a major rainstorm. There was already standing water on the field. This was only a scrimmage, so I remember thinking I might get a reprieve from having to play my second football game in 24 hours. (So much for being sent into panic mode at the thought that I "probably wouldn't play.") After all, this was a freebie for

Green Bay fans, so there wasn't any ticket money to refund, so maybe ...

No such luck: Coach Lombardi said we were going to play, come hell or—well, high water.

What that meant was that the first snaps of my professional career during warm-ups to our All-Pro quarterback would be with sopping wet footballs. Any new center-quarterback combination takes a while to coordinate the exchange, even under the best of conditions. With driving rain, the texture of the football changes, the balls become swollen and slick, leading to sloppy exchanges, or worse. At best, the timing of the play is affected. At worst, I lose purchase on the ball as I snap it and sprain or fracture one or more of the quarterback's fingers.

I stood with awe bordering on reverence as equipment man Dad Braisher handed me my green No. 50 jersey. My helmet looked huge, a funny consequence of the gold color and my massive head. The pads and shoes felt strange. I stood at the opening to the offensive locker room and tried to make myself really believe I was where I was, that I belonged here.

This was my dream come true. Could I handle it?

DAY TWO OF my life as a Green Bay Packer—theoretically, an off day between the Saturday night scrimmage on August 7, 1965, and my first day of practice of Monday—dawned with me in a daze.

Talk about your rude awakenings. Deep, nervous, mental exhaustion had followed hard on the heels of a slight concussion incurred two evenings earlier in the College All-Star Game. A little collateral travel trauma—fear of getting up late, getting to the airport, getting to Green Bay—had contributed to a near sleepless night of tossing and turning in Chicago.

In scientific terms, I'd been rode hard and put up wet.

Then came the big intrasquad scrimmage on Saturday, my first time in a Packers uniform. A night full of memories that would be forever seared into my consciousness, right?

I wish.

Running onto a football field in front of Green Bay fans for the first time? Ritual warm-ups with 39 new brothers, all of us side-straddle-hopping in unison? The center-quarterback exchange drill, a raw rookie snapping balls to one of the game's reigning superstars, the former suppressing a terrifying image of a mangled finger on the throwing hand of the latter? The scrimmage itself?

All a blur. Thanks to a meter-shattering stress spike, I had spent my first three hours in full Packer regalia at Lambeau Field fending off an overwhelming desire to stretch out on the bench, nod off, and sleep for 18 hours. Concussions make you sleepy anyhow, and this turned out to be the one time in all my years in football that two such draining events came so close together.

The only plays of the scrimmage that remain vivid are the ones in which I snapped for field goals at the very end. I recall them as if in a dream sequence, but they are riveted into my consciousness because they were the very first times I had physical contact with Ray Nitschke.

There would be more—many, many more.

After the scrimmage, Lombardi hadn't seen fit to use what I later learned was his favorite quote from one of his favorite people, General George Patton: "Fatigue makes cowards of us all." Good thing, because I'd have been sorely tempted to amend it: "Fatigue makes zombies of some of us."

Somehow, we must have showered and dressed and ridden the buses back to De Pere. All I recall is an odd sensation of being cold on an August night.

Our dorm rooms embodied Spartan simplicity with their bare linoleum floors, spare furnishings, and communal bathroom. As I prepared for bed, I realized for the first time I had no sheets or pillow cases and that I would be sleeping on a bare single bed covered by plastic. I would sleep on that slippery thing a couple of weeks. There simply was not time to go to the store to buy bed linens except on Sundays, but in those halcyon days nothing was open.

Buy bed linens? It was either that or go without. We bunked at St. Norbert College in De Pere, and the school didn't supply bed linens in its dormitories, at least not to summer renters like us. Green Bay veterans, knowing this, brought sheets and pillow cases with them. Green rookies made do without until a care package finally arrived from home, because there wasn't *time* to go shopping, even for basic necessities.

We practiced twice a day, and the yellow school buses that hauled us between Lambeau Field and St. Norbert turned a 15-minute trip back from practice to our dorm into a 1-hour trek, what with waiting for slow dressers and besieged autograph-signers like Bart.

Did I say 15-minute drive? That's what the trip would have been each way if players had been allowed to drive our own cars. Many of the vets had brought their vehicles, but they weren't allowed to drive them to and from practice. *Everybody* took the bus. Maybe it built team spirit. It sure didn't leave time for shopping.

Not that we'd have been able to buy much anyway. Not on the $6 per day, $42 per week that we earned for the six exhibition games before the season started.

That's right, six bucks a day. Even back then that didn't go far. My salary would commence once the season started— *if* I made the team.

Half of my $12,500 signing bonus had gone for a brand new, gun-metal blue, four-door Oldsmobile 98. The rest Carolyn and I stashed to live on for a while if I didn't make the team and had to go into another line of work.

None of that really mattered, though. I would happily have bunked down on the sidewalk if it allowed me to pull on that No. 50 Packers jersey twice a day.

THE MORNING OF my second day as a Packer was a beautiful, crisp, Wisconsin Sunday. Church with the Starrs was perfect. The minister, Roger Bourland, was everything Bart had promised the day before when he asked me to attend. My spacey head was gradually finding some clarity after the muddle of the previous 36 hours.

After lunch, I couldn't wait to get back to my slick mattress and crash again. Dozing off, I heard a resounding knock at my door, but I was too lazy to get up. The best I could offer up was a weak "Come on in." Just one of the other rookies dropping by, I figured. The door opened and there was the last person on earth I expected to see: Coach Lombardi.

I started up out of the bed, snapping to attention out of habit. He smiled at my surprise, then sat me down and spoke earnestly and without wasting words:

> We plan to work you on both sides of the ball, but we need to begin you at center. You'll be our backup at center, middle linebacker, and outside linebacker. If you beat somebody out, then good. You'll also work on all special teams. You're a long snapper—that'll give you another way to make the team. The more things you can do, the better chance you have of staying in the NFL.

So simple, so true. A survival mantra for all marginal players. The most frequent chant of every training camp. Hang on as a utility man and maybe someday, if you stay ready, you'll get a shot at a starting job.

Coach invited me downstairs to the same classroom Ken Bowman had used the day before. There I sat for two hours with the Oracle of Football, Leadership, and Winning. I was lucid for the first time since my arrival and had a notion of just how lucky I was to be getting a private tutorial.

It quickly became apparent that I wouldn't need the playbook I had brought along. Coach left his closed. Instead, he opened a yellow legal pad and began to draw his now famous set of systematized plays in an orderly, concise fashion.

The films, tapes, and DVDs of Coach Lombardi drawing the Packer Sweep on a blackboard are among the most familiar of all instructional images to coaches, teachers, and businessmen to this day. In the "America's Game" series on Super Bowls from NFL Films that made its debut in 2006, the Super Bowl I story features a long segment of him standing at the blackboard delivering his Packer Sweep lecture. Many of today's fans, born long after Lombardi was gone, amaze me by quoting him.

Coach Lombardi began his professional career as a teacher at St. Cecilia High School in Englewood, New Jersey. And the man standing at this blackboard was a passionate, consummate *teacher*. Like all great teachers, he exuded confidence and enthusiasm. Like all great teachers, he made the complex simple. The Vs and Os he drew on the blackboard in rapid-fire succession took on a life of their own.

Vs & Os

Every time I hear a sports analyst remark about a coach's "mastery of the Xs and Os," I know one thing: that analyst has never witnessed the actual diagramming of a football play.

How do I know that?

Because there's no such thing as "Xs and Os" in football.

For the offense, there are Os plus one square. (That would be me, the center.) And for the defense, there are 11 Vs. So the next time you hear somebody go on about "Xs and Os," just smile smugly and nod confidently.

You know the real deal.

His voice was clear and measured. He didn't distract with asides, nor did he make mistakes. His sure hand, orderly mind, and clear language described actions in terms a child could understand.

His only pauses were for me to make notes when a call was required from the center to the offensive line. I can hear him now:

> Obviously, you'll know the play and the snap count when you come to the line of scrimmage. The moment you set up over the ball, you'll actually control one aspect of the defense. When your hands touch the football, that defense has to get lined up! They don't know but what we might go on a quick count; they have to get ready according to *your* timetable. By the simple act of aligning themselves, they'll show you all you need to know to call signals for the offensive line.

The man then proceeded to teach me the famous Green Bay Packer Sweep. He drew and talked, talked and drew, each act seeming to drive the other.

> The sweep's our basic play. Everybody knows it. Everybody expects it. Everybody thinks they can defend against it. To prove them wrong, we have to execute ... *perfectly.*

So, if the defensive tackle on the side we're going to lines up head-up or on the inside shoulder of our guard, you make an "even" call. You'll have to yell to be heard, and you can't turn your head because smart middle linebackers will be watching your every move. If you do anything that gives any kind of hint, they'll overplay that side and stop us cold.

Now, if the defensive tackle lines up outside our guard, you'll shout "odd!"

"Even" means you block the tackle to the play side, and "odd" means you block the middle linebacker. The play side offensive tackle hears your call and blocks the man you don't block.

Got that?

I'm nodding my head up and down, saying to myself, "Yes, I do! Yes, I do!"

(And I really, honestly did. I think ...)

"You have a real important job to do before you ever snap the ball," he said. "Understand? Can you draw the two blocking combinations for me?"

I could, and did, with relish. Great teachers make you want to please them. When you do, and when they acknowledge it, you feel a surge of adrenalin and your senses heighten. Lombardi understood all of this and pressed on.

Having imprinted the Packer Sweep on my memory forever, he began to draw what he called "companion" plays.

For instance, "When we line up in the Red Formation, the defense is going to expect the sweep. We want to take advantage of that with some plays that *look like* the sweep, but in fact are power plays or play-action passes."

Made sense then; makes sense now.

"Our system is complete, simple, and comprehensive," he went on. "We can attack the whole field. We have very little trickery. We really don't need it."

He summarized, "We win with execution. Something works, not because it's a brilliant piece of strategic or tactical thinking, but because our team has practiced the same plays, the same movements, and the same fundamentals over and over and over again."

How great a teacher was Vince Lombardi? The best way to answer that is to tell you that, 43 years later, *I remember each one of the plays he outlined for me that day.* I can draw each assignment, make the calls, and teach their installation. I remember the coaching points for the guards, tackles, and tight ends. I remember it all, as if it were yesterday.

That's how great a teacher Vince Lombardi was.

VINCE LOMBARDI'S APPROACH to football was modeled on the fundamentals of his deep and profound Roman Catholic faith. Every day he reminded us of the priorities that must guide us: "Your religion, your family, and the Green Bay Packers will be your priorities as long as you are here! And in that order!"

As surely as he believed in daily celebration of the mass, he believed in daily practice of assignment, alignment, and execution. Faithful attendance to the details of football liturgy was basic. There was order, a logical progression for every aspect and concept. Salvation was to be found *in victory*, on the gridiron and in life. And just as the Holy Fathers had taught him, there would be no shirking personal responsibility.

The one distinction I noticed between Vince's football religion and the real one is that his was less forgiving of human frailty.

The stark difference between a Packers football service and the Catholic mass that Coach attended so, well, religiously, was that he conducted the former with Pentecostal zeal and Southern Baptist hellfire and damnation. Fear was the dominant theme. He was honest and upfront about it. "I *will* put the fear of God in you! I *will* make you afraid of me! I *will* use fear to get what I want from you! I *will* make you into a football player!"

I once heard him tell offensive tackle Steve Wright, "Wright, wipe that smile off your face! I'm going to make a man of you before I get rid of you!" That took four years, at least two of which were pure hell for Wright. Coach traded him to the Giants after the 1967 season. Steve played in the NFL five more years with the Giants, Redskins, Bears, and Cardinals.

The moral? Never smile unless Coach smiles first.

THE OTHER AND utterly predictable result of my private tutorial was that it heightened my desire to play. Before our encounter, I had waffled, wondering if I loved football enough to suck it up and keep going. After his intervention, I could feel that burn in the gut that drives a person to survive in brutal pursuits. This would be no place for the faint of heart, and mine was feeling a whole lot less faint.

I was the smallest lineman on the squad. That fact loomed larger in my psyche than it should have, mainly because I had been raised in the culture of the weight room by my father. Strength, size, and power were all important, and I was clearly deficient in all three. Strange as it seems, I had rebelled against my father's obsession with strength and was paying for my stand in a definitive way. I had no choice but to find a way to compensate.

The next morning, Day 3, my first at a Packers practice, Coach pulled me aside, noted that I had weighed in at 235

EIGHT DIRTY WORDS

Every pro football fan knows him. Every pro football player has nightmares about him. The Turk is the club employee who pays house calls at least once a week during training camp to utter the eight most dreaded words in the English language: "Coach wants to see you. Bring your playbook."

Camp begins in early July, with 80 people vying for 53 spots, and the carnage begins almost immediately. Early on Monday or Tuesday morning of the second week, there are soft knocks on doors in the dorms. Those are followed by a brief conversation, and often a short burst of profanity. Heads pop out of rooms like mice from their holes to witness the sad procession to the land of crushed dreams. Later, in the locker room, several lockers are vacant, spotless, as if no one had ever used them.

[continued on following page]

The Turk only does the fetching; the assistant coaches do the actual cutting. Coaches never mention the departees. It's as if they never existed.

Just before the third exhibition game, I got an early-morning knock on *my* door. But it wasn't the Turk; it was Rick Koeper, a big, talented center from Oregon State. He and I were competing for the backup job to Ken Bowman.

"How about a ride, Bill?"

A ride? Where? Why? I was dumbfounded.

"The airport, man. They cut me."

Numbed by the news, I threw on my clothes, grabbed my keys, stumbled out to my car—and cried all the way to the airport, with Rick doing his best to console me.

Our Turk was a front-office guy name Pat Peppler. He'd been the one who took me in the 20th round of the draft the year before, when Lombardi called it a night. And he'd signed me to my first Packers contract.

On final cut day, I hear an early morning tap-tap on my door, opened the door, and there was Pat. I felt light-headed, like I was going to pass out. Koeper was gone. I was the only other center besides Bowman in camp. Unless … had they made a trade or something?

"Bill," Pat said, interrupting my runaway train of disastrous scenarios, "have Carolyn call my wife, Lindy. There's a luncheon for the wives this week and Lindy would like to take Carolyn to make her feel welcome."

Dear God.

I had made the *Green Bay Packers!*

pounds, and urged me to put on 10 pounds "in the next month or so."

It would take me five years.

My advantages included quickness, technique, and grit. I knew how to work and I knew how to study. While I improved, I would get by on tenacity and special teams play.

One of my assignments on special teams was wedge buster, the guy in the middle of the coverage pattern who smashes into the big guys in the kickoff return wedge.

The "wedge" on a kickoff return unit is generally made of three or four of the "friendliest" 285-pounders on the kickoff return team. They line up on the 15-yard line and wait for some unsuspecting rookie to show up. Their goal: pulverize him.

I loved sprinting down the field and diving into the wedge to open a hole for teammates or slipping through it to make the tackle myself. More often than not, I succeeded.

If I say so myself, I was an All-Pro wedge-buster.

But the competitive edge I enjoyed on special teams because of my quickness wasn't an unmixed blessing.

Take my wedge-busting experience in an early league game with the Baltimore Colts. I was excited because Ted Davis, a great teammate of mine from Georgia Tech, was the Colts player assigned to block me up front to keep me from reaching the wedge. I would have to get by him to do my job. Ted was one of our best players at Tech, and I wanted to show him my moves.

Assuming I could do that, I looked farther down the field to see how the Colts deployed their wedge blockers.

It wasn't hard to find their biggest guy, No. 77. When I tell this story on speaking engagements, I exaggerate—slightly. "He was so big he was standing in the middle of the field with one foot on each hash mark." But the fact is, he really was big: 6'3", 275—skimpy for now, but huge for then.

I knew if I could deck No. 77 it would destroy their return and make Coach Lombardi proud. When the ball was kicked, I ran left, then cut back, juked Ted, and picked up speed as I headed for No. 77. The closer I got to those two 7s, the more they loomed like something out of a 3-D movie—and that's the last thing I remember about the play.

As I waited for the stretcher to come out to cart me off the field, Ray Nitschke jogged by, nudged me with his toe, and said, "On your feet. We don't waste time carrying rookies off. Get up and walk off this field!"

So I started crawling toward the sideline, when suddenly I had the terrible sensation of having been blinded in one eye and groped for support. I yelled to fellow rookie Junior Coffey, "Help me! That big guy, 77, he blinded me in my left eye!" Junior's response: "Turn your headgear around, man, you're looking out the ear hole!"

The 77 for the Colts whom I had encountered was Jim Parker. Eight times an All-Pro. The first offensive lineman elected to the Hall of Fame. Consensus pick as the NFL's top offensive lineman of the first 50 years.

At least I could say I had been dropped like a potato sack by the best ever.

FROM MY ENTIRE NFL experience I was to learn that for the driven competitor the line between competition and lunacy is very, very thin. I also learned that I was capable of far more than I had imagined.

My first 10 days as a Packer, I was tormented every single day by the fear that at any moment I would be an ex-Packer. But soon, still within those first two weeks, a pep talk given to me by our head coach in the College All-Star Game, Hall of Fame quarterback Otto Graham, finally began to register. Better still, it began to merge with the Packers 101 principles outlined on Day 2 by Professor Lombardi.

The middle of the second week of preparations for the College All-Star Game, Graham had called me into his office between practices in Evanston, Illinois. I showed up as directed, but there was a coaching staff meeting going on. His staff included Marion Motley (Pro Football Hall of Fame) and Howard "Hopalong" Cassady (College Football Hall of Fame), so their presence meant something to me. They sat quietly, smiled, and nodded as Otto delivered his sermonette.

> Bill, you don't always look like you believe in yourself. Let me tell you something. I've played with a lot of fine centers, and I know what I'm talking about. You've got the tools to play this game. You need to handle yourself with confidence, no matter what's going on inside.
>
> We need you to be a leader.
>
> *Will you begin to believe in Bill Curry?*

I had floated out of the room, but after the game and my concussion, Graham's message got tucked away somewhere in my unconscious. There it lay buried in fatigue and self-pity, only to have Coach Lombardi rekindle it with his personal touch.

Within two weeks, Otto Graham and Vince Lombardi had unknowingly combined forces to plant an idea in a fertile young mind. It only required a little time, a lot of focus, and my absolutely undivided intention to come to fruition.

In every life there are moments of truth. When they appear, they are often disguised. People miss them, then look back years later with regret. It would have taken a blind man to miss mine. So eventually I got the message.

I would play for the Green Bay Packers.

I would play for Vince Lombardi.

"SPEED OF THE game" is one of our most misunderstood sports clichés.

Funny, because it means exactly what it says. Players use the term to express how it feels to be forced to adjust to a new, usually heightened velocity during the action.

If a lineman says, "The speed of the game was too much for me," he's telling you everybody else seemed a half-step faster than he was.

A quarterback who's had a great day might say, "The speed of the game was nice today. It slowed down for me." What he's saying is that he could see, anticipate, and perform better because, relatively speaking, everyone else seemed slower.

Its simple meaning has been bludgeoned to death by self-styled "experts," usually sportscasters, who use it for every game situation whether it applies or not. As players we adjust to it, crave it, and then become addicted to it. In the National Football League, you adjust to the speed of the game or your locker is emptied.

The huge leap in speed between college football and the NFL destroys those who can't adapt to it. I've seen rookies shocked, then relieved to be cut, glad at least for the chance to have learned that they don't belong in such hostile environs of speed, collisions, and pain.

For those who do adjust, the velocity itself becomes an integral contributor to the addictive hold of the sport. It's heady stuff to match quickness, speed, and physical violence with other addicts. The allure heightens until we cannot imagine living without it.

Nothing had prepared me for the quickness, speed, and *hostility* of this Green Bay team. Violence, physical confrontation, and outright brutality are the hallmarks of the space between the white lines of a football field. Break the huddle to run to the ball against a great defense and look into the eyes of the opposing players. They aren't smiling. We all know when the ball is snapped all hell is going to break loose. The faster, more hostile, more violent team usually wins.

The 1965 Green Bay Packers were a group of intensely focused men about to embark on a streak of three championships in succession, 1965-67. They could run and hit with such abandon, confidence, and brutal efficiency that they intimidated the league throughout their epoch-making run.

BEEP! BEEP!

Incredibly, the same year (1965) that they drafted Dick Butkus, the Bears also drafted Gale Sayers, who electrified the football world from the minute he stepped onto an NFL field.

My personal opportunity to be embarrassed by Gale came on a punt at Wrigley Field. I snapped, got held up by the nose tackle, struggled to get going, and was in the second wave of the coverage. Behind me was the fullback on our punt team, a linebacker named Tommy Joe Crutcher, who was the last line of defense—unless you count the punter, and most folks don't.

Sayers fielded the ball on the dead run, juked a couple of tacklers, and burst toward the sideline to my right. As he approached it, I could see that I had him hemmed in and that he'd either have to cut back or get bumped out of bounds.

Uh-uh. He simply accelerated, kicked into hyperdrive two decades before *Star Wars* was released, and swooshed by me. Poor Crutcher. His vision impaired by my body in front of him, he tackled me to complete our embarrassment.

It wasn't my finest NFL moment.

Ten men on that team would eventually be enshrined in the Pro Football Hall of Fame:

Coach: Vince Lombardi
QB: Bart Starr
OT/OG: Forrest Gregg
RB: Paul Hornung
RB: Jimmy Taylor

DE: Willie Davis

DT: Henry Jordan

LB: Ray Nitschke

DB: Herb Adderley

DB: Willie Wood

I believe three other members of that 1965 team also deserve to be in Canton:

OT: Bob Skoronski

OG: Jerry Kramer

LB: Dave Robinson

Small wonder that I should be anxious about my chances of making this team, of keeping up with the speed of their game.

THE FIRST PLAY of my first practice is as fresh in my memory as if it had happened last week instead of 43 years ago.

Our practices began with individual drills; progressed to combination drills in which the units competed head to head; and then moved to teamwork, the 11-on-11 scrimmages. The tempo of the team drills was always dictated by the head coach, and could vary from a pace called "thud," in which the plays are run full speed without tackling the ball carrier, to "full speed," which is self-explanatory.

All day long, I had snapped balls without incident to Bart Starr and backups Zeke Bratkowski and Dennis Claridge in drills like center-quarterback exchange. Now there would be full speed contact, but I was ready—or at least I thought I was.

We broke the huddle and I crouched over the ball, my confidence growing. I had become familiar with the snap count, a crucial factor for new players, especially the centers. I looked at the defense, made the right blocking call, and studied the feet and body language of middle linebacker Ray Nitschke and defensive tackle Henry Jordan. I heard Bart's strong commands, and I snapped the ball.

In time I would become able to predict what players were going to do on the snap of the ball by their foot placement and posture. But this time, my first real test of the speed of the game, I was at the very beginning of that learning curve.

Nitschke and Jordan? Gone. By me, just like that. I stumbled. When I looked up from my vantage point of all fours, each of them was mauling the ball carrier. So much for my newfound confidence.

The scrimmage went downhill from there. I missed a couple of snap counts, never picked up Nitschke or Jordan in time, and had my teeth rearranged and nose bloodied when I did make contact.

This was *not* Georgia Tech.

Georgia Tech football was a petting zoo.

This was the jungle.

Lombardi never chewed out rookies. He simply stared at them so that they understood that he'd caught their miscues. Starr went about his business as if he didn't notice. None of my other teammates spoke to me. There were no pats on the butt, not even from other rookies. No direct criticism, but no helpful suggestions, either. I was, for the balance of the drill, simply a pariah on my own offensive unit.

The nightmare finally ended after 90 minutes that seemed like 90 hours, and we all began to make our way back from the practice field to the locker room in Lambeau. A bunch of kids who'd been watching the workout matched us step for step, darting from player to player, asking for autographs on everything from their bike seats to the palms of their hands.

One little fellow approached me, and I was thrilled when he presented his wrinkled piece of green paper and a ballpoint pen. I scribbled something noble, signed my name really clearly and in big letters, and handed it back to him. He grinned, looked expectantly at the autograph, frowned, tossed the paper onto the ground, and ran after Herb Adderley.

My day was complete.

One of our fearless heroes was Max McGee. About five days after I got to De Pere, Coach Lombardi appeared with more than his usual fearful mien when he addressed the squad. He said, "Last night Max McGee decided to leave the dorm after curfew. He said he left to get a pizza." There were a couple of snickers, but trust me, they were muffled. Most everybody looked straight ahead, necks rigid. I glanced over and McGee smirked, looked at the floor, and waited for the Grand Inquisitor to pronounce his sentence.

Lombardi continued, "McGee, the fine will be $1,000. You should know that the next time the fine will be $2,000. And oh, by the way, if you decide to take me up on that one, call me and let me go with you. I'd love to have a slice of any

HIT THE GRASS!

Ever do a grass drill? For your sake, I hope not. But back in the day, you hadn't lived until you'd done one of Coach Lombardi's grass drills. Provided you didn't die trying.

A Vince Lombardi grass drill was, simply put, the most arduous, the most demanding, the most horrific physical test known to mankind. Think I'm exaggerating? If anything, I'm understating.

After a lengthy calisthenics session conducted by assistant coaches, Coach Lombardi would walk to the front of the squad spread out before him, give us a little half leer-half smile, and then—after a slight pause so that the dread could percolate through our bodies—start barking orders and blowing his whistle like a Marine drill sergeant on steroids.

On his first whistle we ran in place, pumping our legs and arms at a rapid pace.

On his next whistle, we fell to the grass—hence the name of the drill—catching ourselves on our hands, heads up, ending in a push-up position.

On the next whistle, we jumped up, resumed running in place, all the while knowing there would soon be another whistle, and another, and another ... for eternity.

As the minutes lengthened into hours (or so it seemed), the pace quickened (*C'mon! Work it! Faster! Faster!*) as the intervals between whistles decreased. Players started gagging and cursing and vomiting. Here and there, one or two would pass out. If they were rookies or marginal roster-fillers, they were usually cut the same day.

My *compadre* Ken Bowman and I kept count, rating the degree of difficulty by the length of rest time on the ground between whistles—usually a few seconds at best—and by the number of reps. I think our unofficial record was 78 repetitions, up and down.

Excuse me, I need to go lie down for a while.

pizza that's worth $2,000!"

Our average salary was probably $18,000, so assuming Max made $20,000, his after tax-hit from the fine was perhaps 6 percent of his net earnings for the season.

A few weeks later, I was alone in the locker room with McGee and his running mate, Paul Hornung. Rookies were not to speak unless spoken to, so I was trying to get dressed and get out without being noticed. But they were getting on each other pretty good, and the subject was religion, so I listened close. Both were Catholics, and they were having a serious debate about sin and forgiveness.

"Listen, Max," said Paul, "you are one sorry SOB!"

"Thanks, pal," countered Max. "What does that make you?"

Paul blasted back, "You run around chasing women, you drink like a sponge, you smoke cigarettes, you cuss worse than Lombardi, and you never go to confession!"

Max absorbed that, then responded, "Lets see, I do all those things, absolutely right, and I enjoy them. Now I get a damn sermon from a hypocrite who does exactly the same things? Just what I need, preaching from you. Every time you walk into a church it ought to fall down on your sorry head. Thanks so much."

Paul was ready. "You don't understand the system. I go out, have fun, and then go to confession and mass. Don't you see? I love to sin, God loves to forgive sin. Pretty good deal, don't you think?"

The crux of the matter was that Hornung wanted McGee to be clear that confession was the only way. McGee was already quite clear that hypocrisy was worse than no confession at all. And on the debate raged, neither side willing to give an inch.

Hornung, who had befriended me from the beginning of the year, spotted me eavesdropping. He had discovered my interest in theology and that I had been active in the Fellowship for Christian Athletes. So he gave me what he thought was a perfect nickname. One that I hated.

"Hey, Elmer Gantry!" he shouted, "Get over here! You're our resident theologian around here. Solve this for us"

"Don't call me Elmer Gantry," I begged. "Please."

He fixed me with a stare and said, "Elmer, listen up, here it is in a nutshell. Is it or is it not true that God forgives sinners who confess their sins? I mean, I know I do a lot of stuff, but I always go to confession, so I'm forgiven, right? And Max here, he does the same stuff and never even feels guilty, and doesn't go close to a church. He's doomed, I mean, really, he's going to hell, don't you think? Come on, Elmer, answer this for us."

I gave it one more shot. "Stop calling me Elmer Gantry, and I'll try."

Later on, I would realize that it was something of an honor for a veteran star to have thought enough of me to give me a nickname. At the time, though, solid Methodist that I was, I was appalled at being saddled with the name of a detestable fictional caricature.

"Just answer the damned question, will you?" Paul persisted.

Cornered, I pulled myself up to my full ecclesiastical height, moved between the two legends, eyeballed each evenly, and spoke from deep in my diaphragm, much like I imagined Moses must have spoken to the sinful children of Israel.

"Now Paul," I said, "listen up. This isn't between you and me. It's not between Max and me. It's not even between you and Max. You know very well who to address with a problem like this."

I was so proud of myself for just a second, until McGee piped up. "Oh, so you want to bring Vince into this thing, too?"

MAX DIED IN October 2007 at the age of 75 when he fell while clearing leaves from the roof of his home in Minneapolis. On hearing the news, Paul said simply, "I just lost my best friend."

If there were a Hall of Fame for free spirits, Max would be in it. And he was also a heckuva fine football player for a dozen years in the NFL.

Trivia buffs already know that Max McGee caught the first touchdown pass and scored the first points in Super Bowl history in 1967—a game that he thought he'd be watching from the sideline. Max hadn't expected to play because he'd spent the previous night partying and had stayed out well past team curfew.

But Boyd Dowler separated a shoulder in the early going and Lombardi had no choice but to send in McGee. Max had to borrow a helmet because he'd left his in the locker room. A few plays later, he caught a pass from Bart and ran 37 yards to score. He ended up catching seven passes and scoring twice.

"When it's third-and-10," Max told reporters after the game, "you can take the milk drinkers and I'll take the whiskey drinkers every time."

Jerry Kramer played 11 seasons on the Packers with McGee, and he said after his friend's death that Max's humor and irreverence managed to defuse tension on a team run by Lombardi's iron hand. "When everyone else was looking down at their feet wondering what to do when Lombardi went off, Max would come up with something to get a laugh out of the room."

KEN BOWMAN DISLOCATED his shoulder in the fourth exhibition game of the 1966 season and I became the starting center on the best team in the NFL.

Thrilling? Sure.

Scary? More than I could possibly have imagined.

To be on the same line with Jerry Kramer, Fuzzy Thurston, Forrest Gregg, and Bob Skoronski was plenty exciting, at least until the blocking grades were posted every week on Tuesday morning. Then it became plenty humbling.

As we approached our second meeting with the Lions on October 23, right guard Jerry Kramer came to me with a plan.

Alex Karras is a great pass rusher and gives everybody fits, but he's got lousy vision and I have an idea. On certain pass plays, you block back on him and he'll read trap. I'll drop and check your responsibility on the middle linebacker. Karras will either spin or try to cross your face, and by the time he figures out what's going on, the ball will be in the air. Ray [offensive line coach Ray Wietecha] thinks it's worth trying.

We tried it, and it worked. Karras spent at least some of the afternoon running in circles, Bart threw for a couple of scores, and we clobbered the Lions 31-7.

After the game, reporters in the locker room complimented Jerry for his excellent pass protection on the great pass rusher, Alex Karras. Jerry responded that the credit should really go to young center Bill Curry, who had helped a great deal. Jerry went on to say nice things about my improvement in just the four weeks I'd been on the job.

On Tuesday in our team meeting, just before getting things under way, Coach Lombardi looked squarely at Jerry and said, "Kramer, *I* will be the judge of who has improved around here. Do you understand? If I need any help in evaluating players, I'll let you know."

Jerry nodded.

Lombardi never looked at me nor mentioned my name.

That's okay—Jerry had noticed.

THE MOST MEMORABLE halftime speech I ever heard from Vince Lombardi—or from anyone else, for that matter—consisted of exactly seven words.

He uttered them on Sunday, October 17, 1965, in the visitors' locker room in the old Tiger Stadium in Detroit, at the midpoint of our first game that season against the Lions.

Packers-Lions was—is—one of the NFL's great rivalries. Two Midwestern teams with rich traditions and reputations for tough, hard-nosed football, Green Bay and Detroit seemed to wear those reps on their sleeves when they went head-to-head. The Packers held a big edge in the mid-1960s—7-1-3 from 1963 through 1967—but those three ties tell the tale. Our games against the Lions were usually a lot tighter and tougher than the final scores would indicate.

The Lions jumped on us early, rushed Bart unmercifully, knocked the ball loose a couple of times, and dominated the first half. We couldn't block Alex Karras, Roger Brown, or their swarming linebackers. We couldn't run against them. And, with the pressure he was getting, Bart couldn't throw against them. As a fitting conclusion to two quarters of punishment, Lions safety Wayne Rasmussen picked off a Starr pass and ran it 50 yards into the end zone to make the score 21-3 with five seconds left on the first half clock.

My place on the sideline was always next to Coach Lombardi when kicking situations were imminent, so I waited for him to signal the kickoff return unit onto the field for the final play of the half. We'd receive the kick and, barring a runback for a TD, head into our locker room with an 18-point deficit to make up.

One eccentricity of the older combination baseball/football fields was that they often had the home team and visitors' benches on the same sideline. As the teams jogged on and off, there was a natural crossover between units, and I noticed one of the Lion players approaching us on the way to his bench. As he walked past us, he caught Coach's attention and asked, "How'd you like that, Big Guy?"

Lombardi's reaction?

He just smiled.

We didn't see Coach at all during the halftime break. We'd been 4-0 coming in, we were big favorites, and here we were getting out butts kicked all over the field. You'd think that any coach in his right mind would storm in, take names and kick ass, and, after a much-deserved reaming, tick off the things we had to do better the second half. Maybe most, but not a coach with Vince Lombardi's mind.

We all sat there, not looking at each other. Not saying anything. What was there to say? We were down 21-3 to a team that, talent-wise, didn't belong on the same field with us.

Meanwhile, the energy built.

There were 10 embarrassed future Hall of Fame players in the room, and the energy built.

There was a 1965 World Championship team in the room, and the energy built.

But there was no Coach Lombardi in the room—and the energy built.

Halftime in the National Football League is only 12 minutes, but on that day in Detroit, down 21-3, it felt more like 12 hours.

Then, with only seconds before a rap on the locker room door by one of the refs would tell us it was time to head out and get our butts kicked for another 30 minutes, Coach appeared. He walked slowly to the center of the room, looked around to make sure he had everybody's undivided attention, and gave us his pep talk:

"Men, we are the Green Bay Packers."

That was it. He was done. And after giving us one last, sweeping look, he walked briskly and purposefully to the door.

Seven words.

Men, we are the Green Bay Packers.

Final score: Packers 31, Lions 21.

MY SECOND YEAR as a Packer, 1966, was marked by one major high and one major low.

1. At the beginning of the season, I was named starting center.

2. At the end of the season, I was unceremoniously dropped from the team.

Shortly after the end of the 1966 season, Coach Lombardi called me and said he had some sad news. He told me that the new NFL franchise, the New Orleans Saints, had claimed me in the expansion draft.

Every existing team (except for the Falcons, an expansion team the year before) froze 29 players on its 40-man roster. The other 11 were left unprotected. The Saints chose one unprotected player from each of the 14 teams. Then, each of the 14 teams put two additional players on the protected list, leaving eight unprotected. From this list, the Saints chose two more. If one was picked, the team that lost him got to pull two guys back. And so it went until the Saints had a core 42-man roster going into the 1967 draft.

Coach also put Hornung on the unprotected list. It was a calculated risk. Paul had been hurt much of the year, and I think Lombardi reasoned that he wouldn't be picked. Coach was very upset when the Saints took him; Paul had been like a son to him. After spending his entire pro career as a Packer, Paul went to New Orleans, but he had such severe neck and shoulder injuries that he never played a down for them. He did stay on to do their broadcasts for a few years.

I couldn't believe it. From starting center in the first NFL-AFL Championship game—it didn't get official designation as Super Bowl I until two years later—to an expansion team? From the top of the heap to rock bottom, just like that?

I was devastated. And furious.

But before I could come down off the ceiling to be measured for a New Orleans Saints jersey ...

... I WAS A BALTIMORE COLT.

You'll hear how that came about a little bit later, but right now let's flash forward to January 6-12, 1969—Super Bowl Week in Miami.

Then as now, the week leading up to the Super Bowl between the Baltimore Colts (NFL) and the New York Jets (AFL) was a huge media circus, especially since this was the first AFL-NFL title game to be called "Super Bowl."

Not surprisingly, I guess, as the only player on the Colts

or the Jets to have played in a previous Super Bowl—the AFL-NFL Championship Game of January 15, 1967, retroactively dubbed Super Bowl I—I received a fair amount of attention from the press.

But as the only player on either side to have played for both Vince Lombardi (whose Packers had won Super Bowls I and II) and Baltimore coach Don Shula (whose Colts were heavily favored in III), I received a whole lot more.

Lombardi and Shula.

Shula and Lombardi.

From the minute we unpacked our bags, reporters bombarded me with questions about their different personalities, their different philosophies, their different coaching styles.

Like an idiot, I answered them.

After a long interview, for example, a reporter for *The New York Times* reported after interviewing me that "Curry does not have a pleasant memory of ... any part of his two-year association with the Green Bay team. The problem was simple—Vince Lombardi."

Yep, that's about right.

"He coached through fear," I was quoted (accurately) as saying. "Most of the Packers were afraid of him, of his scoldings, and of his sarcasm. It's a form of motivation that works for some people. But it didn't work for me."

And I wasn't done.

"Our coach [Don Shula] believes football can be fun," I said. "Don coaches with enthusiasm rather than fear. Oh, sure, he works us. The Colts work harder—have more contact in practices—than the Packers."

Take that, Mr. Block of Granite.

"The Colts have a kind of swashbuckling, hell-for-leather spirit. We're not cautious. We feel if we make a mistake—blow an assignment—the best thing to do is to go and hit somebody anyway. We know we're not going to get chewed out by the coaches."

And how, exactly, did I react to that atmosphere back in Vince Lombard's Green Bay?

"It got so bad I couldn't sleep [before a game], thinking about what kind of mistake I'd make the next day," I said. (Note: not "whether" I'd make a mistake but "what kind" it would be.) "My wife, Carolyn, had to nurse me through the season, and I mean that. At the end I was close to being a basket case."

Any more questions, guys?

The big, bold headline in the January 8, 1969 edition of *The New York Times:* LOMBARDI IS NOT CURRY'S DISH.

And I couldn't even claim to have been misquoted.

A YEAR OR so after Super Bowl III, I bumped into Paul Hornung in New Orleans. He was positively livid about the little speech I had made to the press before the game.

"You had no right to say those things about the Old Man," was his message, delivered with a side of expletives. "No bleeping right!"

For all his shenanigans, Paul loved Coach Lombardi, revered him as a father figure. I countered that not only did I have the right, but the obligation to expose Lombardi's abusive behavior for the world to see. (Thinking back, I must have been going through a high-and-mighty period in my life.) We went back and forth for a while until Paul blurted out that Coach's mother had read my comments in New York, and that they had made her weep.

"And still," Paul said, "if the Old Man saw you right now, he'd greet you like a long lost son."

I lashed back that if the Old Man saw me now, he'd treat me like dirt, just like he had when he screamed profanity in my face, when he humiliated us all in film sessions, or when he once tested my concussion with Ray Nitschke's forearm rather than a medical exam. (More about that in Chapter 6.)

No, I insisted, the Old Man would never be kind to me or anyone else. He was constitutionally incapable of kindness toward his players.

Less than a month later, I was invited to the President's Prayer Breakfast in Washington, D.C. Coach Lombardi had been lured out of retirement to coach the Redskins, and as I started up a narrow staircase I glanced up and there he stood. There was no polite escape route, so I took a deep breath and held out my hand. Vince Lombardi took my hand warmly and greeted me ... like a long lost son.

I felt like I was maybe an inch high. As I struggled for control, he smiled and said, "Bill, maybe you and I need to get together and talk."

A few months later, Coach Lombardi was diagnosed with terminal cancer.

IN THE SUMMER of 1970, there was a lockout by the team owners and I was asked by the NFL Players' Association to man the phones in Washington for a few days. While there, I got a call from former Packers wide receiver Bob Long, who had become a good friend.

Long had been in a terrible automobile accident when he was with the Atlanta Falcons in 1968 and nearly died. As he recovered, Coach Lombardi signed him to come play in Washington, provided therapy and personal motivation for Bob's recovery, and then got him back onto the field in the 1969 season. I hadn't learned of this until much later, when Bob and I became friends. Bob got right to the point: "You and I are going to see Coach at Georgetown Hospital today."

I said I didn't know if I could handle that, and that I was certain Lombardi wouldn't want me coming around at a time like this. "Look, Coach and I have had our differences," I said, "and this isn't an appropriate time to try to deal with that stuff."

Long wouldn't take no for an answer. "Listen Bill, we are going by the church, we are going to light some candles for Vince Lombardi, and we are going to that hospital. I'll pick you up in an hour."

All my bitterness and self-doubt welled up again. Could I have gotten it wrong? How would he greet me this time? What about Marie Lombardi, Vince's wife? That dear lady didn't deserve any of this. Why hadn't I thought of her and the Lombardi family before I shot my mouth off the year before at the Super Bowl?

So we drove by the church and lit the candles. Bob is

Catholic and had to explain the significance of the candles to the Methodist he had in tow.

He also spoke of his devotion to Coach Lombardi, and all I could remember was the day he had been injured at a Packer practice and had writhed on the ground for more than the Lombardi-approved time for responding to pain. In the team meeting Lombardi had stopped the tape, a sporadically used new toy in those days, and said, "Bob Long, the next time you put on a performance like that one, wallowing around on the ground like you are dying, will be your last day as a Green Bay Packer. Do you understand?"

I had been horrified at the time. Since it was one of the moments I remembered most vividly about what I perceived to be Lombardi's cruelty, I asked Bob about it on our way to that hospital.

Bob smiled and said, "He was right. I wasn't very tough. I had to grow up, and that's what he's really all about. When I was nearly killed and had all those broken bones, I lay in the hospital and thought about him. I certainly didn't expect to play football again, but I was grateful he'd been my coach so that I could survive that ordeal with courage. When I got out and started recovering, he not only got in touch, but he gave me a chance to play again. Bill, the guy literally redeemed me. I owe him."

It was my turn to do some grimacing as I grappled with my anxiety. I had been so certain of myself when I had criticized him. But I had made him into a monster without studying his motives or the outcomes of his involvement off the field in lives like Bob Long's.

I was quiet for the rest of the ride.

When we stepped off the elevator at the hospital, there stood Marie Lombardi, as lovely as ever, always perfectly dressed and groomed. There were fatigue lines around her eyes, but she relaxed and smiled when she saw us. Standing next to her was Redskins quarterback Sonny Jurgensen, who would play six of his 11 NFL seasons with the Redskins on his way to the Hall of Fame.

The four of us chatted briefly, and then Marie looked me in the eye. "Now we'll go in and see Vin."

For some reason, it touched me to hear her use the diminutive of his name. I had never thought of him as anything but "Coach" or "Coach Lombardi," and I had never heard anyone call him "Vin."

I have played in Super Bowls. I have made speeches to audiences of thousands. I have coached games in which my future was on the line. I have testified in courts of law and before congressional sub-committees. On such occasions, I have often experienced stage fright, but never anything like this. I have never been more nervous than at the moment we walked into that room.

I must have been in a sort of shock because I can't remember whether Sonny or Bob went in with me. The only person I recall for sure was Marie. She stood to my right and slightly behind me as we approached the bed. She may have nudged me to move closer because somehow I seem to have floated to within a couple of feet of Vince Lombardi. I could hardly breathe.

He was in a state I had never seen him in before: helpless, vulnerable, diminished, and no longer larger than life. He was gray and his body was emaciated. There were tubes protruding from his right arm. It was hard to believe this shell of a human being was Vince Lombardi.

There were an awkward few seconds while I struggled to gather myself. I'm an extremely emotional person, and I never know when I'll be overwhelmed from within. I make no apology about being emotional, but I don't like the fact that I can't talk when I'm in that condition.

There I stood, the penitent sinner before the dying hero.

The great man did as he had always done. He did what I hope to do when I come to my final hours.

He took charge.

He reached me in the only way possible. He held out his left hand. I took it in mine and found the grip was firm, firmer than the right one when I first shook hands with him in the summer of 1965.

His eyes were clear, riveted on mine, and they were warm.

We waited.

At length I managed, "Coach, I have some things to say to you. All those things that you may have read that I said about you last year at the Super Bowl, I have to admit that at the time I said them I was still so mad at you. I was wrong, and I want to apologize. I want you to know that you have meant a great deal to my life."

His eyes didn't waver as he squeezed my hand.

He spoke, and the famous voice was still powerful. "You can mean a great deal to my life if you will pray for me."

My lips began to quiver. "Coach," I responded, "I will do that. I promise."

I kept that promise.

Coach Lombardi forced me against my will to grow up and be a man. He took me places I simply could not have gone without him. I fought him every step of the way, but he was steadfast and confident that his path was the correct path to victory.

He was right.

Vincent Thomas Lombardi died on September 3, 1970, less than two months after I said goodbye.

*The gracious gentleman from Montgomery,
Alabama, took no guff from Lombardi or
anybody else. And he always gave plenty
of himself—still does—to fans, friends,
and perfect strangers. You've got to
love that combo in a man.*

4

BART STARR
LEADER

The Packer practice fields are located about a quarter of a mile from the Lambeau Field locker room. Morning and afternoon during preseason training camp, we'd get on our gear, walk down a gentle grade through the stadium parking lot, across Oneida Street, and enter the practice field through a chain-link fence that surrounded it.

Security? Didn't exist. Our sessions were always open to the public. Especially on Friday afternoons and Saturdays, people gathered around the fence and watched us go through our drills. (Somewhere, Bill Belichick is having palpitations at the mere thought.) As a practice session neared its end, kids would cluster around the exit gate waiting for us to leave. Then, as we began to file out for our return to the locker room, they'd gang around us, asking for autographs or just hanging close to their heroes.

Something like this scene was probably repeated at every camp in the NFL, but Green Bay had a special twist: free bike rides, just for the asking.

I don't know when the Packer Bike Tradition began, but it was in full bloom when I was there. Kids would seek out star players and try to get them to ride their bikes back up the hill to the locker room. Most of the time, the kids found a lot of takers, and you'd have this strange caravan making its way across the otherwise empty parking lot. The players rode, slowly, while the kids jogged alongside, carrying headgears and jabbering every step of the way. Guys like Willie Wood and Paul Hornung were crowd favorites and seemed to enjoy the relationships.

Once we got back to the locker room at the stadium, though, I noticed that some of the veteran players showered and dressed as fast as they could and sneaked out the back door of the building and onto the busses to avoid the autograph seekers, who were mostly young kids. I thought that was a little strange, considering that just minutes before there had been this warm community thing going. I didn't learn until my second year that those guys wanted to get back to our dorm as fast as possible so they could hit the De Pere bars before dinner. They called their daily bar forays The Five O'clock Club, in honor of Vince's daily get-togethers with the press, which took place at the same hour and bore the same name.

The backdoor departure strategy worked early on, when there were 80-plus players in camp and two buses were needed to get everybody back to the dorm. Catch that first bus and you could be back in De Pere before the second bus had loaded the last straggler.

But near the end of camp, when cuts had dramatically reduced our numbers, one bus could accommodate everybody—and one person invariably delayed its departure. Everybody would be on board save that one guy, and there'd be rumblings from first one, then another Five O'Clock Clubber, and then exasperated shouts out the window, "C'mon, Bart! Hurry up! Let's go!"

The exhortations fell on deaf ears. Our starting quarterback, our future Hall of Famer, our future MVP of Super Bowls I and II and five-time world champion, Mr. Bart Starr, had business to attend to.

Every afternoon after practice, Bart would walk straight out of the main entrance to the locker room and stride directly up to the jostling, raucous crowd of kids and more than a few grownups. "Don't push!" he'd shout. "Stop shoving and make a line. Let's help each other here. Be patient, because I'll sign for every single one of you."

After a stunned silence there would be instant order. It was as if a military command had been barked from a public address system. Kids beamed, youth camp directors and parents looked at each other and nodded, and I sat in some more awe on the bus. Bart Starr asked every young fan his or her name, took their tiny pieces of paper or pictures, and carefully signed his famous signature. No kid ever walked away without glancing over his shoulder to get one more look at the famous man who had made him feel so special.

Out in the bus, especially on Friday afternoons and Saturdays, that led to a chorus of groans, even from those of us who weren't planning on any Five O'Clock Club activity but were mighty interested in getting prone in our bunks for a little pre-dinner shuteye.

SINCE BART HAD been the first veteran to befriend me, I thought for sure he would console me when I had begun so poorly. I waited for his approach on bus ride after bus ride.

On the practice field our mechanics of exchanging the ball got progressively better, but I just couldn't block those great players when we scrimmaged. The fact that no one else on the face of the earth could block Ray Nitschke and Henry Jordan never occurred to me at the time. I thought it was just me. That's how deep my insecurity was.

While Bart continued to be unfailing in his courtesy, he maintained an unmistakable distance between us. In my pronounced depression I became bitter. I vacillated between genuine appreciation and absurd disdain. I remember thinking, "If he doesn't want to be my buddy, why in the world did he invite me to go to church with him? He's just another one of those superstars who acts friendly at first and then dumps regular people when they're in trouble."

That attitude, in case you haven't already guessed, was a product of my off-the-charts rookie insecurity. My "reasoning" went something like this: if Bart Starr wouldn't take time to diagnose and fulfill all my emotional needs, he must be a bad guy.

Seemed to make sense at the time.

At Georgia Tech, veteran quarterback Stan Gann had taken to encouraging me early on by making up a chant, which he repeated loudly any time I seemed down. As we passed one another on the way to practice he would sing out, "I don't worrah, I'm Bill Currah!" Others had picked it up until it became a regular mantra from my friends. On rough days when I was struggling, a loud proclamation might ring out, "Currah! Currah! Don't worrah, I'm Currah!"

None of that from Bart. Why could he not provide what I needed? Why couldn't he give me a little boost?

I was becoming a whiner. I never asked Bart about it, but the fact that I became so clingy and dependent was reason enough to avoid me.

Most whiners get cut.

Starr did take notice of me a couple of weeks into camp on one of our daily bus rides between Lambeau Field and De Pere. I had struck up a conversation with another SEC player about Charlie Bradshaw, the Kentucky coach. The player scuttlebutt about Bradshaw had been scathing in its denunciation of his methods. Reputedly more brutal and confrontational even than Vince Lombardi, Charlie allegedly drove his players beyond exhaustion until they couldn't stand up. My SEC compatriot and I were swapping tales, trading second-hand stories, laughing, and dealing in the worst kind of gossip.

"Charlie Bradshaw is a great football coach," a large voice rang out from just behind us. "I don't want to hear another word about him from you guys. He coached me in high school. No one here rips him, understand?"

Did we understand? Yes, we did. Yes, *sir.*

"Just remember," he said, "be respectful of our coaches. Be respectful all the time."

THE ONLY CONSISTENTLY friendly, approachable face on the entire team belonged to my cohort at center, veteran Ken Bowman. He usually sat with me on the bus rides, and he could always make me laugh despite myself. His fun and infectious wit were like a tonic. And in a continuing display of unselfishness, he diagnosed a significant physical part of my problem.

"Do you realize why you're losing vision on the defenders at the snap of the ball?" he asked.

"I'm *what*?" I practically shouted. "How did you know that?"

He smiled, bobbed his head, and pointed it down. "That's where you're looking. When you pull the ball up, you duck your head. It's a natural thing to do, but it's a bad habit. I used to do it, and sometimes still do. When we watch the films of last season, you'll see the times I fell into it. It just kills your start, and you'll never block someone like Henry Jordan when you do it. He's just too fast."

"What do I do?" I asked, relief fighting with desperation for control of my voice. "Can you help me?"

"Yep," he said, "you've come to the right place. Just beg Coach Bowman and he'll help you take his job!"

Later we worked together on the mechanics of my snap, the way I positioned the ball, the pendulum swing of my arm, and the necessity of holding my head up and motionless as the ball smacked into the quarterback's hands. I'd been hiking a football for a solid decade at this point, and I'd never been aware of a habit that could have ended my career before it got started.

Snapping the ball correctly demands a difficult, even unnatural posture. The fact that I executed the move so many thousands of times over the years is one reason my neck aches every time I turn my head today. If this were a television commercial, we would be obligated to add the phrase, Do Not Attempt This at Home.

THE PRECIOUS MOMENTS of the day fell between the morning and afternoon practices, which were critical for more than the obvious: food and rest. I could never eat much because of dehydration, so I quickly retreated to the sanctuary of my bare room to stare at the wall. The chill in the air was just wrong. While I was happy we didn't have the southern humidity, at least it would have been familiar. The incessant wind and overcast skies made me think of black and white World War I movies. The vacant campus was desolate, empty except for our 50 odd souls.

I began to appreciate Carolyn's insistence on flowers and art. I missed her desperately. Even after she got to town, we weren't allowed to live together until camp broke. Cohabitation evidently wasn't appropriate for a band of adult males about to hit the practice field as Green Bay Packers.

What the hell was wrong with me? Here I was with the opportunity most guys would sell their soul for, and I was virtually frozen in self-pity and homesickness. I knew I was sinking into a personal hell, thinking of myself as a sort of tragic figure.

But Coach Lombardi's blaring, repeated admonition to "Suck up your guts!" was beginning to sink in. Every time I did that, every time I quashed my self-pity and sucked up my guts, I knew I was improving the odds that I would do the right thing: stay the course.

That was the No. 1 theme of training camp with the Green Bay Packers: stay the course. Do that and there was almost no limit to what inner strength you would find, what resources you would tap, what heights you could achieve.

You either got that message or you were sent packing.

For us rookies, Lombardi's fire, profanity, and sheer vocal volume dominated our every minute, waking and sleeping. We all agreed that even our toughest college coaches had never approached Lombardi's intensity, nor matched his capacity to flay all-pro egos as if they were tissue paper. Those of us who survived the trial by fire and returned the next year would learn only then that he was intentionally *easy* on rookies.

That's why, when somebody happened to mention that Lombardi went to church every day, I laughed out loud. C'mon, no real Christian ever talked like this guy! At least none that I'd ever met growing up in the WASPy South. How could anybody go to mass every day and talk like that?

Where (and when) I grew up, Catholics were almost as suspect as Yankees, and this guy was both. He simply confirmed the prejudices I had inherited from my forefathers. For my part, I guess I must have glossed over the admonition in the Book of Matthew, "Judge not lest ye be judged."

There was only one person to share my concern with: Bart Starr. By now—we were nearing the end of training camp—my early negative vibe about him (born of me looking for a security blanket and him not offering one) had given way to an appreciation of what a thoughtful, caring, and complex person he is.

On the way back to the dorm from dinner one night, I cornered Bart and laid it out bluntly. "Bart, I really worry about Coach Lombardi. I mean, do you think he's a practicing Christian the way he claims he is? All that profanity, screaming, and humiliating folks ... would a real Christian do all that stuff? And somebody told me he goes to church every day! Could it possibly be?"

"Absolutely," said Bart. "He goes to mass every single morning, and he's very serious about his faith. But there's one thing you have to know. After you've worked under him for a while, you're going realize this man *needs* to go to church every day!"

FOR AN EXHIBITION game on the road against the Browns in Cleveland's Municipal Stadium, which held 81,000 and change, there wasn't an empty seat in the house. One big reason was that people were getting two games for the price of one. That's right—a double header, Giants vs. Lions in the opener and Packers vs. Browns in the nightcap. (Strange as it may seem today, the NFL had to resort to that sort of thing back then to draw fans.)

My role was clearly defined. I would play on all special teams; snap for punts, points after, and field goals; study Ken Bowman playing center; and maybe take a few snaps on offense late in the game.

The game rocked back and forth uneventfully until late in the second quarter, when our offense got a drive going, my signal to go on standby alert. Once we got into field goal range, I was to go to a location next to Coach Lombardi. If he decided to kick, that would be my cue. As we went into a huddle on third down at the Cleveland 4, I got as loose as I could while trying to fight off the hoard of butterflies trying to elevate me. Whatever happened on the next play, I was going in.

Then Bart did something he *never* did: he was late breaking the huddle, and we were hit with a delay penalty. Since he called all our plays, there was no complex system of communication from the sideline to clutter things. That made the delay all the more inexcusable.

As if on cue, Lombardi exploded, "What the hell is going on out there? What the *hell!*"

As usual, his timing was perfect. Coach's vocal tantrums seemed to coincide with quiet moments; he wanted the guys on the field to hear him. The relative quiet allowed his bellow to carry all the way out to the Browns' goal line.

I took a few steps away from our irate boss as the refs re-set the scrimmage line—third and 9—and glanced out at Bart. It was evident that he was not pleased by what he'd just heard. He stood apart from the newly formed huddle and glared over at his coach for several precious seconds. A thought flashed through my mind: was he going to incur a *second* penalty?

Then Bart stepped deliberately back into the huddle, called a play, broke the huddle, lined up behind Bowman, barked out the signals, took the snap, dropped back quickly, and threw a touchdown pass to Boyd Dowler.

"Whew...!" Our entire sideline exhaled a sigh of relief.

All was well, I figured, so I looked to Coach for his nod to the PAT unit, got it, and started to trot out onto the field. Fifteen yards out I stopped dead in my tracks because here came Bart, our holder on PATs, running full steam toward me. As he drew even with me, Bart stopped, glared directly into Vince Lombardi's eyes, and at the top of his lungs let loose a string of profanity that would have been the envy of a street thug.

Pausing like an actor on a Broadway stage just before delivering the curtain line, he stared down the shocked coach for a few seconds, then nodded to me, turned on his heel, and trotted back out to set up for the PAT.

To the raw rookie, to the great coach, to everyone on our bench, the message was unmistakable: there would be *one* master and commander of the Green Bay Packers between those white lines.

Back out to the business at hand, Bart set up exactly six yards, two feet behind me, took a knee, extended his right hand as my target, stationed his left as the kicker's mark, called the signals, took my snap, placed the ball (laces facing out) for kicker Don Chandler, and watched the kick sail through the uprights. As I started making my way to midfield where my next assignment was to bust the Cleveland wedge on the ensuing kickoff, I watched as No. 15 trotted right past our domineering coach to the bench.

Neither offered so much as a glance or a word to the other.

None was needed.

They had already made their points with perfect clarity.

In the wee hours of the next morning, on the drive back in from the Green Bay airport, I tried to get Bart to talk about the previous night's confrontation. He didn't smile or try to laugh it off, as I halfway thought he might have. He just looked at me and shook his head. No.

Looking back, I believe—no, I *know*—that the reason the Starr-Lombardi relationship worked so well for so long is that Vince Lombardi, with all his well-documented virtuosity in the art of intimidation, could only respect those with the inner strength *not* to be intimidated by him. He knew he needed that strength to win.

A REAL LEADER understands when and how to impose his will.

Coach Lombardi was the best I have ever seen at sniffing out moments when discipline might be slipping. He warned us, he *promised* us, that he intended to use fear as a tool if he sensed complacency or felt us losing concentration on details, and then he *kept his promises.*

The man was alert for tiny errors, things most coaches miss. For example, an offensive tackle who steps with the wrong foot can get ball carriers blown up in the backfield. Lombardi never missed those things, and used them to shock us into focus. We bought into his eerie ability to see everything at once. Each guy had a different way to process the tension, but it was a force in every mind.

Coach Lombardi's most powerful tirades will last forever in the collective consciousness of his Green Bay teams. I was a Packer for only two years, ordinarily too brief a time to learn much about a team's culture. But there was nothing ordinary about the personality in charge of the Packers, so the learning curve was shortened—considerably.

In a room of 40 alpha males, the dominant one carried the day. He could do that through the sheer force of his words and will. He was at his most powerful when we played sloppy ball and still managed to win. After one such performance against the Steelers in a 1966 exhibition game, he went with his favorite metaphor, The Whip.

You guys only understand one thing! You don't have the guts to stay after this task on your own! You only understand the whip! And by God, I will bring that whip and drive you every day if necessary! I wish to hell I didn't have to do it this way, I wish I didn't have to go to the whip, but you give me no choice!

He challenged our motives for being on the team. Standing face to face with us in his white, insulated V-neck shirt, his khaki coaching pants, and his black riffle-soled shoes, he started by speaking evenly, "You guys don't care. You don't want to do what's required to win the right way. You aren't responsible enough to take on your share. Why, right here in this room there is only one man who publicly took the blame for the poor performance. Willie Davis is the one leader we have here. He's the only one who told the truth to the press and the public!"

But before he could continue, a voice boomed out from the back of the room. "That's not true!" barked Bart Starr. "If you're going to say stuff like that, get it right."

You could have heard the proverbial pin drop.

"I *said* I made mistakes," Bart went on. "I *admitted* them when reporters asked me questions about the game. I took *full responsibility* for my poor play. So get it right."

The oxygen was sucked out of the room as we waited for the counter, the next eruption. And here was the magic: it never came. The unthinkable happened. Lombardi backed down. Even more, he was actually subdued the remainder of the day.

By Wednesday's practice he was back with his whip. "You guys have no fire, no enthusiasm! You practice like washerwomen!" he shouted at the top of his lungs. I'd heard rougher language in the eighth grade, but when *he* screamed the insult it felt like a kick in the groin. "Washerwomen, I tell you!"

Ken Bowman lurked behind the huddle to mutter to me, "Washerwoman Bill, that's who you are! You ain't nuthin' but a damn washerwoman!" His Lee Marvin chuckle punctuated the attempt at comic relief. I didn't laugh.

Other coaches could have said more or less the same thing and be ignored. You couldn't ignore this guy. There was something about the voice, something about the intensity that hit you right in the gut. Every player was shaken, even the veteran All-Pros. I remember future Hall of Fame defensive end Willie Davis saying he felt like Vince had *hit* him, *stunned* him when the wrath was turned in his direction.

During practice once, a petrified rookie running back named Allen Jacobs was so nervous that he ran over his blocker, Jerry Kramer, missing a perfect running lane.

"Jacobs! Jacobs!" an all-too-familiar voice boomed out. "You are a stupid son of a bitch!" (That's a notch up from washerwoman, I suppose. Or below. I'm not sure which.)

The crestfallen Jacobs, standing with head bowed behind the huddle and barely able to fight back the tears, was approached by the still-seething Lombardi. More of the same? No. Coach as a rule didn't like to jump on rookies, remember? After circling Allen a couple of times, Lombardi said in a conciliatory, "Jacobs, sorry I called you a son of a bitch. [Pause.] But you are stupid!"

The sloppy practice session earned us all a little lecture. "You have to hate your opponents! *Hate them!* Show no mercy! Hell, here we are with this great opportunity to be Champions of the World, and you don't care enough to learn the audibles or step with the right foot. You look like a bunch of cattle out heah! You don't hate enough!"

Then he cranked up the volume. "Let me tell you something, gentlemen! If you don't show me by Thursday that you hate the Colts to my satisfaction, I personally *guarantee* that you will hate me so much by Sunday you will want to kill those guys across from you!"

On the rare occasions we lost, another surprise was in store. I assumed he would attack us and that I would then spend countless sleepless nights agonizing over my errors. But when we got beat, Coach was unfailing in his kindness, patience, and forbearance. Granted, it happened very seldom in my time there, but I was told that he handled things similarly even when there were more than a couple of losses.

The 1967 season, his last as the coach of the Packers, is an example. I was no longer with the team, but Bart says Coach took the losses in stride. The Packers had a 9-4-1 record that wasn't really as good as it looked, but was good enough to get them into the playoffs. They then fought their way to their third consecutive World Championship. I don't think the third title would have happened if Lombardi hadn't been so adept at handling the losses.

Obviously as much a genius at motivation as he was at intimidation, Vince Lombardi was unmatched in the force of his personality, in his belief in his system, in his attention to detail. But he also knew when and how to back off, and when to accept a small rebuke in order to prevent big mutinies.

Starr was one of the tiny group of men who could, and did, take Vince Lombardi on before his team. Deep down, Coach knew it would strengthen the team if he permitted one of its most respected members to take a principled stand against him—and not be punished for it.

On the field, after all, it was Bart they had to rally around, not the guy in civvies on the sideline.

WHEN I VISITED with Bart while doing some research for this book in 2006, he was uneasy when I asked him about his confrontations with Coach. Bart and I have fundamental differences in what we remember. He says he only went after coach that one time in front of the team. I remember seeing him do it twice, and I was only there two years! When I persisted—well, begged—he finally smiled and agreed to get into it.

I asked how he managed to be so bold, regardless, of whether it was one time, twice, or twenty times? Where did that come from, given that it seemed so out of character for the Bart Starr I knew?

Then, for the only time in all our years, he opened up about his father, Ben Starr.

> My younger brother, Hilton, had a tougher, more outgoing personality than I did. I was three years older, and I was more like my

mother—calmer, quieter. Hilton probably had more of a chance to excel in athletics than I did, but he died from an infection when he was 10 years old. And I remember something my father said a few years later that I have never forgotten. I was playing Little League baseball, and I struck out a few too many times to suit my old man, and he said after the game, "Hilton could have done this. I don't think you have the guts to do it."

"He said that to you when you were just a kid?" I asked, instantly comparing Bart's father with my own, who would never, ever have said a thing like that to me.

Bart nodded and went on, "It triggered something in me. From that moment, there was only one way to go: I had to prove Dad wrong. I think—no, I *know*—that those words helped drive me in everything I did in sports from then on. Maybe Dad knew exactly what he was doing. Maybe he said that on purpose to light a fire under me. I honestly don't know."

Bart went on to say that he never feared standing up to Coach Lombardi, but that except for that one time I witnessed ("when I lost my cool"), he always did it in the privacy of Lombardi's office.

One day in practice, Coach chewed my butt out pretty good on a tipped pass that wasn't a clean interception. I mean, he just jumped all over my case. After practice, I went up to his office and said, "Coach, I can take any ass-chewing you want to hand out. That's not a problem. I understand your role. But please do it in the privacy of this office. My role is to lead this team, and it makes it harder if you chew me out in public. I can take it, but please do it in the privacy of this office. That's all I ask." After that, he never again chewed me out in front of the team.

"Didn't he get under your skin and drive you crazy like the rest of us?" I asked.

"Oh, man," Bart said, "after growing up with Ben Starr, Coach Lombardi was no problem at all."

I had to ask Bart the next question because *I* had been asked it so many times. "Do you think Coach Lombardi would succeed today?"

Bart leaned forward and looked me in the eye.

I do, I really do. I've always believed that one characteristic of a successful team is respect for discipline. People with the right makeup *want* to hear a leader with the guts and talent and credentials to stand up and say, "That this is how we do it! This is what I demand! This is what I expect!" No ambiguity, no self-doubt, no mixed messages. Bottom line, a true leader must believe with all his heart that he's right. And Vince Lombardi believed in himself.

You can say that again—and I will: *Vince Lombardi believed in himself.*

So did Bart Starr.

ON DECEMBER 5, 1965, I had my scariest moment ever with Bart, and it came during pregame warm-ups, when I thought I might have ended his career.

A standard drill before a game is for the quarterback to take snaps from his center and throw to his receivers running short and medium routes. Strictly routine, maybe 25 to 30 reps, just enough to get all the parties in synch.

As receivers jogged back with the balls, they tossed them to the manager or ball boy designated to protect us from having loose balls rolling around. If two sets of receivers are running routes, one right after another, a loose ball bouncing around becomes a hazard, a sprained ankle waiting to happen.

Well, on the Sunday in question—our opponents were the Minnesota Vikings, one of the two or three toughest teams we faced that season—a loose ball did get through, and it came close to causing a lot more damage than a mere sprained ankle.

It came close to derailing our run at the NFL Championship.

Somebody let a bouncer get through, and at the instant I was about to make the snap to Bart, the loose ball hit my snapping hand, causing me to hesitate for a split second as Bart called the snap count.

A veteran center wouldn't have snapped the ball. Bart would have pulled out, stepped back, returned to position, and called the snap again. But I wasn't a veteran center. After a nanosecond pause, I snapped the ball, only now Bart was pulling back, which exposed the tip of his middle finger to the football.

I can still hear the awful thud as the ball smashed Bart's fingertip, and his simultaneous exclamation of pain, "Damn!"

Time stopped. In my mind, it was as if every person in the frigid stadium was instantly focused on the mini-drama unfolding on the 30-yard line on the visitors' side. I dumbly watched as Bart shook his right hand and inspected his damaged digit.

As Bart continued warm-ups, I stole glances at him. After every pass, he shook his right hand, opened and closed it, all the while holding it next to his leg so that the Vikings wouldn't spot a potential chink in his armor. He didn't call for a trainer to look at it. He didn't say a word. A Green Bay Packer was supposed to play through pain.

(That didn't stop the next day's headline flashing in front of my eyes: ROOKIE CENTER SMASHES STARR'S FINGER, DESTROYS PACK'S NFL TITLE HOPES. Hey, maybe I could get a job as an assistant coach at some junior high.)

On the opening kickoff I got lucky. As wedge buster, I ran down the middle of the field, avoided the lumbering guard up front, slipped through the wedge, and bore down on the kickoff receiver, Lance Rentzel. As he swerved to dodge me, I stuck my left hand into his midriff and raked the ball out of his hands. We recovered at the Vikes' 20, the crowd went berserk, and Ray Nitschke greeted me on the sideline as if I were a peer.

Then, on the first play from scrimmage, Bart threw a TD pass to Boyd Dowler on a skinny post. I could breathe again. As I trotted onto the field, I was one happy rookie.

After the PAT, I bounced back to the sideline still pumped by my hand in our 7-point lead, and then, before returning to the field for more heroics on the kickoff coverage team, I heard Bart say to Coach Lombardi, "I can't go. This finger won't grip. I'm out! Get Zeke ready."

As usual when Zeke Bratkowski was forced into action, we won. Zeke was a fine quarterback, but he was also our lucky charm. The margin was narrow, 24-19, but it was a W. Fortunately, we didn't have to put our luck to the test the next week against the Colts in Baltimore. In the rain and the mud of Memorial Stadium, Bart returned and threw three touchdown passes.

Recently, I asked Bart if he remembered the time I pretty near destroyed his finger during a warm-up drill. He smiled, and said, "Yes, but it was only a sprain. It wasn't broken. I played the next week. Really, it wasn't broken."

Maybe not, but to this day the thing still looks pretty doggone crooked to me.

OVER THE YEARS, I've fielded more questions about Bart Starr and Johnny Unitas—their similarities, their differences, their secret weapons—than you've had hot dinners.

Rightly so, I guess, since no center of the era snapped more balls to those two superstars combined than I did. I guess that makes me something of an expert, so here goes.

CULTURE SHOCK

Today, Carolyn Newton Curry, PhD, is a lovely, erudite, sophisticated—did I say lovely?—woman who has sustained a successful marriage for 45 years, raised two wonderful children, traveled and studied abroad, lectured extensively, taught at the high school and college level, lived in virtually every corner of the United States, built four houses (general contractor on the last two), and formed a successful not-for-profit foundation (check out womenalonetogether.org) to support women who live alone.

But in 1965, when I took her off to live in Green Bay, Wisconsin, and set her up in a tiny apartment that we affectionately dubbed The Closet, I returned from practice on her first day there to find her quite upset. She has never suffered fools gladly, and does not like being ridiculed.

"They laughed at me at the grocery store!" she announced in her most indignant tone. "All I did was ask the lady at the register where I could find the grits and turnip greens. And those people just laughed at me like I was a freak or something. Then they asked me to talk some more, just so they could listen to me and get some more laughs."

We required periodic care packages from down home to survive during our Wisconsin sojourn. Carolyn continued to do her grocery shopping, but with a withering glance ready for the locals looking for a laugh at her expense.

- Bart kept to himself off the field; John frequently joined the O-line for beers after practice.

• Bart seldom said anything negative about anybody; John was blunt (and sometimes harsh) in his assessment of teammates (to our face), opponents, coaches, and the press.

• Bart was (and is) measured and introspective; John was anything but.

• Bart could seem distant, even aloof-especially to a young center who was desperately trying to win his respect. John was beloved for his candor—beloved, that is, unless you happened to the object of his judgment on a particular day. (He could crush you with a harsh remark, and then five minutes later melt you with that crooked grin, meaning you were okay again.)

How much time do you have? Given my past with those guys, I could go on with the Starr-Unitas for a while. But as I'll be talking about John later on, let me re-focus on Bart.

Bart Starr can be comfortable with intimate conversations, but he is sparing with them. Circumstances have to be perfect and of his choosing. The occasion has to be just right, and a long afternoon sitdown we had in his Birmingham office in June 2006 was just that.

Understand, back in Green Bay in 1965, when I was a terrified kid, I looked on Bart with awe and trepidation. Now I'm all grown up—well beyond grown up, with aching joints to remind me every day.

More to the point, I've become skeptical to the point of cynical about sports heroes (and other kinds as well). I've seen so much that I'm not easily—or at least not automatically—impressed by sports celebrity anymore. But I had never spoken with Bart in such depth before, and I sat and marveled.

Most of us have moments of cowardice in our past, but Bart Starr seems to have taken the courageous road virtually *every time*. In fact, taking the more difficult moral, spiritual, and physical path seems to have been the overriding factor in his life.

I say "seems" because I was skeptical.

Going into our discussion of our shared past, I thought to myself, nobody's *this* good. Coming out, I thought to myself—you know, maybe some people *really are* this good.

EARLY IN MY rookie year of 1965, Carolyn's parents, Weyman and Frances Newton, came up from Georgia to Green Bay for a game. Autumn in Wisconsin meant the weather was cool, the leaves were beautiful, and the Packers were winning. Their son-in-law was on the most famous team in the world, their young daughter was happy, and as they sat in favored seats, they witnessed a victory. What could be better than that for the quiet couple from College Park, Georgia?

Let me tell you.

On Monday morning, our day off, we piled into the new Oldsmobile I'd bought with some of my bonus money and toured the orderly, Norman Rockwell town. As we drove around town, we noted the distinct similarities to the neighborhoods we were familiar with in the South: mostly small frame houses, neat lawns, and nice public parks. Except for the crispness of the autumn air and the constant wind that made it feel even crisper, we might as well have been in College Park instead of Green Bay.

I knew where Bart's house was, and I figured the Newtons would like to be able to say they had seen it, so I drove over there. Bart's house was no different from most of the rest, unpretentious in every way except that the yard man was an All-Pro quarterback.

The day before, the same guy had led us to a 27-10 win over the San Francisco 49ers. Today he was raking leaves. "Well, I'll be darned," observed the normally taciturn Weyman Newton.

Bart spotted us as we sat at the stop sign. "Hey, Bill," he shouted, those familiar tones ringing across the yard. Everybody in Wisconsin knew that voice because they heard him bark signals year after year. "Get out! Are those Carolyn's folks? Let's go in the house!" The Newtons, unaccustomed to hanging out with famous people, protested, but Bart insisted.

He opened the car door, helped the ladies out, and led us across the spotless lawn into the little house. After being greeted by a beaming Cherry Starr, we sat down in the living room and accepted coffee (and declined a piece of pie). Bart and Cherry put the Newtons at ease, asking about their backgrounds and talking about sites to see around Green Bay. They bragged on Carolyn and predicted a bright future for the Newtons' blushing son-in-law.

Weyman and Frances told Bart and Cherry how much they appreciated their kindness toward Carolyn earlier that year. Because of a misunderstanding, Carolyn hadn't been able get into the apartment we'd rented in Green Bay until the first of September. I had been too preoccupied with smashing my face into Ray Nitschke and Henry Jordan day after day to find a room for Carolyn at any of the outlying motels around Green Bay. My only recourse was a dark, dreary, downtown establishment, the Northland Hotel. (I learned later that someone had recently been murdered there.)

One day, about four weeks into camp, Bart pulled me aside and asked me if Carolyn was staying at the Northland Hotel. Yes, I told him, we have no other choice right now. His response: "Yes, you do, mister. Cherry will pick her up this morning. Call her *right now* and tell her to be ready at 10 o'clock. She's not staying at that place another night. She'll be staying with us."

That act of kindness was but the first of many to be bestowed upon the Currys by the Starrs. Carolyn stayed with the Starrs for a little over a week, until our apartment was ready. During that time, she was undoubtedly the envy of every other Packer wife. Cherry even took her to play golf with the Starr boys.

Our visit concluded with a short tour of the house, and I have one abiding memory. On the kitchen table was a neat stack of pictures next to a pile of manila envelopes. They were autographed photos of Bart throwing a football, each with handwritten messages above the autograph. I flipped through few and noticed that each message was different, personalized for the individual recipient, usually with a word of encouragement.

"Bart," I asked, "do you get thousands of these?"

"No, not thousands," he laughed. "Maybe hundreds, and I figure these are the folks that allow us to play the game. I like signing them, and Cherry addresses each one."

"Well," observed Weyman Newton, "I'll be darned."

IN THE NFL, best friends can become worst enemies with a change of shirts.

After the Saints traded me to the Baltimore Colts in 1967, Bart was one of very few Packer teammates to make a conscious effort to stay in touch. That was pretty rare in the NFL. After all, I had gone over to "the enemy." Not only that, but I had gone over to a team that beat the Packers every time we played them in the six seasons I was in Baltimore.

That didn't matter to Bart. Whenever we bumped into one another, we'd always shoot the bull for a while, checking in on each other's families, asking after mutual friends. Then, as his career was winding down, he'd ask me about my plans when my playing days were over. I didn't have much to say on that score, because like most professional athletes in their prime years, I figured they would last forever.

But once, a few years before he retired, he told me something both startling and serious. "Bill Curry, if I ever get a head coaching job in football, I'm going to hire you right away."

Now, you hang around the game long enough, you hear talk like that from a lot of people, and most of it's just that— talk. How often does anything come of it? I recall being skeptical, not because Bart was a promise-breaker, but because I figured the odds against the stars ever being aligned properly for that kind of thing to happen were pretty high.

Bart took over as general manager and head coach of the Green Bay Packers after the end of the 1974 season. One of

SETTING A STANDARD

"Did I ever tell you my Bart Starr story?"

An old and dear friend, Scotty Dodson, put that question to me when he learned I was writing this book. Scotty, who died in January 2008, had been an airline pilot. He was a gruff guy, not given to sentiment, and my first thought was that he and Bart had once had some sort of run-in. I was so wrong.

"On a flight one day, the flight attendant came into the cockpit all atwitter, asking if we knew who was on the plane," Scotty began. "I didn't know and didn't much care, and so said something smart, but she was breathless. 'I think it's Bart Starr,' she said. 'I think it's that football player, Bart Starr.' "

That got Scotty's attention. Turns out that Bart was one of the few public figures he actually admired. So he went back into the cabin, introduced himself, shook Bart's hand, and returned to the cockpit.

A few minutes later there was a tap on the cockpit door. This was before 9/11, things were looser, so Scotty opened the door to see Bart Starr standing there. Scotty invited him in and they struck up a conversation. Both had grown up as Air Force brats, so they had something in common. Bart asked about Scotty's family and asked for his home address.

"A few days later," Scotty told me, "two autographed Bart Starr pictures arrived for our sons, and naturally we were all blown away. But there was one problem. Starr had misspelled one of our sons' names. I figured we would let it go, but I remembered how gracious this guy was, and so I finally just sat down and wrote a letter, very apologetic and all, but pointing out the misspelling. A couple of weeks later, a corrected autographed picture arrived—with an apology."

The best thing, Scotty said, is that his sons learned a great lesson in life about what it is to be a man.

his first calls was to me. He asked me to play one more year, since he desperately needed a center, after which I'd join his coaching staff.

Where do I sign?

Only one problem: my left knee, which I'd torn up in 1973 while I was with the Houston Oilers. The next year, after a 24-day players' strike was resolved, the Oilers released me without allowing me to practice with the squad. Dumb move. After all, I was the former president of the NFL Players Association, so the NFLPA filed an unfair labor practice suit with the NLRB faster than you could say "Bud Adams."

Meanwhile, I cleared waivers and signed with the Rams, for whom I played 10 games in 1974.

But at the Packers training camp in the summer of 1975, even though my spirit was more than willing, my knee announced that it was ready to retire. Without so much as blink, Bart told me he'd make me a Packers scout for that season. Fine. Good. I was a Packer again, working with Bart.

Eventually, by the way, the Players Association prevailed in my lawsuit. The settlement of the case before the NLRB required Bum Phillips to call me in 1976 to offer my job back at full salary. By then I weighed all of 208 pounds.

Bum and I couldn't keep from chuckling as we played out the charade.

In 1977, Bart named me his offensive line coach. I had exactly one year of coaching experience under my belt. *One year.* I had worked in 1976 after my year of scouting for the Packers as the line coach at my alma mater, Georgia Tech.

So how did I land such a plum job? One reason: Bart Starr. He had promised me that if he ever got a head coaching job in pro football, he would hire me. He had given his word. Period. End of story.

Bart caught a lot of flack from the media for selecting me. After all, there were a lot of qualified guys available with a whole lot more experience. Because he'd stuck his neck out for me, I made up my mind that I owed him a good offensive line. When I was introduced, I made no grandiose promises. What I did do was assure one and all that we would have a tough, smart, well-conditioned OL that could come off the ball, hit the right opponent, and protect the passer.

In my three years with Bart, we got that done.

Bart had a plan for the 1977 draft. He wanted each of his assistant coaches to fan out across the country and ID the top players at the position he was responsible for. It was an unusual game plan at the time, but it eventually paid off for the club. I don't know how many teams do it now, but it is really smart.

Think about it: If the guys manning the position you're in charge of—say, linebacker—turn out to be marshmallows, you'll only have yourself to blame. No, "Gee, Coach, I did the best I could with rubbish you and your scouting combine gave me to work with." That might hold a little water your first year on the job. After that, the buck stops with you.

"Look at as many available offensive linemen as you can between now and April. Work them out. Talk to them. Talk to their coaches, See what they're made of," Bart said. "Look at all the other scouting reports we have coming in. And then give me a list of the top 50, in order. On Draft Day, I'll call you to the board and you'll make our selection if we're going with an offensive lineman in that round. You will *personally* be selecting the Green Bay offensive line of the future. Do you understand?"

I understood. And I made a vow to myself that I would justify Bart's confidence in my judgment and that every single OL pick Green Bay made that year *would play* for the Packers. I worked as hard as I'd ever worked before in my life. I traveled far and wide. I got to be on a first-name basis with just about every warm-blooded, able-bodied big guy in America. I internalized every detail of personality, physical ability, potential, and most important of all, productivity, for every lineman we had on file. I even checked out certain defensive linemen who didn't figure to play the D-line in the NFL but might have potential on the other side of the ball. I looked in every nook and cranny of the country for any prospect who might be able to help us.

One of the first things I learned is that no matter how hard you work, and no matter how good you think you are at something—in my case, evaluating offensive linemen— you're going to screw up sometimes.

Two examples that proved that point still make me cringe—for different reasons: Joe Klecko, the best of the "non-traditional" prospects, and Rick Scribner, a third-round selection.

Klecko was a college nose guard at Temple, Scribner a serious, thoughtful offensive guard from Idaho State.

I thought Joe was too short and rotund, although he ran well. He went on to become an All-Pro defensive tackle for the New York Jets, a charter member of the Jets' Sack Exchange (with Mark Gastineau, Abdul Salaam, and Marty Lyons.)

Joe was one of those players who matured quickly after college. While he didn't always go full speed at Temple, he learned to do it in the NFL. If I could have gotten inside his head to see what he might become, I certainly wouldn't have rejected him. You have to learn how to scout *potential*—and you'll never do that without making some painful mistakes.

I thought Scribner's work ethic and natural strength would guarantee success as an offensive guard in the NFL. I was wrong. He simply didn't live up to his obvious potential when big guys knocked him around. He wouldn't defend himself. We'd never have taken him so high if all the other scouts hadn't rated him high as well. It was just one of those things where a nice kid didn't want to get as violent as you have to get in the NFL We had to let him go in the final cut before the season began.

I felt terrible about both of them.

OUR BEST OL pick in that 1977 draft was Greg Koch, a great hulk of a kid at 6'4", 270, who played high school ball in Houston before going to the University of Arkansas. An All-Pro in 1982, he started nine straight seasons for the

Packers before moving on to Miami and Minnesota to finish out an 11-season NFL career.

The thing that impressed me most about Greg, besides his talent and his raw strength, was his willingness to learn. He'd played the wishbone at Arkansas, and he had a devil of a time early on learning to pass block for us. Time after time at the end of practice, he'd holler at me to come teach him. "Bill, Bill! Come back! Just help me here. I know I can learn to do this thing."

That kind of request is always sweet music to a teacher's ear, so I'd cajole Ezra Johnson, a lightning fast pass rusher, to stay out with us and go at it with Greg, rep after rep. In time, Greg became one of the better pass blockers in the game.

Now flash forward 22 years to late December 1999. I was in Houston at the Astrodome, alone in the broadcast booth, two and a half hours before game time, preparing to broadcast the Houston Bowl for ESPN. I like to be early on game day so I can watch the crowd filter in, see which players come out early, and get a feel for the competitive scene.

The acoustics at the Dome are weird. When it's empty, you can hear things from far off, like echoes in a big canyon. Anyway, I heard a familiar cry reverberate through the empty Astrodome from somewhere well below me in the stands, eight or ten rows up from the field, around the 30-yard line on my side. "Bill, Bill! Come coach me! I can do this!" It was coming from a distinguished, slightly graying middle-aged gentleman.

It was Greg Koch, who's now a successful attorney.

We had a wonderful reunion, laughing about our idiosyncrasies from so many years before. Unlike most

NFL experiences, both coach and player had been rookies together. I had driven Koch and his O-line mates unmercifully, and Greg had become the mouthpiece for the unit. They called me Mr. Bill, after the cartoon character. I never did bother to learn exactly who Mr. Bill was, but I got that they were not complimenting me. I let it go because I knew I was being overly demanding and they needed the comic relief Greg provided.

We had a tough job to get done in a hurry. We were successful, in part because Greg had the capacity to be a leader in work ethic and to deliver his wisecracks with good timing ... most of the time.

MY MOST VIVID memory from the three years I coached for Bart in Green Bay had nothing to do with football—and yet everything to do with Bart Starr.

At a difficult moment for our team, Zeke Bratkowski and I were sitting in the Starr living room working with Bart on problems with our offense. When Cherry answered a knock at the front door, Bart called to her to ask who was there. Cherry called back that she didn't recognize the gentleman. When she opened the door, we could hear a halting voice asking a question. "Mrs. Starr, I am embarrassed to be doing this, but my dad is in serious trouble. He loves your husband so much! Could you get Coach Starr to sign this piece of paper?"

As Zeke and I rolled our eyes, Bart excused himself, got up and walked to the door, and invited the intrusive fan into the house. The guy was horrified and protested, saying that all he wanted was an autograph for his ailing father. Bart stepped outside to talk with him on the porch, and Zeke and I—by now hovering around the door—heard our boss ask where the gentleman's father was located.

This elicited another round of protests, with the young man begging that Bart simply sign the paper and let him be gone.

Bart asked again, this time sharply, "Where is your Dad?"

The reluctant intruder said, "Coach, he's sitting in the car in front of your house."

Hearing that, Bart said, "Go get him."

Presently, a frail old man entered the front door as if stepping into a cathedral. Bart and Cherry greeted him as if he were a dear friend, and then Bart took him by the arm and gently escorted him into the den, which contained all sorts of Packers memorabilia with special meaning to Bart. Tears began to stream down the old gentleman's face.

After a time, when the Super Bowl MVP trophies, the five championship rings, the civic awards, and the team pictures had been reviewed, the old man pulled himself together. He held out his hand to Cherry, then Bart, and said in a clear voice, "Mr. Starr, I can die in peace now. My life is complete. I am deeply grateful to you, sir."

And then he and his son made their exit.

When the door closed behind them, Bart turned to me and Zeke and said, "Now, where were we?"

IN 1988, BART and Cherry Starr endured the most shattering loss imaginable. Their son Bret was found dead at age 24 in Tampa of a drug overdose.

The Starrs were devastated. Everyone who knew them and Bret were devastated. I spoke with Bart many times. Finally, I asked them what they planned to do to try to get beyond this tragedy.

Bart answered that when they were ready, he and Cherry would try to prevent this happening to other families. "We'll go to the young people, tell Bret's story, and beg them not to make similar mistakes."

I asked if they might find it therapeutic to speak to our football team at his alma mater, Alabama, where I was head coach. He said he would think about it. Six months later he called. "We're ready to speak to the team. Cherry and I will come over next week if you still want us."

I called a team meeting and worked to gather myself. When the Starrs walked into our office, I said to Cherry, "I cannot believe you are doing this." She looked at me and said, "I can't either."

When I introduced them to the team, it was Cherry, not Bart, who stood up to speak. I will never forget her words, and neither will our players. "Bret was a good boy, a very good boy, much like each of you. He was not a bad person and only wanted the best for everyone. He worked hard at his rehab and at his job. We thought he had come through the worst when he was straight for three years, but ..."

And she faltered.

Bart stood, and I assumed he would take over. But he walked to her side, put his arm around his wife, smiled at her, and waited until Cherry gathered herself.

After a few minutes, she continued. "When you think things are unfair or too demanding, think about your mother, your dad, and everybody that loves you. But more importantly, think about *yourself,* and all the value you bring to life. *Cherish* each day and each moment. Do the hard things right, and hopefully you will not end up in an impossible situation. *You can do it.*"

Bart followed with a discussion of the realities on the street. His experience as a head coach, general manager, and personnel director of the Packers had given him a streetwise understanding of the drug and alcohol culture and the way it penetrated locker rooms all over the country. Bret's experience had only reinforced the horror that can bring.

"Men," he said in strong, measured voice, "those guys who say they can fix you up with some 'really good stuff' aren't your friends. They want to get you hooked and to become your personal dealers. If you think you may have a problem, see Coach Curry. If you are uncomfortable talking to coaches, see the drug and alcohol counselors here on campus. You have great resources here that can help you manage your lives properly, get your education, and play great football."

He paused for a moment, then concluded, "If you ever think Cherry or I can help you, just call us. We're in the phone book in Birmingham."

And they still are.

Dr. Feelgood was my go-to guy when things got bumpy in Green Bay. On top of being the best DE ever to play the position, Willie was also a pretty doggone good therapist.

5

WILLIE DAVIS
COUNSELOR

A great teammate and a great man, Hall of Fame defensive end William Delford Davis played a key role in a life-changing period for me during the two years I played for the Green Bay Packers.

I'm not sure that I would have understood and accepted what Willie Davis had to teach me, though, had it not been for an unassuming, unknown construction foreman from Hapeville, Georgia, who touched my life and awakened something in me six years earlier.

THE FIRST SUMMER I had a driver's license, I took a full-time construction job. I had no choice. My father had a rule for his three children: once you turned 16, you had to get a job in your time off from school. My two sisters—Linda, who is four years younger than me, and Deborah, who is 12 years my junior—had similar responsibilities later, at least in theory. But they got away with things I could never have dreamed of. I think it had to with them being girls.

That meant that at Christmas and Easter breaks until I graduated from high school, I worked as a shoe salesman at the Thom McAn shoe store or as a stock boy at Rich's, the department store where my dad was the sporting goods buyer. And it meant that in the summers, I worked full time.

My job résumé tracks back even earlier. (This was the 1950s, and we weren't rich.) At age 14 during the school year, I sacked groceries on Saturdays at the local grocery store for 50 cents an hour. That summer, I worked as a day camp counselor under Coach Badgett for $15 a week.

The summer of my 15th year, I worked at Stephenson's Chemical Company with Ronnie Jackson, bagging pesticides—maliathon and other toxic chemicals—and loading the bags onto big trucks. Theoretically, we were supposed to wear masks, but often a handkerchief over my nose was close as I came. Nasty work, good money, 75 cents an hour.

I also washed windows for an apartment developer near the airport on a per job basis, but ran afoul of him when I neglected the windows with wasp nests attached. I still have a phobia about those critters from having been stung badly several times as a kid.

Then, between my junior and senior years, my ship came in. I landed a job in construction.

Construction was a high school jock's dream summer job. Not only did it pay the princely sum of $1 per hour, a good 20 cents more than I could have commanded in any other summer job, but because it was hard work outdoors, it would be help me stay in shape.

The job was an hour's drive away in Chamblee, on the northeast side of Atlanta across town from our home in

College Park, which then was a suburb of about 25,000 people on the southwest side.

Bob Scruggs, a close friend since first grade, was my connection. His dad, a Delta pilot and the coach of our American Legion baseball team, was a co-developer of the construction project, an apartment complex of four buildings, each with eight tidy two-bedroom apartments that are still in use. I drive by at least once a year, just to be reminded of some important lessons I learned there.

Bob was 5'11", all of 125 pounds, and cared not a whit about football, but he could flat out hit a baseball and shoot jump shots. His sardonic sense of humor had earned him the nickname Sunshine. He was reasonably tough, but worked very hard at disguising it. His breakfast most mornings was chocolate ice cream and PepsiCola, because he didn't give a rip about what he put in his body or how his body looked.

We made up television commercials on the trips back and forth.

> What does a rugged construction worker eat for breakfast? Wheaties? Hell no! Why, he knows he will never resemble the great Bob Scruggs, never conquer the women like Scruggs, unless he chug-a-lugs Pepsi and scarfs down rapidly melting chocolate ice cream! Pepsi and ice cream—the real Breakfast of Champions!

The first day at the job site, Mr. Scruggs met Bob and me to lay out the general rules and procedures, talk some about job safety, and introduce us to our foreman, a man named James Harvey. Mr. Scruggs told us in no uncertain terms that he would be in complete control. He looked Bob dead in the eye when he said that, making sure his son understood that it didn't matter who your daddy was on this job.

The place smelled of wood shavings and creosote. The large rectangle defined by the four foundations for future apartments was pure Georgia red clay and was packed hard on the dry June morning. The concrete blocks were going onto the foundations, the cement trucks were downloading their "mud" into wheelbarrows for the brick masons, and the framers were at work with their hammers and electric saws. There were six or eight brick masons, an equal number of carpenters, and a small gang of common laborers that included one foreman and three flunkies, of which Bob and I were two. The other was a chubby country boy named Wayne, maybe 25.

All the while, Bob and I were separately taking the measure of our new boss, the foreman James Harvey.

He was 33 years old. (To kids our age, anybody over 25 was old.) He was muscular, very thick across the upper body, with huge biceps. He went about 6'0", 220 pounds. He wore bib overalls, a tee shirt underneath, and large brown brogans with thick soles, and sported a nondescript baseball cap with no logo, cocked at an odd angle.

A hearty smile prominently displayed a gold front tooth. A handshake with him was akin to grabbing hold of a wide, rough stone with five stubby protuberances made of angle iron. (I noticed in that first handshake that they jutted out at odd angles, much the way mine do now.)

Oh, and there was one other thing about James Harvey, our new boss.

He was black.

BLACK! OUR BOSS on this job was *a black man!*

I was stunned.

All I knew about people of color in those days was that they were inferior to us in intelligence, morals, education, and ambition—just about anything that mattered. In our culture in Georgia back then, they were lumped just below Yankees, Catholics, and New York Jews, people I had rarely encountered the first 18 years of my life. (Southern Jewish people were fine, since my dad worked for Dick Rich at Rich's Department Store and Mr. Rich and his colleagues were wonderful people.)

A strange contradiction prevailed in our home: it was okay to tell "nigger jokes," and my father did from time to time, but it was not okay to be cruel or abusive, even to black people. The real sin was cruelty; jokes were "harmless." We should have known better, but we didn't.

I don't need to tell anybody with any sense of history at all how deeply cruel the culture in the Deep South was in those days when it came to race. We were only a little ways beyond Brown vs. Board of Education, the federal orders to integrate schools and public facilities were being ignored, and the rumblings of the civil rights movement were beginning to be heard big-time. The old post-slavery relationships between white and black were coming unmoored, and the backlash by many Southern whites was mean and ugly.

Not surprisingly, the purveyors of hatred were even busier than usual. I saw the Klan marching in Atlanta. I heard the whispered tales of lynchings in the rural areas. I heard remarks like "over my dead body" from white classmates when integration was discussed.

The "good old days?"

Not unless you look at them through rose-colored glasses.

FOR SOME REASON, James Harvey decided within a couple of days that he liked these two white knuckleheads from College Park and that he was going to take care of us. Work our butts off? You better believe it. But if we delivered, and we did, he was also going to take care of us.

Why, I don't know, but I will be forever thankful that he did.

Most of the carpenters and framers we were there to serve came from Paulding County, a rural area just west of Atlanta proper. They were stereotypical good old country boys with shaggy hair, dirty fingernails, bad teeth, long sideburns, pickup trucks, chaws of Red Man in their cheeks, and Rebel flags on the antennas of their pickups. Not mean to us or anything, but you got the feeling there would be no buddy-buddy stuff with the boss's son and his companion.

They hollered things to me like, "Hey, son, you ought to be a pro rassler with them shoulders you got!" I smirked under my American Legion Post 50 baseball hat. I was still pretty sure I would be pitching for the New York Yankees soon. No Gorgeous George antics for me.

Mostly they nagged Bob about being skinny and frail, like a "tall girl."

They cut Wayne slack because he was from their world, a Paulding County boy through and through.

I knew guys like them at our high school, and I'd encountered plenty at filling stations and barbershops and feed stores around College Park. They talked football, women, car racing, and "shine," their four favorite subjects, in no particular order. The humor was routinely sexist, sexual, homophobic, and—when it came to black people—always racist.

There was one preacher among them—there always seems to be one in those bunches—and the language cleaned up some when he walked by. He sat alone at lunch, reading the scriptures from the King James Bible, mumbling to himself.

Our first assignment was to move some huge stacks of 12-foot-long 2x4s, 8-foot 2x4s, and joists, which were 2x10 and 12 feet long. We had to tote them over to where the framing out of the first apartment was under way. I started off carrying two boards at a time, an easy load for someone my size. Bob and Wayne were taking one at a time.

It was still passably cool at 7:30 a.m. when we started moving the lumber, but Georgia summer mornings have a well-deserved reputation for sliding up into the low 90s by 9:00 a.m.—and then it gets hot. As the first morning matured into a full-fledged scorcher, Wayne sweated through his overalls, slowed his pace, and started grumbling. After a while he approached me, leaned close in with his noxious breath preceding him, and said, "You don't need to carry no two boards at a time."

I didn't understand at first, so he explained that me carrying two boards each trip made him and Bob look bad. The implication was that I had better cut back on my load. I pointed out that we'd finish the pile sooner if we carried more at a time. "That don't matter," he said. "We got to work eight hours anyways, so why kill ourselves carrying two at a time?"

At a break, I pulled the foreman aside and asked him what I ought to do about this two boards business and what Wayne had said. Mr. Harvey had a severe speech impediment and stutter that caused him to use a colorful array of unique pronunciations, so that my name came out *"B-b-beel."*

"B-b-beel, y-y-you keep c-c-c-carrying two if you w-w-want," he stuttered. "And a nuther th-th-thing. You w-w-watch out for this W-W-Wayne. You k-k-keep to yourself and do your j-j-job. I won't let those guys b-b-bother you."

(He also corrected me when I addressed him as Mr. Harvey: "N-n-naw, B-b-beel. You j-j-just, c-c-call me J-J-James.")

When I told my buddy what James had said, Bob allowed as how he agreed with Wayne and he thought one board at a time was just about right. We just laughed and got back to work. I carried my two, and so did Bob.

Wayne's work ethic applied to all his endeavors. At breaks, designated to be 15 minutes, he hung out in his truck, dozing with the doors open, extending each rest period by several minutes. He showed up just a few minutes late most mornings and left a few minutes early most afternoons.

One day, Wayne didn't show up for work at all. When I asked where he was, one of his Paulding County buddies snarled, "He got fired."

THE HOTTEST, DIRTIEST, and toughest assignment I had all summer was to dig out an area in the crawl space under one of the apartment buildings. (I drove out to it the summer of 2007 and showed the very spot to Carolyn. The apartments are in good condition, and they're still occupied.)

The building shells were scheduled to be wired by electricians, and there'd been a screw-up. The building code required that Georgia Power have reasonable access to a building's electric meter—that is, a GP rep would be able to read the meter standing up, rather than having to lie down in the dirt under the building. Problem was, no such space had been provided in this one unit when the shell went up.

James took me over, handed me a small shovel with a short handle, pointed to the dark space inside the small door, and told me to "Kinda f-f-fold up and d-d-dig about a six f-f-foot hole."

You ever try to dig so much as a soup-bowl size hole—much less one that's six feet deep—in hard-pan red Georgia clay in mid-July? While folded up like an accordion in an airless trap?

I sure hope not.

Thick-headed me, I got into the challenge part of the project, deciding that if I was going to scrunch up and work in the heat and dark, I was damned well going to get it right.

I had just enough space to sit on my heels, hunker over at an oblique angle, and pitch tiny shovels full of dirt out the small door. The very thought of it today causes every muscle in my body to spasm.

My pal Bob's idea of a joke was to sneak over now and then, squat by the door, and make loud noises or toss pebbles down at me, hoping to startle me into jumping and bumping my head on the sub-floor joists.

At least *he* was having fun.

Other than Vince Lombardi's grass drills, digging that damned hole in that damned red Georgia clay was the toughest damned physical labor of my life. But it was there in that dark, airless, oven that I earned the respect of my boss. And it was there that he got my attention, first as a leader, and then as a force of nature.

James Harvey got me through it.

Every time I began to get discouraged by not being able to crack root systems that were as hard as iron with my shovel, or by being nearly blinded by the sweat pouring into my eyes, or by the dirt down my shirt that turned into gritty mud, that strong, dark face would pop into view. James would offer some bit of advice about squaring off the corners, or ask how I was feeling, or hand me the water jug.

The hole took me nearly a week to finish because from time to time I'd get called away to do other things. As the hours wore on and the hole gradually began to take shape, James began to kneel just a little longer, asking questions about my family, my baseball passion, or my latest girlfriend.

Finally, after a few short conversations through that tiny door, between shovel-loads of red dirt, he leaned way down, got my eye-to-eye attention, and said, "B-b-beel, you a d-d-damn good worker."

Never in my entire life, before or since, have I appreciated a compliment more.

After what seemed like a couple of lifetimes, the hole became deep enough for me to stand erect in, which enabled me to accelerate the excavation and begin to believe that someday soon my ordeal might come to an end.

And then I came to the big rock. A *really* big rock, the size of an asteroid. I carefully dug around it, measured it to be sure it would fit through the door, and got myself set to left it up and push it out. I squatted, bent my knees, kept a flat back the way Dad had taught me to do when lifting, grasped the thing under its smooth bottom, and began to straighten my legs. Nothing. I couldn't budge it.

Try as I might, I could *not* budge the monster hunk of granite. It might as well have been Stone Mountain, which was about 15 minutes away and came by its name righteously. I couldn't even make it rock back and forth to loosen it. After what seemed an hour, I did the one thing I detest doing more than just about anything else in all the world.

I called for help.

"Hey, James!" I shouted.

Nothing.

I clambered out of my boiling office and took off across the yard in search of him. I was soaked, filthy, exhausted—and furious at myself for not being to take care of business.

He was unloading sheet rock from his truck, so I helped him finish as I breathlessly described the size of "Stone Mountain" and told him we'd need a winch to get it out.

He smiled and muttered, "We s-s-see about th-th-that."

We walked back to my own personal hellhole, whereupon James stepped in, bent over at the waist with utterly improper lifting technique, picked up Stone Mountain as if it were a pebble, and carefully laid it outside the door. He then pulled himself up and out the door, rubbed his hands against his pants, picked up Stone Mountain again, pivoted, and tossed it underhanded a good five yards into the adjacent yard.

"B-b-beel," he said, a big grin splitting his face, "that's one d-d-damn b-b-big rock!"

"HEY, BOY, GET me some water."

The call rang out from one of the carpenters about 2 o'clock on a particularly hot, humid day—miserable even by Georgia summer standards.

Even though two white boys were on the premises, the call for water could only have been intended for one person—James.

James seemed not to hear.

The next time the call rang out louder and carried an edge. *"Boy, I said get me some water."*

James stood where he had been working next to the water bucket, which contained a large dipper. He was, of course, the one person on the premises who wasn't allowed to drink from the ladle. He could carry it to somebody else, but not drink from it.

I wish with all my heart I had owned a movie camera for what happened next. It is riveted in my consciousness like few other moments in my life.

James Harvey moved a step or two in the direction of the framer, folded his arms in front of his massive chest, smiled, and spoke. "H-h-how old d-d-do a m-m-man have to be b-b-before he not a b-b-boy?"

The hammering stopped. No one said a word. Just silence in the blazing sun. The framer glanced at his companions, who were all staring in his direction, looked at the hammer in his hand, and looked up at his implacable questioner.

"I'm sorry James. I'll get my own water."

A little while later, when James and I were off by ourselves at another part of the site, I went up to my boss and practically shouted, "James, won't that get you in trouble?"

James smiled his biggest, warmest, smile, threw his big sweaty meat hook of an arm around my neck, pulled me close as we continued to walk, and said, "B-b-beel, w-w-we j-j-just go ahead on. W-w-we don't w-w-worry none about it."

"Go ahead on?" I asked.

"Dat's right," James said in a firm voice. "W-w-we j-j-just go ahead on."

AT HOME THAT night, I breathlessly related the story of my new hero to Mom, Dad, and my sisters. My parents listened, then looked at each other and nodded.

After a while, Dad said quietly that James was a brave man and that he had handled himself well.

That summer of 1959, James Harvey taught me as profound a lesson as any I ever learned from another great teacher in my life, Vince Lombardi. My construction boss assumed a powerful presence in the Curry family mythology.

Decades later, for instance, after a particularly painful loss for one of my teams at Ole Miss, my Mom sidled up to me and whispered, "We just go ahead on."

More recently, Mom, who lost her life companion in October 2007 (she and Dad had been married 66 years), has had to draw on her inherent strength and courage to get through some tough days. Fortunately, she has plenty of both. The Christmas following Dad's death, I went down to Auburn, Alabama, to bring her up to Atlanta, where Carolyn and I live. I remarked to Mom about how hard it seemed to be for her to walk. (Two hip replacements, a bad knee, and being 85 will slow anybody down, even my mother.)

Mom just smiled and said, "We just go ahead on. We don't worry none about it."

And so we do.

We just go ahead on.

We don't worry none about it.

Thank you, James Harvey.

TRUE, I WAS the last draft choice of the Green Bay Packers in 1964, but that wasn't my biggest problem in training camp the following year.

Yes, at 235 pounds I was grossly undersized for an offensive center, even back then, but that wasn't my main issue.

Sure, I was trying to earn a spot on the team that was already being called the "greatest professional team in the history of sports."

But—believe it or not—that wasn't my overriding concern.

My biggest obstacle, hard as it may be to comprehend in 2008, was that I had never been in a huddle on a regular team with a non-Caucasian. Or, as my colleagues of that era would have said, if they were trying to be polite, with a Negro.

My brief stops at the Senior Bowl, the Coaches' All-American Game (long since defunct), and the College All-Star Game (also discontinued), had only increased my discomfort about the social barrier I would face. The few black players in those games seemed to hang together, and while they were cordial, they kept their distance from the white guys. White guys roomed together, and black guys roomed together. We ate in the same dining halls, but the tables were invariably all black or all white.

It never occurred to me to take my tray and go sit at a "black" table. And why should it have?

True, James, Bob, and I had eaten bologna sandwiches together sitting on sheetrock stacks on that construction job in the summer of 1959. But my boss couldn't go to the men's room I used at a nearby filling station because there was only one.

The sign on the door said Men.

As there was only one, it didn't need to say Whites Only.

That was understood.

WHEN I GOT to Green Bay in 1965, I had no basis for social ease with Negroes outside the narrow confines of that construction yard. I had no black friends. I had never paid much attention to the civil rights movement or its implications.

TEN MEN YOU MEET IN THE HUDDLE

What James Harvey had implanted in my tender mind seven years earlier, though, was the beginnings of a social conscience. By now I at least understood that something was terribly wrong, dangerously off kilter in American society. But I didn't know what to do about it, so I just kept my head down and I went about my business.

Learning the offense? Difficult, but only because the Packers system numbered holes with odd to the right and even to the left. To this day, I have never seen anyone else do that.

Blocking Ray Nitschke? Impossible.

Pleasing Vince Lombardi? Even harder.

And so it seemed to me that adjusting to playing and dressing and showering and eating with Negroes—the term "African-American" hadn't been invented yet—was just one more problem to deal with. Since I was on new turf, I began to obsess over the issue—that's my nature until I get a handle on something.

Early mistakes only made things tougher.

Tight end Marv Fleming was one of the more sociable veterans on the team. Born in Texas but raised in California, Marv is bright, clever, and curious about every detail of life, a ready and stimulating conversationalist.

We bumped into each other at a local restaurant one day, and I was pleased when he invited me to join him. He asked about my wedding ring and my Georgia Tech letterman's ring, asked to inspect each, and complimented me on both.

Desperate to forge a closer connection, I decided to tell him about James Harvey, so that he would know for sure that I was no racist redneck and that I had at least one friend with darker skin than mine. I said, "I worked construction when I was in high school with a great guy named James Harvey. He was my *boss*, Marv. And he was a *colored guy*."

Marv stiffened, and while I didn't understand what my blunder might have been, I could tell immediately that I had screwed up.

"What did you say, Bill? Did you say *colored guy?*"

I nodded yes, that I had said James Harvey was a colored guy.

"Really?" Marv pressed.

"Yes, really," I responded. Things weren't going well for the kid from College Park, Georgia.

"What color, Bill?" Marv asked. "Tell me, Bill, exactly what color was this colored guy?"

Marv waited while I absorbed the lesson. And it penetrated. I broke into a cold sweat and found myself struggling to control my voice.

"Okay, Marv, what exactly am I supposed to say?"

"*Black* guy. *Black* man. *Black* woman. *Black* person," Marv Fleming said, fixing me with those gentle, steady eyes. "That's what you say, Bill. Black. Not that old 'colored' garbage."

Then he let me up off the mat. "How could you have known?" he asked, smiling. "It's not your fault. It's okay."

I could breathe again, but I was still shaking a little when we left the restaurant.

ONE NIGHT, ABOUT midway through the exhibition season, I commenced my now-customary solitary walk around the campus after our regular post-dinner team meeting. The nightly meetings were short: we studied film, broke into groups, and went over the next day's plays and practice schedule. I'm pretty sure Lombardi held them mainly to drill home the idea of "team."

It was close to 10 o'clock and I had some time before curfew. As I was walking along in the darkness, a voice suddenly boomed out from behind me. "Bill! Hold up. I'd like to talk with you."

I was startled. I mean, it sounded like the voice of God. When I turned, there was Willie Davis, the most intimidating Green Bay Packer of them all. Willie was an All-Pro from Grambling, the defensive captain and a future Hall of Famer. Not only that, but he was working on his MBA at the University of Chicago. At 6'3" and 243 pounds, he was on the small side for a defensive end, even back then. But I have never known a man, before or since, who had more *presence*.

I stopped and turned toward him. I still remember his great smile and his fatherly eyes. But what did he want with me? Willie waited, sensing my discomfort. Then he spoke—and changed my life forever.

Despite the 42 years that have passed since it took place, I believe this is close to verbatim what he said to me that night.

> Bill, I've been watching you at practice. I like the way you try so hard. You're improving. I think you have a chance to make our team, and I want to help you."

I remember when I felt the same way you do now. I was stuck in Cleveland, playing offensive tackle for the Browns, and Coach Lombardi traded for me and gave me a chance to play defense. I was really happy, but insecure about changing sides of the ball. But he gave me a chance, we became a good team, and the insecurities started to fade.

When we made it to the NFL Championship game against the Eagles in 1960, it was a thrill, but we got beat and I had a horrible feeling about my performance. I wandered out of the locker room and back out onto the field. There were newspapers and popcorn boxes blowing around, but I knew there was more than newspapers and boxes on that field.

There were regrets. I had left regrets on that field, because I hadn't played my very best. I made up my mind in that moment that this would never happen to Willie Davis again.

Bill, at practice tomorrow, and every day after, leave no regrets on that field.

Leave no regrets on the field!

I listened with rapt attention, and Willie continued, "When you think you can't take it anymore, when Coach Lombardi is screaming in your face and Nitschke is breaking your nose, you look for me. *I'll get you through it.*"

Willie's nickname on the team was Doctor Feelgood, and for good reason. The man had the most upbeat, positive, supportive attitude of any person I ever met. Sure enough, when the blood and tears flowed, when Lombardi screamed loudest and Nitschke smashed hardest, I'd find myself searching out No. 87.

"How you feel, old man?" I'd ask him, trying hard to sound casual.

"*Feel good, man!*" was the invariable response, accompanied by that brilliant smile of his. "*Feel real good!*"

To me, Willie Davis embodied the Platonic Ideal of Team Captain. While it may be a bit much to canonize him here, I can state with absolute confidence that the lesson he taught me applies in some way to every person in every calling, regardless of one's station in life.

"*Feel good, man! You can do it! Feel good!*"

THE ONLY TIME I ever saw the team leaders go after Lombardi was during the Tuesday team meeting following

---

TEAM PLAY

The players' wives all sat together in Lambeau Field, which made for a rare sight in those days: white faces and black faces commingled in what was, essentially, a social event. Back then, we played together, but we didn't *play* together.

Carolyn often sat with Barbara Adderley, and at one game Barbara's husband was the subject of a loud, profane, and borderline racist attack from a rude fan seated nearby.

What made it so weird was that this guy was a crazed Packers fan and Herb Adderley was one of the crown jewels of

---

our defensive unit, the top-ranked outfit in the NFL. Herb was in the middle of a five-year run as a Pro Bowler, on his way to his third of four selections as a first-team All-Pro. (The Hall of Fame would come later, in 1980.)

Look, a fan's got a right to yell at anybody, so long as he keeps it reasonably clean. But *Herb Adderley?*

Know this about my bride: she's never been afraid to speak her mind. So at the end of the first quarter, she leaned across the aisle, got this particular fool's attention, and—with Agnes Scott-ingrained charm—said, "Hello, my name is Carolyn Curry. How are you today?"

The oaf smiled, nodded, and said he that he was just fine.

"Good," Carolyn smiled.

And then, "I'd like to introduce you to someone. This is my friend Barbara Adderley. Her husband is number 26."

The idiot mumbled a hello, turned back to the game, and never raised his voice again that day about one of the five best cornerbacks in the NFL.

Score one for Southern charm.

But players' wives at games aside, we didn't begin to mingle socially with African-American players until we got to Baltimore. The Packers went their separate ways off the field; the Colts were always getting together in various groupings.

John and Sylvia Mackey led the way by organizing functions that included all segments of the team. Big John simply would not allow cliques to develop. And Sylvia was an All-Star organizer and hostess with the mostess.

It was a lot more fun to be a Colt.

an especially painful 21-10 loss to the Rams at Los Angeles the Sunday after Thanksgiving in 1966. The loss hurt because we were in a tight race with the Colts, who were 9-1-1 after a Thanksgiving Day tie with the Lions. Our loss put us at 8-3.

The young Rams front four—Lamar Lundy, Rosey Grier, Merlin Olsen, and Deacon Jones, already being touted as the Fearsome Foursome—had stopped our running game cold: just 22 yards on the day.

Bad enough, but on the flight home, Coach heard some laughter coming from the players' section of the plane. That simply was not done after a loss, especially not one with such an impact on the title chase.

At our regular team meeting Tuesday morning, Coach Lombardi broke with his policy of kid gloves after losses and he began a powerful, profane tirade. In loud and ugly terms, he questioned our manhood, our desire, and our courage. About the only quality left untouched was our patriotism.

Suddenly, we heard someone cursing in the back of the room. We turned and there was usually the reserved future HOF tackle Forrest Gregg—on his feet, red-faced, veins bulging, being restrained by teammates. He launched into Lombardi, loudly defending the team against all the charges Coach had lodged against us. Running mate Bob Skoronski quickly joined him. They countered in terms just as powerful, just as profane, that the team felt every bit as bad as Coach did and that Lombardi had no right to rip us the way he had.

When they were done, the room got quiet, and after a long pause, Coach said, "Now, *that's* the attitude I'm looking for. Who else feels that way?"

Willie Davis, who had been nervously rocking back and forth in his metal folding chair, lurched forward as if he had been catapulted onto his feet. "Yeah, man! I feel that way, too!"

Then Lombardi did something I have never seen before or since, from him or any other coach. He walked up to each of the 36 veterans in the room—skipping the four rookies—and, eyeball to eyeball, he asked the same question 36 times: "Do you want to win with me?"

After 36 affirmatives, he walked back to the front of the room. He turned and faced us. Then in a slow, steady voice he said, "We... will ... not ... lose ... another ... game."

And we didn't.

We won three of our next four games—including a 42-27 thumping of the Colts—and tied one as we won the last NFL Championship before that newfangled season-ender was inaugurated, the game that would eventually be called the Super Bowl.

IF JAMES HARVEY made it possible for me to respond to Willie Davis, then Willie Davis just as surely prepared me to respond to Herb Adderley.

A Hall of Fame cornerback, Herb took on the persona of the brash, confrontational defensive back long before it was fashionable. He could run stride for stride with the fastest wide receivers, and he could intimidate tight ends with his violent collisions. He was utterly fearless, and he was one of the three or four players Lombardi never seemed to criticize.

The first time he took notice of me was one day in 1965, during the long lap we were required to run before specialty period. Centers and other specialists were required to be out fifteen minutes early and to warm up by running a lap around both practice fields. Since Adderly was a kick returner, he came out with the centers, kickers, and punters.

Jogging behind Ken Bowman and me one day, Herb shouted, "Hey, Bowman!" When Ken turned toward him he said, "No! Not you, the other guy!" Ken corrected him about who was who, and Herb said loudly, "Aw, all you guys look alike to me." We got it, laughed, and when practice was over I approached Herb for the first time.

"Did you mean you wanted to talk to me?" I inquired.

"Yeah, I do," he said. "I want to ask you a question, and you better tell me the truth."

"Sure," I said. "What's the question?"

He fixed his eyes on mine and said, "If I come to Atlanta during the off-season, will you take me to lunch in a nice restaurant downtown?"

I had been around a few weeks, and by now I knew better than to hesitate. I returned his stare and said, "Herb, I'll be delighted to take you to one of the best restaurants in Atlanta. Just call me up when you're coming to town."

He smiled broadly, the first such smile I had seen from him. That smile could light up a room. He held out his hand, we shook, and he said lightly, "I'm going to hold you to that promise."

He did. The following March, I got a call from Herb telling me that he was going to be passing through Atlanta and how about that lunch? So I arranged for us to have lunch at the

Magnolia Tearoom, Atlanta's spiffiest restaurant. Located on the top floor of Rich's Department Store, the Magnolia Tearoom was the place to be seen in Atlanta. My father and a friend of his, Al Fain, joined us. As always, Herb was utterly engaging, and I think he got a special kick out of being on this stage with three white sons of the South.

We all had a great time.

We even enjoyed the stares.

FEBRUARY 24, 2007. I'm sitting at a table in the Marriott in Vail, Colorado. I have just spent two days at a leadership conference with Willie Davis. Almost 42 years have passed since we first met, and the only thing that has changed between Willie and me is that our bodies are older. I had come to this meeting to listen a lot and contribute a little, but—more important—to visit with Willie.

He brought along a DVD of the show recently aired by NFL Films to celebrate the 40th anniversary of the NFL-AFL Championship game on January 15, 1967, in which we beat the Kansas City Chiefs 35-10.

(Remember, that game retroactively became Super Bowl I.)

Two obvious interview choices for the show from our team had been our quarterback, Bart Starr, and our defensive captain, Willie Davis. A surprise pick for the third interviewee was the second-year offensive center, Bill Curry.

The show was a remarkable evocation of that historic event. We met again the dominant personalities of that team and that era—Lombardi, Starr, Nitschke, Jordan,

Adderley, and Taylor. But to me, it plays like a Willie Davis highlights video.

The defining ability that set Willie Davis apart from defensive ends before or since was on vivid display in the Super Bowl I DVD. I'm talking here about C.O.D., or Change of Direction.

C.O.D. is normally used to evaluate defensive backs, who have to be able to backpedal, stop, break left, break right—that is, change directions—in an eye blink if they hope to play in the NFL. Defensive ends and tackles need to be agile, but the principal criterion used to evaluate that position is strength.

Willie Davis had C.O.D. skills that rivaled top defensive backs. The old cliché "stop on a dime" might have been coined especially for him. Only he could also start on a dime, cut left on a dime, veer right on a dime, backpedal on a ... well, you get the picture.

To illustrate Willie at work, the producers of the Super Bowl I film even cut in some footage of him chasing and catching Fran Tarkenton, who of course wasn't present that Sunday. Why? Because KC's Len Dawson rivaled John Unitas in being slow of foot, whereas watching Willie track the greatest scrambler in NFL history like a heat-seeking missile was a lot more revelatory, not to mention a lot more fun.

And now, back to the game ...

In virtually every replay, the film captured Willie D nailing a Chiefs ball carrier, harassing or sacking Len Dawson, destroying blocking schemes, and redirecting the flow of the play. I can say with absolute confidence that on that day, Willie Davis left no regrets on the floor of the Los Angeles Coliseum.

WILLIE AND I spent the afternoon viewing and dissecting that golden day 40 years ago. Not surprisingly, we talked a lot about Vince Lombardi and what he had meant to us. That always happens when old Packers get together. Willie's feelings about the man, like mine, are complex. Also par for the course among old Packers.

Willie said he dreaded the Old Man's "acid tongue." Nobody was immune, said Willie, and if you were the target, it felt like a hard shot to the face. But Willie also expressed his deep and profound respect for Coach Lombardi, and became emotional when talking about a personal reason for revering the man.

"When I got to Green Bay in 1960," Willie said, "there was only one other black player, Emlen Tunnell. Bill, when you got there, there were something like nine or ten, right? I respected Coach Lombardi for many reasons, but one of the most important was the fact that he had such a progressive social agenda."

After that conversation with Willie, I just counted from my team picture. Willie was right. There were nine African-Americans on the Packers roster in 1965:

> Lionel Aldridge, DE
> Herb Adderley, DB, Hall of Fame
> Junior Coffey, RB
> Willie Davis, DE, Hall of Fame

Marv Fleming, TE
Bob Jeter, DB
Elijah Pitts, RB
Dave Robinson, LB
Willie Wood, DB, Hall of Fame

The one aspect of Vince Lombardi's greatness that may have been given short shrift in the many examinations of his career was his awareness of racial reality. The fact that he actually used the narrow prejudices of other clubs to load his roster with great talent speaks to his social conscience and his willingness to judge people on their merits, not the color of their skin.

Willie introduced me to the members of the leadership group. In doing so, he noted that in addition to my college football analyst work for ESPN and my teaching in the leadership program at the Baylor School in Chatanooga, I also did a lot of public speaking. (Check me out, if you wish, at billcurry.org.)

Willie concluded with an admonition, "And please, Bill, stop saying in your speeches that I'm like God."

"I do *not* say you are *like God*," I replied, referring to our long-ago-but-not-forgotten exchange one night during training camp in 1965. Willie knew that the story of that encounter was one of the staples in my repertoire, and that I'd told it hundreds of times in speeches around the country.

"I say that there in the dark that night I thought you *sounded* like God. Besides," I went on, "it's my story and I'll tell it exactly like I want to tell it."

Not only that, I pointed out, but I had been instructed by a distinguished man of the cloth to do so.

Bishop L. Bevel Jones, former Bishop of the Methodist Church and a powerful influence on me for the last 45 years, listened to me speak some years back. "Bill," he said to me afterwards, "the church is not doing the job in the racial arena. You have a moral and spiritual obligation to tell your Willie Davis story every day for the rest of your life. It will be a beacon for many who are stuck in racist attitudes."

Bishop, I haven't told that story every day, but I have told it a lot and I'm going to continue telling it.

Hear that, Willie?

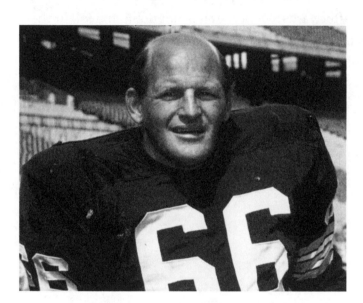

The man made my life miserable for the two
seasons that we were teammates. And the
thing I regret most today is that I never
found the will to apologize to him
until it was too late.

6

RAY NITSCHKE
INTIMIDATOR

R ay Nitschke was an intimidator. No surprise there. You expect middle linebackers who play their way into the NFL Hall of Fame to be intimidators. And you expect them to look the part.

But Ray had a cover. In street clothes, he looked dapper, sharp, like a page out of *Esquire*. He wore glasses that gave him a professorial look. He kept the light blond fringe on the sides of his otherwise utterly bald head neatly trimmed and brushed. His expensive front teeth came courtesy of an expert orthodontist. Add a cap and gown and he would blend in seamlessly in a procession of distinguished scholars at a university graduation ceremony.

The first time I saw him play on TV was in the NFL Championship game at Yankee Stadium in 1962. The Packers were defending their title in a rematch of the 1961 title game in which they'd annihilated the Giants 37-0 in Green Bay. Once again, the Packers defense dominated the Giants, and Green Bay won 16-7 on the margin of three Jerry Kramer field goals.

My dominant memory of the game was No. 66 in the white jersey. He seemed to be in the middle of every pileup.

He scuttled from end to end, looking like a giant fiddler crab in a football helmet. When blockers tried to take him high, he flicked them aside with his forearm, a legal and formidable weapon in our sport. When they went at his legs, he seemed to sprout extra appendages to maintain his balance as he slid off in pursuit of the ball. Then, when he reached the hapless ball carriers, he didn't just tackle them—he obliterated them.

Play after play, always on the move, No. 66 ripped the heart out of the Giant offense that day. Everything my coaches had demanded of us on our Georgia Tech team was present in his performance: intensity, lateral movement, power, balance, speed, and absolute absorption in the moment.

I was awed by what he did to the Giants. So was everyone else. After the game, Ray Nitschke was voted the Most Valuable Player.

That very night, Nitschke appeared on *What's My Line*, one of the most widely watched shows in the early history of network television. The format, for those of you youngsters scratching your heads right about now, required a witty, clever, four-person panel (including, at one time or another, Manhattan luminaries Dorothy Kilgallen, Arlene Francis, Steve Allen, Bennett Cerf, and Fred Allen) prompted by a moderator (John Daly) to guess the occupations of guests. The panelists were allowed to ask probing questions, short of the name of the occupation itself. Ten "no" answers and the guest won the grand total of $50.

The night Nitschke appeared, his name was withheld (not uncommon if a guest's name but not his face might be recognizable). All the panel members knew, before they started grilling him, was that he was poised, physically imposing, and respectable looking in his horn-rimmed glasses and Brooks Brothers suit. A lawyer? A professor? A literary figure?

No one guessed his occupation, and the Manhattan-based panelists were star-struck when they learned that their guest had just three hours earlier ravaged their beloved Giants. Bennett Cerf, who had been at the game, let the others go through their customary drill for a few minutes, then ID'd him.

Yes, that Ray Nitschke.

TWO YEARS LATER, I sat in the Cotton Bowl in Dallas with my wife, Carolyn, and Marie Lombardi before a Cowboys-Packers game. That day, I would sign my first professional football contract.

Aglow from the thrill of being there, I scanned the field during warm-ups looking for that double-digit number of the man they were now calling the Bald Eagle. When I found him, I was surprised that he had no shoulder pads or helmet. He was casually throwing a football back and forth with Lee Roy Caffey, another starting linebacker.

Some people who inspire from afar seem to diminish when one encounters them in person. Not Ray Nitschke. He seemed to have increased in size, stature, and presence. Even without pads he was big: 6'3", 245 pounds of destructive force. Add a couple of inches of height with cleated shoes and the crown of the helmet, increase the already astounding shoulder width by six inches with the shoulder pads, and the effect was overwhelming, especially on first encounter. He towered over the proceedings with his size, presence, and talent. And that's without taking into consideration his aura.

Oh, and one other thing: When he opened his mouth to smile at Caffey, the expensive front teeth were missing. That gaping hole between incisors dramatically altered his appearance. The gentle professor I'd seen two years before on *What's My Line?* was now a warrior.

WALKING INTO THE Packers locker room for the first time in July 1965, I instinctively turned to locate Ray Nitschke.

There he was across the room, laughing, waving his arms, and talking in a nasal Chicago accent. He was wearing only a tee shirt, jock, and flip-flops, and holding a cigarette. Huge in the upper body but surprisingly slender legs. He exuded power and force, even while near naked.

Yet something about him seemed sinister. He was too ... something. I couldn't put my finger on it. But I decided then and there that I didn't like him.

Understand that one characteristic of highly competitive people is a tendency to form snap judgments about one another. Imagine large rooms filled with alpha males. We decide on the spot, based on factors we might not even understand, just who is—and isn't—a threat. In NFL locker rooms, I have seen friendships formed in a matter of minutes and enemies created even faster. It comes with the turf, I guess. In the jungle, there's no place for nuance and no time to weigh pluses and minuses. He who hesitates is eaten.

That day, my first in the Packers locker room, I quickly sensed that Nitschke would become a problem for me. It was completely visceral—but also correct. Ray Nitschke did become a problem for me. But oddly enough, our relationship began with a kind gesture from him.

The day of my arrival in camp, since I hadn't practiced with the squad, all I could do was long-snap. We trotted out for a few field goal attempts near the end of the scrimmage, and as I assumed my stance over the ball, Ray stepped up to me.

My imagination went into high gear. Here I was, in my first play ever with the Green Bay Packers, and Ray Nitschke was about to launch my butt into the holder, who happened to be Bart Starr. I breathed deeply, focused on Bart's hand, extended as a target, and figured that at least I would make my one professional snap a perfect one.

Just then Ray leaned down and said in a clear voice, "I won't hit you full speed. Brace yourself, and I'll just bump you so you can get adjusted."

As a wave of relief washed over me, I snapped the ball back, braced myself—and took a light tap on the shoulder pads from the great Ray Nitschke. His message, "Welcome, rookie. We'll go easy in the beginning. I don't need to tell you that this is going to change the instant we're at full speed."

And change it did when we got to the practice field two days later. Unconsciously, I guess I had the infantile notion that Ray would continue to help me make the transition from college to pro and help me make the team. He helped me stay a Packer, alright, but his method was more Jungle Law than Sunday School Lesson.

Given a choice back then, I'd have opted for the gentle method. Now, of course, I know that if Nitschke had babied me along, it would have been the end of me as a professional athlete.

It was from Ray Nitschke that I learned the practical application of The Law of the Jungle. I had read Rudyard Kipling as a boy and had reveled in Mowgli's adventures. Each rite of passage, each scrape with death was essential to his survival:

> Now this is the Law of the Jungle, as old and
> as true as the sky.
> The wolf that shall keep it will prosper; the
> wolf that shall break it must die.
> As the creeper girdles the tree trunk, it
> runneth forward and back.
> The strength of the Pack is the wolf; the
> strength of the wolf is the Pack.

The moral? In the jungle one must risk death in order to learn how to live. Think of pro football as the the jungle.

To have any hope of survival in pro football, you've got to be willing to confront extreme risk. You need to thrive in a hostile world of giant bodies colliding at full speed. You've got to go to a place rational people avoid at all costs. And you've got to learn to love it.

The first time I snapped the ball in an 11-on-11 drill a few days later, my assignment was to block Nitschke. I never saw him. I'm not exaggerating; I never saw him. Because of a flaw in my snapping technique, I lost sight of him on an off-tackle play and he smashed the ball carrier to the ground.

Following the play, I heard from just behind the huddle the patented Lombardi bellow, "What the hell's going on out heah? Who the hell's got Nitschke?"

Lombardi, of course, knew perfectly well who "had" Nitschke, but he had a policy of never jumping rookies. So he just glared directly at me, set the huddle, and gave Bart the next play. I was struggling with the new play nomenclature, and it took me a couple of seconds to realize that on this play I was supposed to block ... Ray Nitschke.

At this juncture, I should tell you that I fully expected to block him. After all, I was a competitor, and that's what competitors do. We thrive on the opportunity to match wits, power, leverage, and courage with a worthy opponent. We adjust our inner computers to aim a little lower, drive a little harder, and thrust with a more balanced base. We harden our resolve, and we attack.

But I could have watched a hundred Nitschke performances on TV. I could have studied him for hours on film. I could have memorized his stats. I could have seen a season of his games live. I could have done all these things and more, and nothing could have prepared me for what happened next.

As the snap count commenced, I saw from Nitschke's feet that he was about to come straight at me. Middle linebackers' feet and toes tell centers virtually all we need to know most of the time.

But once again, the flaw in my technique betrayed me. Utterly unaware of what I was doing, I bobbed my head downward slightly as I made the snap. That gave up precious hundredths of a second as well as sight of Ray's toes, so that those big feet I'd noted a second earlier were on me before I could get maximum explosion.

Outsmarted and out-techniqued again, I remember seeing him burst from his coil—how did he get so low?—and bring his heavily padded right forearm into a cocked striking position as I hurled myself into him with all my might. With one mighty blow, he knocked me out. My knees buckled. I'd never been hit so hard in my life. I was semi-conscious, on all fours, instinctively shaking my head to try to clear it, when the ball carrier arrived. Nitschke smashed him, picked him up, and drove him into my lower back, pancaking us both us into the turf.

There we lay, a three-man pile with a near-comatose center at the bottom.

As we unpiled, Ray looked into my eyes with evident contempt, and my real hatred of him began. At some level I must have known that this was only going to get worse. As I continued to shake my head to get clarity, I sensed a strange looseness in my equipment. Reaching up to the left side of my helmet, I found that my chinstrap had been snapped and my facemask had detached from my headgear.

I didn't hear any birds chirping, but I most assuredly saw stars, and they stayed with me all the way back into the huddle, accompanied by a new kind of hysterical fear: I could not block Ray Nitschke.

Every day after that was a nightmare. I would not quit, but from that day until the day I left the Green Bay Packers two years later, I lived in a state of suspense and anxiety. I would never earn my teammates' or coaches' respect this way. More important, I would never regain my self respect unless and until I could handle the great Ray Nitschke.

EVERY TIME AN NFL team puts on full pads in practice the week before a game, it means one thing: blitz drill. The goal? To hone the offensive line's ability to protect every NFL team's most precious asset, their quarterback.

In a blitz drill, the idea is protect the passer from the normal rushers—defensive tackles and ends—as well as from blitzing linebackers, who can drop into coverage or explode toward the line of scrimmage, depending on the defensive call.

When a blitzer does come, any blocker assigned to a linebacker—most often the center—is expected to pick him up, set his feet, explode into the onrushing freight train, and stop him in his tracks.

A blitz pickup guy has an obvious and highly visible responsibility. The relative anonymity that comes with being an offensive lineman—especially a center—goes by the wayside when a blitz is missed. When does a TV analyst ever mention a center's name? Always after he botches a long snap, of course. But also, if the analyst is sharp and understands the consequences if a center fails to pick up a blitz. "Well, folks, Butkus seldom blitzes, but when he does, he's the responsibility of Bill Curry. Too bad for Starr. Curry just got beat, and Bart took an incredible shot!"

The blitz drill is the most important component of a practice session in the NFL. Coach Lombardi wanted it to be

ALERT THE MEDIA:
LOMBARDI ADMITS HE WAS WRONG

Speaking of great linebackers, Dick Butkus came into the league in 1965 with a huge reputation, but he wasn't at all graceful or fluid, and he looked awkward at times.

As we studied film of the Bears before our first game of the season with them, Coach Lombardi noted, "That Butkus guy, number 51, he doesn't look as good as I'd heard. Looks like he's just a big stiff that will end up as a defensive tackle."

Coach was right: Butkus didn't look good on film.

But as the season progressed, we watched Butkus do things like force six turnovers in one game against the Baltimore Colts. And in our second meeting of the year with the Bears, on October 31, we saw him systematically take apart our ground game.

The most vivid Butkus Moment I recall from that season came as I looked on from the sideline in Wrigley Field. Jimmy Taylor took the handoff on our patented off-tackle play to the weak side. Forrest Gregg and Paul Hornung executed their blocks perfectly, the hole opened just as it should have, and Taylor tore through it, the most punishing runner in the NFL, running to daylight.

Then he disappeared.

Butkus had materialized out of nowhere, as if by magic. He exploded out of the mass of blockers and defenders inside the play and hit Taylor with such force and velocity that Jim's headgear spun off. Butkus stripped him of the ball and in the next instant was running toward our goal line all alone, waving the football over his head in exultant triumph.

> It stands to this day as the single most violent, most shocking one-on-one tackle of a great back I have ever seen.
>
> In the film session of the game the following week, Coach Lombardi stopped the film at that play. "I was wrong about that guy."
>
> No kidding.

as trying as possible for the offense so we would be ready to execute our protection schemes to perfection on Sundays. If Ray Nitschke was his weapon of choice on Sundays, he was Lombardi's training machine on Tuesdays.

I dreaded Tuesdays.

To save time, we didn't huddle between plays during blitz drills. Standing at the line of scrimmage, Bart would call out the formations, the pass plays, and the snap count. That meant the defense knew when the ball was to be snapped. This was part of Coach Lombardi's genius. He wanted to make it harder for the OL by giving blitzing linebackers an edge they would never have in true game action.

The point? If you could pick up the blitz in practice, it ought to be a snap in games.

A typical play would have us at the line of scrimmage, me watching Nitschke's feet, Bart calling the cadence, and Nitschke beginning to move toward his blitz gap. My job was to sit in there, wait until the proper snap count, pop the ball back, dart backwards to a depth of three and a half yards, move over into Nitschke's path, bend my knees, and explode into his chest.

Too often, way too often from my perspective, Ray would hit the gap at the snap of the ball—remember, he knew when that would be—before I could get over and get set. The resulting collision was a pitiful mismatch in which I was knocked reeling, either into the quarterback or at the quarterback's feet.

But that wasn't the hard part. The hard part was the silence. The disdain. The snickers from some of my teammates. The sneer from Lombardi. The humiliation every single Tuesday.

The hard part was that even when Nitschke smashed me with his forearm, hit me late, shoved me to the ground, and I came up swinging, he'd show his disdain for my ineptness by not even doing me the honor of whipping my ass. He'd just hold me at bay with one hand as I flailed away, grin his awful toothless grin, and mutter, "Come on, kid—you gonna get hurt out here."

It didn't help that I was constantly being compared to Ken Bowman, our starting center. As polished technically as I was crude, Bowman always beat the blitzer to the intersection spot between the line of scrimmage and quarterback, always with enough time to set his feet, drop his butt, keep his head up, square his shoulders, and nail Nitschke right between the sixes.

Tuesdays never changed during my rookie season. The blitz drill never changed. Nitschke never changed. If I did improve, he just kicked everything up a notch and ran over me again. I seldom slept on Monday nights.

EVEN AS WE moved through a very good season on our way to another NFL Championship, even as I proved my mettle on special teams, and even as other veterans accepted me, the Nitschke thing only got worse.

Once I was eating lunch with Elijah Pitts and Ray came up and sat down across from us. A terrific running back and great competitor, Elijah was also one of the nicest human beings ever to grace the earth, and he turned to me from time to time to include me in what he was saying. Ray and Elijah had both served in the Army, and the subject turned to KP. As they laughed over the grief dealt out by the NCOs, Elijah turned and smiled at me as if to say, "Jump in, you're one of us."

So I did. I blurted out something about advanced ROTC camp, and the big guy who once took me into the latrine at Fort Bragg at midnight, handed me a toothbrush, and told me he wanted to "be able to eat [bleeping] chop suey off the [bleeping] floor without a [bleeping] germ in the place."

But Ray turned slowly my way, looked me squarely in the eye through those thick, horn-rimmed glasses, and said, "Nobody asked you anything, so keep your [bleeping] mouth shut. Understand?"

Elijah was horrified. "Hey, Ray! The man's just trying to be friendly. C'mon, be a teammate!"

Ray now turned to Elijah. "I don't want him in our conversation. I'm talking to you, not him. Understand?"

As I hastily picked up my tray and stood up, Elijah just shook his head and said to me, "I'm sorry Bill. I really am."

It would be 32 years before I could forgive Ray Nitschke.

THE NEXT YEAR, 1966, when I reported on the first day of training camp, I was thrilled to find a white number 50 jersey in my locker along with my green one. Our consistent practice colors were green for the offense and white for defense. That meant that I was going to split time between linebacker and center.

Great! Linebacker was more fun than center, and the move would save me from being on the wrong side of the line on those dreaded Tuesdays. Furthermore, I'd be behind the great Nitschke, and I might learn to be the intimidator rather than the intimidated.

Throughout the exhibition season, I mostly played linebacker behind Ray. It was the most fun I'd ever had playing football. I covered all kicks, played on special teams, and played a little on offense but more on defense.

I began to fantasize about becoming the next Chuck Bednarik, the extraordinary center/linebacker for the Philadelphia Eagles who'd played both ways on the 1960 NFL champions, the team that had given the Packers their only playoff loss in the Lombardi era.

But one day after practice, Coach Lombardi called me over. "Bill, I'd hoped to leave you on defense, but we just learned that a backup center we'd signed won't be reporting. You've got to begin on offense until we can make some adjustments."

Then, in an exhibition game against the Steelers, Ken Bowman dislocated his shoulder and I took over at center. All I remember about what happened next is that, a few plays later, I was kicked in the side of the head. The hit was unintentional, but it dropped me like a gunnysack.

Adhering to the NFL code of courage, of course, I refused to leave the game.

What happened next is muddled, but it's been told to me by teammates enough times that I have a fair handle on the facts. We broke the huddle, came to the ball, went on the correct count—and got hit with a five-yard penalty for an illegal shift when I failed to snap the ball. People asked if I was okay, and I nodded sure, let's go. But the same thing happened on the next play, so the trainers came out and walked me off the field.

Following the game I hadn't been able to dress myself, and Carolyn had to come into the locker room to retrieve me. My only recollection of that phase of the evening is of looking at the scoreboard when we walked outside and wondering where on earth we were. She then drove us to the postgame team buffet at St. Norbert, where Coach Lombardi stood up across the room and yelled out a few questions:

"Curry, do you know where we are?"

"No, sir."

"Do you remember how you got here?"

"No, sir. I sure don't."

"Curry, who won the game?"

"We did, Coach."

"Good!" he yelled back, and everyone broke out laughing.

Hey, I knew two things that night. I knew who Vince Lombardi was and I knew we won the game.

What else could have mattered?

MY BIG CHANCE

Our first league game was a 41-9 blowout of the hapless Pittsburgh Steelers. That meant many kickoffs to cover (one of my main jobs), and the temperature was in the 90s.

Late in the third quarter I was put in the game at offensive center. Other reserves were playing as well, so we didn't move the ball. I snapped for and covered the punt (my other main job), and remember being surprised at how tired I was. The cool weather in Green Bay the previous six weeks vs. the extreme heat and humidity in Pittsburgh, the number of 50-yard sprints on kickoffs and punts, and unadulterated rookie anxiety had sapped me even though I hadn't been playing offense or defense.

When I started to the sideline, line coach Ray Wietecha signaled to go back onto the field. Ray cupped his hands and shouted, "Stay out there! Take over from Caffey!" I'd practiced just a little on defense, maybe two or three days total, and here I was being sent in to replace Le Roy Caffey at left linebacker.

Wow! What an opportunity! I much preferred playing defense, and here I was, being showcased at LB!

Much as I like to project possibilities, though, I didn't have time to dream about playing next to Ray Nitschke—as opposed to across from him in practice—because our first play called for a blitz, and I had business to attend to.

At the snap, I hit the line full speed and had the quarterback in my sights when a little tailback named Cannonball Butler stepped up and stuck his Riddell headgear in my sternum, which I hadn't bothered to protect. It was a hell of a shot, and made me feel like puking.

So here I was in my first game ever, the most famous coach in the world trusting me—albeit in a blowout—to play offense, defense, and special teams, and I can't breathe, I'm tired, and I'm on the verge of throwing up. Yet I played most of the rest of the way, so happy to be on the field that I got through the nausea, lowered my shoulder on my next blitz, and made no assignment errors.

On the plane ride home, Lombardi came by my seat, observed that it was unusual for a rookie to do what I had done, and that he was glad he had a chance to get the experience for me.

I was giddy.

Then I started fantasizing about playing next to Nitschke at LB.

Postscript: The rest of the season, I played only on special teams.

THE FOLLOWING MONDAY morning, I sat in the locker room with a splitting headache. A severe concussion will do that to you.

Coach Lombardi came in and called for Ray Nitschke and me. "You two dress in pads and go on out to the field with Ray." (That would be assistant coach Ray Wietecha.) And Lombardi turned on his heel and went back into his office.

Pads?

On Monday?

When Nitschke and I reached the field, Wietecha told us to stretch. Then, for the only time in all my years of football, two lone players engaged in a full-speed, one-on-one drill. After several smashes, the results of which I do not recall, Wietecha stopped us and told us to go back to the locker room.

The next day was the Tuesday before the last exhibition game. That's when the final cut was announced, meaning the roster for the season had been selected. Only then did it dawn on me: The final phase of my "medical exam" to see if I was fit to play was to see if I would willingly, enthusiastically smash my face into the meanest, hardest-hitting linebacker in the game, who also happened to hate my guts.

I passed.

I know now that, because of the severe concussion two nights before, I was at risk in that one-on-one drill of suffering a career-ending injury. Or even death. Know now? Hell, I knew then.

Was that drill dangerous? Very.

Was taking part in it courageous on my part? No, it was stupid.

Who deserves the lion's share of the blame? Me.

I was a grown man and understood the system. I crossed that line of my own volition. In retrospect, I feel like I was compelled more by something within me than by Lombardi, by Nitschke's presence, or even by my desire to make the roster.

Most professional athletes are faced with a similar decision at some point. We praise them, we reward them, and we even worship them if their timing is right. We mourn them if it's not.

Normal people may well question my sanity.

Others will challenge Lombardi's principles.

Some will ask whether, during my 22 years in coaching, I ever put players to such a test. (The answer: no.)

What I did do as a coach, though, was to test the mettle of thousands of young men by driving them beyond their perceived limits in extreme physical and emotional circumstances. My assistant coaches and I did our best to prepare them to play an emotionally and physically demanding game. We prepared them to perform with courage, perseverance, and grace under fire. Under close medical observation, we took them to places they thought impossible, and made them continue.

We taught them that virtually anything is possible when a determined group of people refuses to be divided or to quit.

I LEFT GREEN Bay with some heavy baggage. Deep in my soul was an antipathy the likes of which I had never known—and would never know again. An antipathy toward a single man: Ray Nitschke.

As a Colt, I would see Ray across the line four more times. We won all four games, and he never once laid a hand on Johnny Unitas.

Since my life revolved around winning and losing, I convinced myself that I had somehow prevailed in the Nitschke Affair. My personal vendetta became complete in my mind when George Plimpton and I wrote *One More July*, which was published in 1977. In it, I pilloried Nitschke, insinuating that when I was with the Colts we had manhandled him and that I had repaid him for his sin of disrespecting me.

The minute the book came out and I saw my words in print, I regretted them. There's something about black type on a white page that drains nuance from what, in this case, was a gut feeling in the first place. Plus, I was a rookie at the writing game.

Excuses, excuses ...

But there it was in black and white: CURRY GETS EVEN WITH NITSCHKE.

I had several chances to make amends, the first one coming just a few months after the publication of *One More July*. Bart Starr had just hired me as the new offensive line coach of the Packers. Soon after I came on board, the whole staff attended the Packer Hall of Fame Annual Banquet held in the Brown County Arena, which sits adjacent to Lambeau Field in Green Bay. The atmosphere was festive and I was heartily accepting congratulations for my new position from throngs of the Packer Faithful when Ray appeared.

Ray usually brought with him a whiff of danger—or so it always seemed to me—but this time was different. I experienced none of the fear or intimidation of past years, and I was conscious of my newfound bravado, which I interpreted to be courage ... and just a bit of the benevolent conqueror surveying the vanquished foe.

Ray didn't mince words. As we shook hands, he said, "You never handled me like that." I smiled broadly and said nothing. In my secret thoughts I glowed, remembering the scores of our games and feeling my most recent Super Bowl ring on my right-hand ring finger. I may have remembered a block or two in which Ray had been on the ground.

When he got no response to his first provocation, he pressed on in this new kind of game we were playing. He leaned closer, glanced across the room, and muttered, "Jackie didn't like that stuff you wrote about me."

"Good," I thought. "I've embarrassed him in front of his wife and family. Just the thing to teach him a lesson." What I said was tongue in cheek, designed to give him no personal satisfaction, but to demonstrate that one could win a duel, then be a good Southern gentleman in the aftermath.

"Okay," I said. "I'll apologize to Jackie. Where is she?"

He nodded in her direction and I turned on my heel and walked directly over to Jackie Nitschke, who was engaged in conversation with a friend. I waited in my best Southern gentleman fashion until she paused. Then I stepped a bit closer and she sensed my presence. When she turned and saw my face, she went pale. I felt genuinely sorry for her and quickly sought to put her at ease. I took her hand in mine, looked her in the eye, and said, "Jackie, Ray says I hurt your feelings and I want you to know I am really sorry. I didn't think about your family, and that was wrong on my part."

Now, Jackie Nitschke was known to be plainspoken, and her unhesitating response remains one of my greatest surprises to this day. With just a moment to recover her poise, she took a deep breath and said evenly, "Well, don't worry too much about it. Ray loved it. He loves anything that is written about him."

Now it was my turn to be dumbstruck. I was relieved that Jackie was going to let me off the hook without a tongue lashing, but I sure didn't want Ray to be happy!

I let it drop and headed for the open bar.

My next move should have been to invite them to dinner, where I could set things right in a more relaxed, less impersonal setting.

It never crossed my mind.

I AM ASHAMED now that I wrote what I did about him. I am more ashamed that I could not make myself do the right thing even after I realized what that right thing was.

When I left coaching for good in 1996, I began to keep a personal diary. The worthy habit didn't last, but it did help generate certain positive ideas. One of those ideas was to call Ray Nitschke, fly to his home, and do the right thing. I would apologize for what I had written, put this thing behind both of us, and permanently heal the open wounds that had been re-opened so many times. I promised myself I was going to do it ... as soon as I could get around to it.

Then, on March 9, 1998, I opened my newspaper and a headline screamed out at me: "NFL Hall of Fame Linebacker Ray Nitschke Dead at 61."

Ray, I am so sorry.

Coach Shula could turn the tiniest spark of a player's desire to contribute into a flame. I know, because he did it with me. For the first time, I came to love the football field as much as I once had the baseball diamond.

7

DON SHULA
TEACHER

B ill, this is Don Shula."

The call came out of the blue on March 4, 1967, so I decided to listen a minute to see which of my buddies was messing with my head. It was a prank, I was sure of it, conceived and executed by one of my pals who knew how crazed I was by what Lombardi had done to me.

"I'll get right to the point," the voice said. "Would you like to play for the Baltimore Colts?"

Play for the Baltimore Colts? As opposed to playing for the certain-to-be-hapless New Orleans Saints, a first-year team that took me in the expansion draft when Vince Lombardi put me on the unprotected list? Was this guy kidding? Ah, well, I'd go along with the joke.

To "Shula," whoever he was, I said, "Why, yes, Coach, I would very much like to play for the Colts."

To myself: "I'd walk from Atlanta to Baltimore to play for Don Shula and the Colts."

The voice on the phone then told me that he respected my special teams play. He was considering a trade that might include me. If it went through, he'd like to give me a shot at playing linebacker.

Uh-huh. Yeah. Sure.

Wait a minute ... linebacker?

All along it had been my dream to play defense in the NFL, the way I had at Tech, so this guy's words kicked in like a shot of adrenalin. And then the voice and the message sank in, and I practically yelled into the receiver, "You really are Coach Shula!"

The voice at the other end laughed and said, "Just call me Don."

"Coach, I can't possibly call you by your first name, at least not yet," I said. "But I swear I would hitchhike to Baltimore to be on your team!"

He laughed again—after all, he'd been bounced around the NFL a little himself in a seven-year career with three teams. But then he tried to calm me down. "The deal isn't final, so don't get too excited just yet. Somebody from my staff will be back in touch if we can pull this thing off."

They did pull it off, and I became a Baltimore Colt.

The way I saw the deal, I'd died (New Orleans) and gone to heaven (Baltimore).

MY CONSIDERABLE RELIEF at moving from an expansion team (without even slowing down) now teamed up with unbridled elation: Carolyn was expecting our first child. The next few months became one of the more wonderful periods of anticipation in our lives. New team and new member of our family.

As Carolyn's pregnancy progressed, and as I worked hard to get my body and mind prepared for my first Baltimore training camp, it became clear that this was going to be a large baby. Carolyn isn't very tall—around 5'4", tops—and she carried the baby straight out in front. She could have used her belly as a food tray for Sunday dinners.

The Original Pregnant Lady, as we took to calling her, continued doing her beloved yard work against my explicit but futile protestations. We had purchased our first home in Atlanta, and Carolyn delighted in her azaleas, dogwoods, and ivy.

The good news was that she was due well before training camp was to begin. The bad news is that the due date came and went, the baby decided to bide her time, and we approached my departure date.

It was during this period of anxious waiting that we chose—what were we thinking of?—to attend a football game, of all things, at Atlanta Stadium. The Coaches' All-America Game was played annually in Atlanta at that time, and Francis Tarkenton had tickets. Fran and his then-wife, Elaine, were dear friends, and they were simply trying to distract us from our obvious concerns.

Anyway, before the game, I dropped the nine-month pregnant Carolyn and the Tarkentons as close to the entrance of the stadium as I could manage, parked the car, and joined them. Following the game, they were to board a bus and ride to a common area, where I would pick them up. As they boarded the full bus, there was instant recognition of the famous Bulldogs star and a fascinated audience watched as he dragged my cumbersome bride up the steps and into the aisle. When Fran noticed the attention of all those people, he turned to Carolyn, whom he called Giggles, and said in a loud voice, "Don't you worry, Giggles. We'll find you a husband yet!"

The whole bus burst into laughter. My scholarly, blushing bride—a graduate of Agnes Scott, thank you very much, the college of preference for proper Georgia women—was mortified. Fortunately, she has a great sense of humor and was soon able to ... well, giggle about it.

Training camp or no, the baby wasn't cooperating. I reported the second week of July, went to work with my new team, and lay awake nights the next two and a half weeks, awaiting news of the blessed (if delayed) event. On July 24, 1967, at 9:30 p.m., the wall-phone in our dorm rang and I grabbed it, as I had been doing since we arrived. It was Carolyn.

"I'm in labor," she said calmly. "Daddy's here to take me to the hospital. Dr. Gillespie is on his way there right now. Everything's fine. Now, I want you to take two aspirins and go to bed."

Yes, m'am.

But before following her orders, I called Coach Shula with the news and to tell him I'd like to go be with my wife. It was at this point that I came face to face with the famous Shula Focus.

"One day," he said. "You get one day. Go see your wife and baby, call and tell us what you have, and don't miss a practice after tomorrow. Good luck. And congratulations."

With considerable assistance and kindness from roommate Mike Curtis, which included the use of his brand new Thunderbird, I headed for the airport at 5:00 a.m. I had reservations for a 7:30 flight. I hadn't slept a wink. No cell phones, of course, and no way to get through to the hospital waiting room.

Panic and Curry: both five-letter words.

That night and the next four hours would be the most harrowing of my life. When I ran off my Delta flight, stumbling over other passengers, half apologizing, half expecting them to understand my plight, I spotted my Dad and younger sister Debbie across the gate area. They were smiling broadly and holding up cigars ... with pink wrappers.

Kristin Carolyn Curry had decided to show up at 5:29 a.m., fully three weeks late. She was perfect, healthy, and weighed in at nine pounds, six ounces. My beautiful Carolyn had come through just fine, although Dr. Gillespie could not recall such a big baby from such a small woman. When I arrived at Carolyn's room and Kristin was placed in my arms, it was one of the two most powerful moments of my life.

The second was the birth of our son, Bill Jr., three years later. Carolyn went into labor during *Monday Night Football* on ABC. The only problem was that I was in Milwaukee and she was home in Baltimore. We beat the Packers 13-10, and I flew directly back to Baltimore following the game. When I walked in the door around 4:30 a.m., Carolyn greeted me not with "Hi, Hon," or "Good game, Bill," but "Let's go to the hospital!"

Billy was born 19 hours later after a very tough delivery for Carolyn. He weighed nine pounds, two ounces, and was two weeks early. The doctor said that had he gone full term, he would have been a 10-pounder. I ran into the recovery room laughing and crying, "It's a boy! It's a boy!"

"That's right," said Carolyn groggily, "and that's it."

I got the message, loud and clear.

MY FIRST LEAGUE game as a Baltimore Colt was against the Atlanta Falcons—on national television.

Midway through the third quarter, I was called for a clip on our sideline, negating a long punt return. Coach Shula ran onto the field, grabbed me by the shoulders, and laced into me with a verbal barrage that would have made Coach Lombardi proud. I was certain I hadn't clipped, and because I was in my hyper-competitive mode, I yelled back at him with similar enthusiasm—and language.

On the following Tuesday morning, as we watched the special teams films, assistant coach John Sandusky asked, "Curry, is that a clip?"

"Yes, I suppose it is," I answered.

Big John then said, "Well, in that case, let me make a suggestion. The next time you decide to dog-cuss the head coach on national television, you make damn sure you don't clip."

I had been sent packing by the Packers. We had a five-week-old baby to support. And now I was staring the possibility of a one-game career with the Baltimore Colts dead in the eye.

There was only one thing to do.

I went and found Coach Shula, asked to speak to him privately, and followed him into the tiny equipment room at Memorial Stadium. He shut the door, turned, and eyed me, waiting.

"Coach, I was wrong to yell at you on Sunday," I said. "I thought I had a legal block, I was upset, and I made a bad mistake. I'm sorry."

Shula smiled and said, "I kind of like that spirit. Just don't clip the guy next time, okay?"

In that instant, I understood a bit of Don Shula's greatness.

Aggressive, competitive men are drawn to aggressive, competitive men. He expected performance and results, not conformity. It became clear in time that he found ways to breathe spirit and dedication into most of his players.

I would fight for him—and I would not clip.

ONE OF THE shocks of my career—the memory of which still gives me the shivers—was the length and ferocity of Don Shula's training camp practices.

We were taped, dressed, and in meetings by 9:00 a.m. After a review of the practice schedule, we were on the field by 9:45, just as the punishing heat of a humid Maryland mid-summer morning began to make its presence felt.

Welcome to another 95-degree day.

The morning practice was devoted to the running game, featuring the Nutcracker Drill, in which one defender attacked one blocker, with one ball carrier running behind the blocker, the three of them confined to a narrow space by two tackling dummies. A center was there to snap the ball and a quarterback to hand it off, but then their duties were done and they stepped back to observe the mayhem that followed.

The Nutcracker was the basic macho confrontation of our sport, done before the entire team. There was adrenaline, drama, and injuries galore, as we learned who would—and wouldn't—attack another man again and again. Technique was a factor, but sheer brute force and will to win were important elements.

To many a high draft choice, the Nutcracker was his first sign that he was in a whole new league.

Group work came next, emphasizing techniques by position, and then combination drills against the defense. In combination drills, we were divided into groups, usually of three on each side of the ball.

In Middle Drill the center and both guards worked against the two defensive tackles and the middle linebacker.

In Half Line the center, guard and tackle on the right side would take on the middle linebacker, defensive tackle and defensive end, followed by the left side in alternating repetitions.

The effect was to get in maximum reps of full-speed hitting with a minimum of risk because of the small number of players in each drill. Very efficient—and very exhausting.

Finally, 11-on-11 pitted two full teams, and included audibles, sophisticated defenses, and our full offensive playbook.

Morning practice was two hours long, and was full-speed hitting every step of the way.

It's hard to over-emphasize the effects of full-speed hits on the psyche and body, both for the hitter and the hittee. In an NFL camp, where the competition for jobs is a survival thing, there are mostly two hitters in each encounter, thereby doubling the force generated by the speed and power. I can still hear and almost feel the power of the blows when men like our left guard Glenn Ressler smashed into defensive tackle Fred Miller.

Damn, those guys could smash!

Each hard hit takes a toll, traumatizing the entire organism. The legs wobble, the head spins, the eyes blur, and the hope is that by the time the next collision occurs, some degree of normalcy will have returned.

Not all hits are created equal. I remember angering defensive tackle Billy Ray Smith once. I had shoved him after a play or some such thing. Normally a good-natured guy, Smith, an ex-Golden Gloves boxing champ, knew how to use his hands, fists, powerful arms, and shoulders. On the next play he made no effort to rush the passer. As I set up, he simply rocketed his huge paw into my forehead. His fist was open so he could use the base of the hand against my Rawlings headgear, and he sprung my neck back like a bobblehead. Knocked out momentarily, I dropped to a knee and took a few seconds to recover, then walked back to the huddle.

On the next play he came sashaying in to rush the passer, and while I kept an eye on his awesome hands, I settled in my stance until he got real close. At just the right moment I exploded that same headgear into his lower jaw, driving with all the force my legs and torso could muster. He staggered back, shook his head, and looked me in the eye.

"Son," he said, "I think you just might have broke my jaw. But I cheap-shotted you, and I'm gonna let it go—this time. You understand?"

My answer, "Don't ever hit me like that again. Do you understand?"

He nodded. Just like that, we had a respect thing going.

If you could be intimidated, somebody in a Shula camp would find you out and he'd send you packing.

A huge difference between the three Shula preseason training camps I endured—which were a lot tougher than the two I experienced as a Packer—was that the Colts had two-a-days for six weeks, right through exhibition season, while Lombardi's lasted precisely 10 days.

Oh, and, one more thing: during the two, two-and-half-hour practice sessions for six August weeks in Baltimore, there was no water on the practice field. That's right—no water. Hard to imagine nowadays, when the importance of hydration is a given, but back then the conventional wisdom was that water was for weaklings and that real men—real football players—could do without and be the tougher for it.

It's just amazing nobody died.

DON SHULA UNDERSTOOD something about hitting. He understood that over the course of the training camp, those of us who survived developed the ability to recover more quickly from the blows and fatigue. And he knew that would give us a competitive advantage over our opponents once the season got under way.

Our morning reps ran into the hundreds, wearing 14 pounds of equipment, in literally every kind of weather—except lightning. Fortunately, Don Shula was terrified by lightning. If so much as a tremble of thunder rippled through a morning or afternoon, he exploded up the hill toward the locker room, waving feverishly for us to follow. In the three seasons I played for him, no one ever caught up with him.

The afternoon session was devoted first to the kicking game and then to the passing offense and defense. It began about 2:30 p.m. and lasted an eternity. It was hotter, you were barely recovered from the morning drill, and the reps were again endless.

Coach Shula was far ahead of his peers in three ways. First, in his emphasis on ball security, the single most important aspect of winning. The team with the fewest turnovers usually wins games. Second, the Colts devoted concentrated practice time to special teams, whose success (or failure) usually determines field position. (Other NFL coaches, including Coach Lombardi, devoted very little time to the kicking game.) And third, we were indoctrinated every drill of every day on the foolishness of penalties.

Practice began with Pat and Go for the first couple of weeks. In this drill, the entire team formed two lines on each the 20-yard lines facing the opposite goal line, on the hash. The quarterbacks took a position on the 20, and on the "pat" of their hands on the ball, the man at the head of the line would "go," exploding off the line of scrimmage, running straight down the field, and the quarterback would hit him with a pass. Every player—including offensive and defensive linemen—was expected to learn to catch and tuck a football. The idea was that every player on the team would have at least cursory experience handling a football.

Coach Shula had veteran wide receiver Raymond Berry explain the art of catching, securing, and locking in the football, so that even offensive linemen learned how it felt to take care of the ball. Raymond, who really did resemble a college professor, glasses and all, took the entire team through the components of seeing the tip of the ball, opening the fingers just so, watching the ball into the hands, clamping it against the ribs, and covering it with the other hand.

The drill might have been funny looking, with lumbering lineman running deep patterns and many a dropped ball, but I can't help but believe it won us a couple of games when tipped balls were bounding around.

For backs, tight ends and receivers, there was another ball security exercise—a daily gauntlet drill, in which each player ran through a tunnel formed by two lines of five players each, on either side of the ball carrier. As the teammates in the gauntlet line reached out to rip at the ball, the ball carrier learned to secure it with his fingers, hand, ribs, and forearm. It was to be "riveted to the ribs."

As long as Pat and Go was in the schedule (the first two weeks), the second period of afternoon practice was punt coverage. Long snappers and punters lined up in the middle of the field, with two lines of coverage people—linebackers, defensive backs, and receivers. They were on either side, spread out just beyond the hash marks. Punt returners stationed roughly 50 yards down the field were expected to cleanly field every punt, make several moves, and run 30 of 40 yards back toward us. The coverage men were to release, sprint toward the returner, come under control, and then tag him. The returner's job, of course, was to keep from being tagged.

Interspersed with the punt drills, receiving roughly one fourth as much time, was kickoff coverage, done much the same way as punt with different positions covering on alternating kicks. Punt protection and kickoff return were added in so that every aspect of special teams was covered every week.

Extra point and field goal work was done after practice, and usually involved only the centers, kickers, and holders. At certain times, once or twice a week, the offensive and defensive units stayed out for protection and field goal rush.

All I had seen of Don Shula up to this point was the driven taskmaster who demanded more on the practice field than anyone I had ever played for or ever heard of. He had us in pads, smashing every drill, all day every day. He promised that we would be the most aggressive, hardest hitting team in the NFL. He told us he wanted a loud, raucous sideline during games, contesting every official's decision that went against us. No sitting on headgears. No butts on the bench. We were to be fully engaged ... every second of every game.

And with all that aggression and hard hitting, there was one more non-negotiable demand: we would be the least penalized team in the league.

During each practice, there was a premium placed on following the rules in every drill. The idea was hammered into our consciousness that we would be the most ferocious, physical, nasty football team in the league—while also being the least penalized.

Obviously, a contradiction in terms: most aggressive and least penalized? I didn't think so. I snickered (quietly, to myself) when he said it the first time at a team meeting.

Only that's the way it worked out. The three years I played under Shula, the Colts out-hit people and were at or near the bottom of the charts for penalties incurred.

Passing offense drills included route running, one-on-one pass rush and protection, full-speed blitz drill, 7-on-7 passing (backs and receivers vs. linebackers and defensive backs), and then 11-on-11.

Finally, each workday ended with gassers, a drill that was the heart and soul of the Donald Francis Shula Conditioning Philosophy.

In a gasser, each position group had to run four widths of the field—over and back, over and back—in a specified time. (The times varied according to position, naturally, but none allowed for jogging.) Those four trips constituted one gasser. On most days we ran four gassers, with one minute of rest between them.

That would be 852 yards, a little shy of half a mile.

After five and a half hours of football.

In the blazing sun.

And you know what? The gassers delivered the goods.

I have never played on—or coached—a team more superbly conditioned than Don Shula's Baltimore Colts.

THE GREAT THING about Coach Shula is that he got so much out of his teams without resort to the iron hand.

He had rules—you coach an NFL team, you have to have rules—but he had a relaxed attitude toward their enforcement. For instance, Jim Parker regularly walked out of the dorm after curfew to sleep at home. Shula knew. We knew that Shula knew. And Shula knew that we knew that he knew. Shula's logic: no big deal, and so no fine, because Jim Parker—10 times an All-Pro, 8 Pro Bowls, eventually a Hall of Famer—was a big deal.

Double standard? Sure. Bad for team morale? No.

Think about it. You have the best offensive lineman in football, maybe the best offensive lineman of all time, and he breaks a few curfews to go home to his wife. You can slap him down (metaphorically speaking), sock him with a few fines, and turn him against you, or you can turn a blind eye and ... well, I think you can see where this is going.

(PS: fines handed out to mere mortals who broke the curfew were in the $100 range, not the $1,000 crushers that Lombardi loved to levy.

Shula treated his players like grown-ups—grown-ups he liked. Occasionally, when he would get too serious for too long in a team meeting, official team jester Tom Matte would shout from the back of the room, "Hey, Shoes, if you can't take a joke, then bleep you!" Invariably, Don would lighten up and laugh.

One night, backup QB Earl Morrall went missing post-curfew, and when coach Don McCafferty came around with clipboard in hand, Earl's roomie said he'd gotten overheated and was taking a shower. Sure enough, when Mac pulled back the shower curtain, there stood Earl, fully clothed and wobbling slightly, the shower going full gush. Seems that while he was out, Earl had gotten a little, ah, over-filled, not overheated.

Rookie shows were commonplace in the NFL. The one in Green Bay always veered toward slightly irreverent, but there was the ever-present risk of angering or offending Vince. At any step near the invisible line, all heads jerked to see Lombardi's reaction. If he didn't smile, the skit was over.

Baltimore's rookie show, by comparison, was sheer mayhem, with grossly scatological, politically incorrect, unbridled "locked-up male" humor. Shula, his assistants, all the veterans, and members of the front office were fair game. Owner Carroll Rosenbloom was usually present, and even C.R. took an occasional dig.

The year new assistant coach Hank Bullough joined us, he got the bright idea of teaching the team the Colts' fight song. (There was an official one. Still is, so far as I know. Nobody knows how it goes, except for a few rabid fans.) After singing the Michigan State song (he'd been a Spartan), Hank started in on the Colts song, which he'd memorized for the occasion.

To an accompanying chorus of boos, the determined Bullough pressed on. After several minutes of catcalls and shouted obscenities, tackle Bob Vogel, who never swore, walked up to Hank, who was conducting away with waving arms. Bob smiled, and since Bullough thought he was being encouraged, he picked up the volume. At this point, Bob took the full pitcher of beer he held in his right hand and carefully poured its entire contents over Bullough's sputtering head.

End of fight song.

DURING THE 1967 season, my single campaign as a linebacker, I demonstrated to my own satisfaction and to my coaches that I had the potential to be a … pretty good center.

Or maybe a banker.

That winter, confused and anxious, and wondering whether my future in professional football might be behind me, I returned to Atlanta and got a job as a management trainee at the First National Bank of Atlanta.

The Baltimore organization had been generous when I arrived, upping my salary from $13,500 to $20,000 a year. But with Kristin now a vibrant, cheerful six-month old, our expenses were increasing and we needed the money. More important, I needed something to fall back on in case the football thing didn't work out.

Hard as it may be to believe for fans of today's game, virtually all NFL players back then had off-season jobs. And mine was a good one.

The First National Bank abbreviated their training program for me, and after a couple of months they allowed me to take part in a complex analysis of a new checking account system under the direction a creative young vice president. Next I worked in the credit review department, sitting behind a desk writing credit reports on companies. Finally, I was put on the street to sell a brand new product called BankAmericard, the first plastic bank card in our area. We sold to skeptical local merchants, and it was tough marketing.

All in all, my brief foray into the world of banking and finance was a good, solid experience. No two-a-days, no gassers, and no danger of a concussion. But no adrenalin rush, either, and so I was hoping not to have to give up my Sunday job.

MY COACHES IN Baltimore had done their best, especially Chuck Noll, then our defensive coordinator. I had been given ample opportunity to prove myself at linebacker. And I had, but not the way any of us had hoped.

I had always preferred defense to offense, every bit as strongly as I had initially preferred baseball to football. But I lacked a basic ingredient required to be a great linebacker in the National Football League: feel.

Talk to a top NFL linebacker and you'll find he has football instincts that enable him to make plays without being able to tell how he did it.

Question: "Why did you scrape off one time and come underneath the block the next?"

Answer: "I really don't know," a Ray Nitschke, a Dick Butkus, a Willie Lanier, a Ray Lewis, or a Brian Urlacher might respond. "I guess I just felt the play. I never thought about it."

In my case I could read, think, and react to a play. And I could then run to the ball and perform well as a linebacker—at the college level. But in the NFL, I read, thought, reacted—and found blockers all in my chest, or my butt on the ground. I simply lacked the intuitive and physical components of a human heat-seeking missile. Good NFL linebackers all have it. Great ones have it along with superior size, speed, anger, and an uncanny knack for angles.

That's why it's so much fun to watch them, and so much fun—yes, I mean it—to try to block them. One reason to keep playing was to match wits and intensity against the greatest opponents.

When I knew the snap count—meaning, when I was

playing center on the offensive line—I beat most everybody to the punch, including the top middle linebackers of the day, a fair amount of the time when they were my blocking assignment. I worked hard, and I got better. It's the story of my life. I'm a plugger, and I will outwork most folks.

It's been pretty much the same at everything I've tried to do.

After one particularly disappointing performance against the Philadelphia Eagles during which I'd been dominated by Jim Ringo, the perennial All-Pro center sought me out after the game. We'd won handily, 38-6, but I hadn't been happy with my play. Ringo was in the last of 15 illustrious seasons in the NFL, 11 of them as a Green Bay Packer. For me, it was like talking to one of the faces of Mount Rushmore, and I was touched by the fact that, after kicking my butt all afternoon, he wanted to talk.

"How did the Old Man treat you at Green Bay?" Those were the first words out his mouth, and I was caught off guard. Not wanting to offend, I offered up a throwaway lie, "Aw, he was great."

I have no idea why I couldn't make myself tell one legend my true feelings about another, but it didn't matter, because that line of conversation ended there. The future Hall of Famer and I spent a few more minutes gabbing about our days as Packers, Green Bay cold vs. East Coast cold, nothing in particular. I felt privileged.

As a parting shot, Jim Ringo looked over his shoulder, as if in a Coca Cola commercial and called out to me, "Hey kid, don't tip your blitzes!"

After the Eagles game, I played a grand total of 10 or 12

more plays at middle linebacker the rest of the year. All of those plays came in the closing minutes of games we'd already wrapped up. I continued to play special teams, but that was about it. In November, when we steamrolled over Atlanta—Colts 49, Falcons 7—I got a start at outside linebacker. But I looked (and felt) as lost out there as I had in the middle, and once again I got knocked around pretty good.

The experiment was over. Obviously, Shula and his staff shared my assessment of my performance and promise as a linebacker.

I knew I could play, just not at linebacker in the NFL.

What about my old position, center?

SITTING AT MY desk in proper bank attire in January 1968, I wrote Coach Shula a letter asking him what his plans were for me. It was the beginning of the Tet Offensive in Vietnam. It occurred to me that I might well have been there had it not been for Packers assistant Pat Peppler "having some fun" in the last round of the 1964 NFL draft. Here I was, a year after I was sent packing by Vince Lombardi, having disappointed Don Shula—not to mention myself—in stage two of what looked like it might be a very short football career.

A week or two later, I received a call from Coach Shula. "We're moving you back to center. I'm going to find a way to get some football out of you. And you'll continue to play special teams as well."

"Wow," I thought to myself, "if this guy thinks I can play, I have to find a way to play for him."

He promised nothing except one more chance. Why? I think it was because if Don Shula ever spotted a spark in a player, a deep desire to contribute, he became determined to find a way to turn that spark into a flame. I knew he had seen that spark in me.

THAT SUMMER, WHEN I reported to camp raring to justify Don Shula's trust in me, chomping at the bit to become a center who could anchor one of the best offensive lines in football, I faced a little challenge that I had never encountered in my worst nightmares: hemorrhoids.

Go ahead, laugh. People who've never experienced them always do when I tell this story. And I'm not talking about just any old garden-variety case of hemorrhoids. I'm talking about Hemorrhoids from Hell.

The act of bending at the waist was horror enough. But the act of exchanging the ball with the quarterback, the notion of his hand placement, the requirement to drive off the ball once I'd snapped it? Trust me, you don't want to know.

The pain was searing and constant. The bleeding was nasty. Then there was the pain when I sat down on a hard chair at team meetings—and had to stay seated for 45 minutes ... an hour ... a month?

Fortunately, I had plenty of brilliant medical advice from teammates, most of whom struggled to hold back guffaws as they delivered it.

Split end (ouch!) Jimmy Orr sidling up beside me on the field to whisper "Preparation H, Billy. Preparation H."

Kicker Lou Michaels, walking by me as I sat gingerly on a set of stone steps, calling loudly enough to be heard in downtown Baltimore, "Bill! Bill! Come on, Bill! Those things are hitting the steps before you do! You got to carry a pillow with you! Listen to Louie, I know!"

Offensive tackle Bob Vogel, a gentle soul, actually trying to be helpful. "Get one of those small, inflatable inner tubes. My grandmother uses one and it helps."

Halfback and designated team needler Tom Matte, "Get'em fixed, Curry! You're embarrassing us, bleeding all over the damn ball! Get'em fixed and you'll be a perfect asshole!"

By now, Coach Shula had determined that I might actually be serviceable as a center, and he wasn't about to let me disappear into a hospital. He called me into his office and said point-blank, "I don't want you to have the surgery. Not until off-season. Do you understand?"

Yes, I understood. I told him that I'd dealt with this, ah, condition before, and that I'd get through it without missing a practice. That's what he expected to hear, of course. That's SOP for the NFL, a culture of Spartan discipline and toughness, in which the "small hurts" must always be endured with stoic calm.

"Small hurts," of course, are hurts that somebody else has.

My stiff-upper-lip braggadocio lasted exactly one day, when team doctor Norman Freeman asked to see me. He never minced words. The next thing I heard was, "Pull your pants down. Bend over, please. Now, let's see what we have here."

And then, "Good God almighty, Curry! You're going to the hospital right now!"

I told Doc Freeman that I had no intention of going to any hospital, and that I was going to play in the game. He told me that if he had to call an ambulance and personally drag my (literally) bleeding butt to it, I was going to Union Memorial that very night.

We stood eyeball to eyeball, and I knew I was beaten.

"What about Coach Shula?" I asked.

"Don't you worry about Shula!" Doc Freeman practically shouted. "This isn't Shula's business! This is my business!"

Next stop: Union Memorial.

There Dr. Freeman packed my "affected area" with ice for two of the more excruciating days of my life, and then examined me again. "They're not receding," he said.

"What's not receding, Doctor Freeman?" I asked, maybe the dumbest question of my life.

"Bill, don't be stupid," he said, calmly this time. "Do I have to draw you a picture?"

I began to protest, invoked the Shula doctrine, and was interrupted again.

"Do not mention Don Shula's name to me. Just do as I say. And I say you are going into surgery tomorrow. Understood?"

Yes, Doctor Freeman.

"The procedure is called a hemorrhoidectomy," he said. "It will be performed first thing tomorrow morning."

How extensive would it be, I asked. Is this one of those deals where we snip a couple of loose ends off, something quick and easy?

"No Bill," he said, "this is the Roto-Rooter deal. The hemorrhoids will be taken out from the inside of your rectum. A circle will be cut all the way around it and every problem will be removed. I promise, once you recover, you will never have this issue again."

"Once I recover?" This was sounding serious. "What does that mean?"

He paused a few seconds, and then responded, "Well, if we don't have bleeding issues, you will be able to get out in a week or so."

A week! I couldn't spare a whole week of training camp under any circumstances. I was converting back from linebacker and trying to win the starting center's job. Out a week? No way.

I took one last shot. "Well, Doc, has Coach Shula been ..."

He interrupted me. "Coach Shula has been briefed, and he understands that there is no choice. He said he would hold your spot on the team."

Yeah, sure. Every injured player who's not an established veteran has gone through the same onslaught of fear that I was experiencing.

Surprisingly, a phone call from old friend Fran Tarkenton and my former teammate Steve Wright the night before surgery eased my ... well, anxiety, if not my pain. They listened to my explanation of my condition and the procedure I'd have the next morning, and they laughed hysterically for several minutes. "You've got what? They're gonna cut where?" And then more laughter. Believe it or not, that cheered me up.

AFTER THE SURGERY, the next couple of days were a blur of anesthesia and pain, made worse by the frustration of having to listen to our exhibition game against Oakland on the radio. Four days had passed after the surgery. I was getting antsy, a good sign, but Doc Freeman had said a week to recover.

A very nice lady came by to tell me she had birthed two babies and also endured a hemorrhoidectomy. She wanted me to know that the hemorrhoidectomy was much worse. I thanked her and felt maternal. I had a private room, but several Colts fans came by once they heard I was there.

After a long week of pain, reflection, drugs, and kindness from every angle, I got sprung. I hitched a ride back to Westminster with a young doctor heading that way and walked into training camp feeling pretty good about myself.

That didn't last long. Don Shula was waiting.

"Curry, I told you I did not want you to have the operation."

"I didn't want to have it either, Coach!"

There we were, five days after I reluctantly went under the knife, and we were back in each other's faces on a matter that should by now be behind us.

(Behind me, at least.)

I wasn't smart enough or confident enough about my own abilities to interpret his remark as indicative of my value in his plans. I did, however, get another message from his demeanor. "If you want to play for me in the National Football League, you will show up for work every day, no matter what."

The trainers wouldn't let me practice, but I walked over to the track adjacent to the practice fields and ran three miles in the heat of the day while the team worked out.

The next day I was in full pads for both practices.

THE FOUR WEEKS remaining in training camp after I got back from my little procedure gave new meaning to the word tumultuous, at least in the Bill Curry unabridged lexicon.

For one thing, I'd been on the other side of the line for a year and I'd sort of gotten used to being a linebacker—the position I'd always wanted to play—even though that hadn't played out the way it had in my dreams.

But the main problem was that I had just days to master an offensive system that was radically different from the one I'd grown accustomed to in Green Bay. How different? Both involved a football—that was about it.

And how many days would I be allowed to get a handle on it? In an NFL training camp, you just never know.

Every night the coaching staff meets to talk personnel and check the day's waiver lists containing cuts from all the clubs. On that list may be players that play your position and who have already been rated by the sophisticated systems in the scouting combine. So, if you are struggling with the play calls and audibles, someone from the waiver wire might look more attractive. They claim the other guy; they waive you.

My challenge was that the Green Bay offense was famous for being a model of simplicity, while the Baltimore system was anything but. It had been built over nine years by Weeb Ewbank, amended with a few bells and whistles by current offensive coordinator Don McCafferty, filtered through the creative imagination of Don Shula, and tinkered with extemporaneously (and continually) by John Unitas.

For me it was, literally, a whole new ballgame.

Start with the nomenclature for the basic formations and assignments, which as offensive center I had to have down pat in order to make calls to the linemen on either side of me. For instance, RED RIGHT in Green Bay was OUT LEFT FLANK SPLIT RIGHT in Baltimore. Just a matter of learning a few new names? Easy to say, harder to do in a tight time frame, especially since the consequence of the center calling out the wrong line call was four teammates going "huh?" and a blown play.

Assignments for the running plays were relatively simple and straightforward, but pass protections were complex, with certain "exceptions" that required the center to make very quick mental and communicative adjustments. The audible systems were of entirely different natures, and even the hole numbers were flopped: the Packers used odd numbers for the right, the Colts for the left.

Having dealt with Bart Starr's lightning-quick adjustments, I should have been ready for Unitas, but the system was new and I hadn't played offense in 18 months. I struggled mightily with assignments. Several times I went the wrong way, made the wrong calls, or simply froze.

Then came the greatest shock of all.

Nobody yelled. Nobody embarrassed me in front of my peers. The clock was ticking to the season opener and nobody—not my fellow linemen, not my coaches, not my quarterback—exhibited any signs of distress.

One time during offensive drills well into the fifth week—less than 10 days before our first game of the regular season against the 49ers—I broke from the huddle, moved crisply to the ball—and froze like a statue. My mind went totally blank. Grinning his crooked grin, Unitas nudged me to get over the ball, patted me on the butt, leaned over me, and mumbled in a low voice, "Billy, I said 68 Dig. That's one of the exceptions. And remember, white's our live color, so the audible was a dummy."

I nodded and got into position, never to forget 68 Dig or the live audible color again.

After coming out of the drill, I glanced over at my position coach, John Sandusky. He crooked that big, gnarled finger of his and beckoned me over. (An offensive tackle for seven years with the Browns and the Packers, his hands were mangled from hundreds of helmet slaps delivered to guys trying to invade his space.) I jogged over and he asked, "Learn anything?"

"Yeah," I said, "I got it now."

Then he added a technique note that made me know he had been watching me for years. "Your problems in Green Bay had a lot to do with your footwork. In our individual drills today, I want you to step with the opposite foot when you have Middle to Strong responsibility. Not far, just six inches or so. You get out a full count quicker. Bill, you're quick, and you can do this stuff."

Bill, you're quick, and you can do this stuff.

How many high-strung kids have longed to hear words like that? How many lives have been altered by one positive truth at a time of self-doubt? Don Shula and John

Sandusky had seen aspects of my potential that I had not. They had decided to make the difference when I could not do so alone.

That, my friends, is coaching.

My first start at center for the Colts came against the Dolphins in the next-to-last exhibition game before the season began. For me, it might as well have been a playoff game. Sandusky called me from my room that afternoon before the game that night, sat me down in hotel lobby, and asked, "Bill, can you be a starter and keep playing on most of the special teams? We'll take you off kickoff coverage, but we need you on the others."

I was overjoyed. I assured him I could. And I did.

Rep by rep, literally step by step, moment by moment, the Shula/McCafferty/Sandusky trio brought me along, with each contributing something different: Shula's stern demeanor coupled with his surprising light moments ... McCafferty's tactical genius and wry humor ... Sandusky's huge presence on the field, and the fact that he'd been there, done that.

For the first time in my life, I began to love the football field the way I had loved the baseball diamond. I went to practice anticipating the whole thing rather than praying for its end. I picked up my playbook at odd hours rather than just studying it the minimum required time.

I was, in every way, a happy camper.

TO ME, SUPER Bowl III will always seem like an entire season of Rod Serling's *Twilight Zone* compressed into 60 minutes.

FLARE SCREEN RIGHT

As I became part of the offense, Tom Matte became a huge presence, not only because of his wacky jokes and sense of the absurd, but also because he understood everything on the football field.

Tom could also do everything on the field. Already famous as a stand-in quarterback for the Colts in 1965 in the playoff game against the Packers that went to sudden death, he was critical to us in helping Earl Morral with the play-calling, in carrying or catching the ball, and in keeping up the morale of the offensive unit.

Once, before a game with the Dolphins, he sat me down and talked to me about a specific play, a flare screen on which I was his only lead blocker.

"Billy," he said, "when you get out in front of me, you have to give me a chance by bellying back, giving ground to be behind the line of scrimmage. You've been running straight down the line, and I'm too far behind you. That lets the linebackers and defensive backs get by you and nail me. If you'll belly back like this"—he drew a kind of backward arc in the dirt—"I can get on your butt, and we'll be impossible to stop."

I didn't quite get it until we were in the Orange Bowl playing the Dolphins. The play was called and I came down the line of scrimmage, bellied back, and felt Matte on my hip. Nick Buoniconti, the Hall of Fame middle linebacker for the Dolphins, came whirling at us, all quickness and intensity, like a bird of prey. He was always tough to hit in the open field, but because of Matte's proximity to me, he had only one route to Tom. I knew it, and Tom knew it. If Nick tried to juke me, Matte could simply make a cut in the opposite direction. Nick was forced to come through me, and I was much bigger. Down he went.

That's the night I learned how screens work. Matte popped a long gain, jogged back, patted me on the butt, and smiled.

I felt like a million bucks.

My Colts teammates and I played in a football game that day that revealed and explored human hopes, fears, and despairs in a surreal, sci-fi world. Like Serling's characters, we were trapped in a horror of our own making, destined to re-live it forever.

Super Bowl III was the third AFL-NFL Campionship Game in professional American football, but the first to bear the name "Super Bowl." (The 1967 and 1968 Championship Games would retroactively be called Super Bowls, but those of us who were there know that III was really I.)

We were 24-point favorites over the New York Jets. Many of us privately figured it would only be that close if we got bored. The NFL and the AFL had merged three years before, but everybody knew we were still the dominant league—by far.

Joe Willie Namath had other ideas. The Thursday night before the game, speaking to the press, he guaranteed a Jets victory. We read that prediction with our morning coffee on Friday, and we just laughed. We knew that we were going to make Mr. Namath eat his words.

After all, despite losing John Unitas in the last exhibition game to an elbow injury that kept him out all season, we had gone 13-1 with Earl Morrall at QB, and we avenged that one to loss to Cleveland by trouncing them 34-0 in the NFL Championship game. The highest ranked passer in the league, Earl was voted the NFL's Most Valuable Player. Six Colts were All-Pros that season, the most from any team. We ranked second in the NFL in points scored and first in fewest points allowed.

We were the best team in pro football by a wide margin.

Most experts in the sports media called us the best team in pro football history.

Final score: Jets 16, Colts 7.

THE BEST WAY to recall a football game in which one played is to re-read the official play-by-play chart that each team keeps. Even better than a videotape, a play-by-play record on paper of the actual down and distance, time in the game, and result of each play has the power to evoke distinct memories, emotions, sensations, and "feel" of an experience that transpired in a blur.

After doing that—reading the play-by-play—to prepare myself for telling this still-painful story, I confess that the hard facts of that darkest day in my football career forced me to confront something I have never admitted to myself, much less to anyone else:

It could have been worse.

We began the game by ripping off long gains, running and throwing. The Jets looked and felt tentative. Yet each time we approached their goal line, we turned the ball over, or missed a short field goal, or did something that kept us off the scoreboard. And each time that happened, the eyes of the Jets players changed, their body language livened, and their pace grew quicker.

Just before the end of the first half, the definitive play of the game occurred. Trailing 7-0 with 43 seconds on the clock and operating from the Jets' 42-yard-line, we called the Fleaflicker.

Great call. Perfect field position. The Fleaflicker almost always produced a touchdown for the good guys.

The play began as a sweep by Matte, who pulled the entire defense to the right. At the last moment, he stopped, turned, and threw a perfect backward pass to Morrall, whom I was protecting on the opposite side. I peeked into the end zone, where Jimmy Orr was standing by himself with no one within 20 yards. At the last instant I spotted defensive tackle John Elliot coming inside out, turned, hit him, and waited for the roar and touchdown signal.

There was a roar, but no touchdown signal

Earl had thrown a perfect spiral to ... Jim Hudson, the Jets safety, smack in the middle of the field. Hudson was the guy who'd been 20 yards from Orr, the guy who was desperately trying to recover once he saw the play unfold, the guy who'd been totally and utterly beaten—until the ball landed in his hands.

It was our third interception ... in one half. All from a guy who'd thrown only 17 INTs in 14 regular-season games.

At the beginning of the second half, we fumbled the ball away on our first offensive play.

Combine four turnovers with two field goals missed in the first half and you've got six blown scoring opportunities in two quarters plus one play. Do that against a good team—and the Jets were certainly that—and not even the greatest pro football team in history is going to win very often.

Yes, it could have been worse.

No, it doesn't get better with time.

We created our own Twilight Zone.

They won.

We didn't.

We need to get over it.

I haven't.

AT TRAINING CAMP in 1969, near the final cut, Coach Shula called me into his office and said, "Bill, I want you to

---

EARL OR JOHN?

Earl Morrall started every game, literally learning our system on the job, after John Unitas tore a muscle in the elbow of his passing arm in our final exhibition. John Unitas came back at the very end of the season and was cleared to go for the big game in Miami, but Shula started Earl.

He should have—Earl had brought us all the way. As the saying goes, "You got to dance with them what brung you." Everybody on the team, including John, believed that Earl deserved to start.

But in a decision he later publicly questioned, Don Shula left Morrall in even though he was having a truly horrible game.

Unitas sat until the score was 13-0, with four minutes remaining in the third quarter.

A lot had been written about John's probable lack of arm strength, rustiness, tentativeness after the layoff ... so much blah-blah. When he stepped into the huddle, it was the same old John. "We need two touchdowns. We've plenty of time, Let's get to work."

(Much later, Joe Namath told me he nearly panicked when he saw No. 19 jog out. Joe says he said to himself, "We don't have enough points with that guy on the field!")

One question I've been asked by people who saw the game on TV is why I broke the huddle and ran to the ball with such enthusiasm as our chances waned. Well, I'd always been taught that how the center breaks the huddle is the first indication of the team's attitude, both to his team and to his opponent.

A good habit, but there was more.

The man at the helm in our sport, the play caller, inspires something with every word he speaks, with his body language, and with his eyes. He also brings a track record into each huddle. His history steps in beside him. We popped up to the ball because we knew that with John Unitas at the helm, we were going to win.

Except we didn't.

In our previous 30 games, we'd lost just twice. We'd come from behind again and again. The thought of losing with John Unitas back where he belonged, taking my snaps, never crossed my mind.

Except we did.

know I'm not keeping another center this year."

I nodded sure, fine, that was okay by me.

He smiled and said, "Wait a minute. Don't be so casual. Do you realize what I'm saying to you?"

I thought I did, but obviously he thought I didn't.

He leaned across the table and said, "I'm telling you that you will be playing every snap of every game. Do you understand now?"

"Oh, I see," I mumbled. I didn't remember anyone who had ever done that, but thought it was a neat idea. It became an exercise in gut-checks, and it worked. I found a part of myself I had not known existed. I played harder, expected more, and gave in less.

I was proud of my season.

After the last game of the year in Los Angeles, Coach brought us all together and called out the Pro Bowl selections. My name wasn't among them. I hadn't given much thought to whether I deserved consideration, and I was walking out with the rest of the guys when he called me over.

"Bill," he said, "you played every play of the season and you deserved to be in the Pro Bowl. You did everything I asked of you, and you should be there."

I thanked him and floated from the room. It was one of the signal moments in my career, and the last time I ever played for Don Shula. He went on to spend the next 25 seasons as coach of the Miami Dolphins

Under him, football had been full of joy and fun, the polar opposite of the deadly serious, tension-filled existence I had known under Vince Lombardi. I have tried to employ Don Shula's approach to the game from that day to this.

My appreciation for what he taught me is boundless.

Coach Shula built our team by force of personal will, by building personal relationships with each team member, and by allowing autonomy to his staff.

He did it without the distance and aloofness of Bobby Dodd, or the anger and cruelty of Vince Lombardi.

To me, Don Shula was the model of what an NFL coach ought to be.

He was the best.

*The 1958 NFL championship game between
the Baltimore Colts and the New York Giants is
commonly known as The Greatest Game Ever
Played. To me, it was even bigger than that:
It was The Game That Changed My Life.*

8

JOHN UNITAS
WINNER

T he genius and magic of John Unitas—of all the qualities of all the men examined in this book, that is the most difficult to describe and comprehend, even for someone who spent five years in his huddle.

A comparison? I remember walking into St. Peter's Basilica in Rome, gaping in every direction amidst the throng of tourists, when one object caught my eye, then my soul. Michelangelo's Pietá sent chills deep into the fiber of my being before I could even register what I was seeing.

Scholars call that feeling "a moment of esthetic arrest." An object or an action penetrates to one's soul without passing through the brain's prejudices. I could study that work of genius the rest of my life, and I would never be able to fathom—much less explain to another person—what that thing of beauty means to me.

I saw John Unitas' athletic artistry do that very thing to people. I saw Unitas performances bring tears to the eyes of people who knew nothing about our sport. Artistry accompanied No. 19 when he crossed the white lines.

(For the record, I always called him John. Most people, of course, called him and remember him as Johnny. Maybe my preference for John come from liking Bill better than Billy. Sounds more grown up.)

Outside M&T Bank Stadium in downtown Baltimore, home of the Ravens since 1998, there is a huge statue of John. I stopped by recently to get a solo look. At first I wasn't sure why, but the body proportions didn't look quite right. Maybe no statue of a close friend ever looks right; it is, after all, an artificial representation.

But then I saw it—the arm angle is ever so slightly off.

WORD

This is the inscription on the 13-foot-tall statue of John Unitas at Ravens Stadium in Baltimore. It says it all ... and yet it only scratches the surface:

In memory of Johnny Unitas (1933-2002)
The Golden Arm
Led Baltimore to many winning seasons, including 2 NFL Championships in 1958 and 1959, and a Super Bowl in 1970.
Threw touchdown passes in 47 consecutive games.
Johnny Unitas will forever remain the yardstick by which all other quarterbacks are measured.
NFL Hall of Fame, 1979
Greatest player, first 50 years of NFL
Quarterback, 75th Anniversary Team
Quarterback, All Century Team
Sculpture by Frederick Kail
October 20, 2002

I hung around for a while, deeply saddened by the fact that John had died on September 11, 2002, just a month before the dedication date on the pedestal. As I turned to leave, I took one more backward glance, looked up, and into the eyes. I had looked directly into those eyes across a huddle for five campaigns. Those eyes always told me one thing: "We are going to win."

Memories flooded in from old Memorial Stadium, the one that stood for half a century on the other side of town on 33rd Street—The Old Gray Lady of 33rd Street, aka The World's Largest Outdoor Insane Asylum. It was there that John Unitas spent 17 glorious years as a Colt. It was razed in 2001, 17 years after the Colts decamped in the dead of night for Indianapolis.

The new stadium is a fine, modern facility. But the only bit of magic remaining from the Unitas Era is the statue outside. If you go there to visit the heroic statue—and I know that I will return—be sure to look into his eyes.

They're the eyes of a winner.

SO MANY WORDS have been written and spoken about the greatness of John Unitas that it's hard to know where to begin to look for the key to that greatness.

He didn't have the strongest arm, the quickest release, or the best of any of the other usual measures used to rate quarterbacks. He was certainly not a great scrambler. He did have wonderful field vision and could improvise like a jazz pianist. He had an uncanny ability to look one way and throw the other—with accuracy. His knack for making creative on-field adjustments to the game was unparalleled. But there was no single attribute that could account for his command of the game.

The key to John Unitas' greatness, in my view, came from somewhere inside his soul, from his utter, absolute confidence that he would find a way to beat you.

One time in a game against the Rams, DT Merlin Olsen sacked John for a loss. No big surprise there—that's how Merlin made it to the Hall of Fame, by sacking people. And there was probably not a quarterback in NFL history who was slower afoot, less nimble, than John Unitas.

Later, during the off-season, I ran into Olsen and he harkened back to that game and that single sack and said, a bit of wonder still in his voice long after the fact, "I hit Unitas with *all my might.*"

I was all-too intimately acquainted with Merlin Olsen's 6'5", 285-pound "might." It essentially ended my career as I attempted to block him in the Astrodome in 1973. As he trampled me, my left knee exploded into tiny fragments.

My first memory after the play is of Merlin's anxious, pale face peering into mine as he kept asking, "Bill, are you alright? Stay down! Don't try to get up! You're badly hurt." (Anybody else would have said, "You're hurt bad!" Merlin said, "You're badly hurt," with his characteristically thoughtful, grammatically correct speech.)

He held me down until our trainers arrived. They took one look and called for the ambulance.

Yes, I knew about Merlin Olsen's "might."

Well, in that otherwise forgotten game that Merlin couldn't get out of his head, he had hit John Unitas with *all* his might. "I drove my shoulder pad into his sternum, picked him up, and drove him into the dirt. A sack like that, most quarterbacks will go skittish on you, at least for a while."

"So how did it work out?" I asked, although I pretty much knew.

"Nothing," Merlin said, with a shake of his massive head and a grimace. "I got *nothing*. Just those cold eyes glaring into mine, waiting for me to get off him. I got to tell you, it was unnerving. I knew—*we* knew—he was going to get us sooner or later."

That, in my view, was the key to John Unitas' greatness.

The man loved every tiny, obscure, mundane detail of the game he played at the highest level for 17 years as a Baltimore Colt. He loved everything about professional football from the first moment he saw it and felt it. He is the only football player I have ever known who loved, even craved, every sordid detail of our existence. I swear to you that he even he seemed to like the pain. At the very least, he didn't let it distract him from the business at hand: finding a way to win, to make the other guy pay.

In football, each of us is broken at one time or another. I've seen powerful All-Pro players sobbing into their hands. I've watched the best of the best drop to their knees, hang their heads in pain, and allow themselves to be carried off the field—beaten, at least for the day.

Personally, I was broken, battered, and beaten by our sport's demands so many times that I shudder to confess it. My consolation is that just about every other driven competitor who played the game any length of time would have to confess the same.

All save one.

PRACTICE MAKES PERFECT? Not quite.

One late afternoon after practice in my first training camp as a Colt, I left the locker room on my way to the dining hall. I was exhausted. Shula's two-a-days had a way of doing that to you. My only goal was to stay upright until I could sit down in front of a very large plate of food.

Light was fading and practice had ended 45 minutes or so earlier, but I heard voices filtering up from the practice field, down a hill and roughly 80 or 90 yards away. Someone was still down there, obviously, and I assumed it would be kids, maybe some of the children of players. But I took a closer look and saw that there were two players, still in full pads.

Raymond Berry and John Unitas.

Raymond had been a Colt since 1955, John since 1956, and here they were, stealing the last few minutes of light over a decade later to fine-tune a passing combination that had ranked among the NFL's best since John first hit Raymond on an out pattern.

Frail of build, Raymond was the slowest wide receiver in the NFL, couldn't see a lick, and one of his legs was shorter than the other. It's a wonder he was able to find the Hall of Fame and walk into it when he was inducted in 1973.

Almost as slow and equally un-athletic as Raymond, John would win his third NFL MVP award that year.

And here they were, running posts, digs, flys, drags, and outs after all their teammates had showered and dressed— and they were doing it with the focus of a couple of rookies working to avoid a visit from the Turk.

To this day, I get chills remembering the scene, because

it exemplified the enthusiasm and the commitment those two guys brought to their profession years after both could have gotten by on cruise control.

From those two, I learned that an old adage needs amending.

Practice doesn't make perfect.

Perfect practice makes perfect.

JOHN MACKEY ONCE said that being on the field with Unitas was like getting in the huddle with God.

I think that's going too far.

God? No, John, that's over the top.

Superman ... yeah, that's more like it.

Start with the locker room. That was like being in the phone booth with Clark Kent. One of John's guardians on the offensive line, Danny Sullivan, regularly had fun with John's physical limitations. (Actually, Danny Sullivan had fun with all our limitations, all the time, but that's another story—much of it unprintable in a family publication.)

Just before it was time to head out onto the field, defensive captain Freddy Miller would make an impassioned appeal, and then turn to his counterpart on the offense, Captain Unitas, positioned in his customary station next to the door leading out to the tunnel.

John Unitas led the Colts through the valleys and up to the peaks for a lot of years. And we always did as he admonished us to do in his pre-game speech, which had become virtually written in stone by the time I joined the club in 1967.

As we all turned toward No. 19, he would survey the room, make eye contact, and say, "Talk's cheap. Let's go play."

It was his mantra, and ours.

Talk's cheap. Let's go play.

EVER WITNESS 80,000 raucous, hostile, screaming fans go dead silent? Then you never saw John Unitas work in an enemy stadium.

Let's say the home team's up by a field goal in the middle of the fourth quarter, we have third and long on their 44, and the crowd decides to take over. Down on the field, it sounds like 100 747s are revving up for simultaneous takeoff.

"Listen up!" John shouts at us in the huddle. "We're going to shut those people up right now! Out Left, Flank Right Split, 68-Y Delay—on Goose. Ready ... *Break*!"

Let me translate.

John's been filing away coverage data and play possibilities since the opening kickoff. Many of our biggest plays resulted from two or three quarters of patience. You start with a game plan. Then you let a John Unitas adapt it in real time as he sees fit.

If a corner bites on an out or a dig from man coverage in the second quarter, John waits for just the right time to call an out and up, or a post corner to get an easy touchdown. All good quarterbacks do this; John simply does it better than anybody else.

This time, he smells blitz, which means the free safety's going to be covering John Mackey—a physical mismatch in our favor. Hence Y Delay.

HOLDING ON NUMBER 19

The Packers were always tough, but somehow they seemed harder to beat in County Stadium in Milwaukee than in Green Bay. In 1970, we were in a brutal defensive battle with them on *Monday Night Football.* Since our best backs were injured or gimpy, Coach Don McCafferty had devised creative ways to move the ball on the ground: stack formations, getting receivers Roy Jefferson and Eddie Hinton into the fray with Wing T counterplays, and all manner of exotic stuff.

One play came from Coach McCafferty's son's high school playbook. It was a reverse to Sam Havrilak, our dentist/wide receiver/jack-of-all-trades guy. Sam had the option to run or to throw. On this occasion, he threw it to Ray Perkins, who took it down inside the 10-yard line.

Then came the moment all linemen dread—hostile crowd cheering at the wrong time. That could only mean one thing: a yellow penalty flag on the ground.

Who did it? What fat slob screwed up the play? We five interior guys instinctively gather like hogs in a sty at such times, furtively checking the officials, hoping against hope someone else is the guilty party. We look like a bunch of nine-year-olds denying responsibility for busting out a picture window with a baseball.

"Holding on Number 19!"

Number 19? Aw, come on guys—get it right! Who really did it?

The referee looked us in the eyes. "I said number 19. I mean number 19!"

[continued on following page]

> We jerked around to see an unrepentant Unitas, standing with hands on hips. He clued us in on what happened.
>
> "The damn guy was right in the middle of things. I grabbed him by the shirt and jerked his ass on the ground. If you guys did what you were supposed to, I wouldn't have to do things like that. Get in the huddle!"

We can't go on a quick count; I wouldn't be sure of hearing it, much less our tackles. We can't go on a timed silent count; too much risk of somebody jumping offside. So we go on Goose.

Up to the line. Get set. John tucks his hands under my butt. We check the location of the blitzers. John starts calling signals. Mid-call, he snaps his right hand up against my butt. ("Goose," get it?) I snap the ball and move to pick up the blitzing linebacker.

Meanwhile, Mackey blocks two counts, releases, takes the short toss from Unitas, tramples the free safety, shakes off a pursuing linebacker, then outruns one corner and stomps the other into the turf as he twists into the end zone, 44 yards away.

The crowd goes silent and stays that way the rest of the game.

The Man with the Golden Arm?

Johnny U?

Sure, but I have another nickname that fits him like a glove: The Silencer.

EVER BEEN GOOSED? If you're a male, chances are about 99.5 percent that the answer is yes.

Think back to when you were, say, nine years old. Little boys seem to have a genetic predilection to poke one another in the butt at the least appropriate times. No doubt you were a victim from time to time. No doubt you were a perpetrator. But the purpose behind (sorry) the act itself, whether you were gooser or goosee, was always the same: to get somebody to jump, drop his lunch tray, yelp loud enough to earn a hard look from a teacher, or all of the above.

Well, think of professional football players as a bunch of nine-year-olds trapped in huge adult bodies. Got it? Then you'll quickly understand why the aisle of an NFL team bus or plane is a constant gauntlet for anyone who has flunked the Goose Test.

Never heard of it? Not exactly like the PSAT, perhaps, but still a means of determining who shrugs off a sharp jab into the business end (sorry) of his backside and who goes a little Unitas.

Let's say you're making your way down the aisle of a team plane or a bus, looking for a seat (sorry) next to a back or a receiver rather than a wide-body lineman or linebacker, and trying to avoiding sitting next to the guy who's been kicking your butt (sorry) in practice, whom you now hate with all your heart. As you ponder your choices, there is an inevitable sharp jab into the lower zone of your backside. What do you do?

If you stop, turn slowly, survey the all-innocent-but-snickering group of teammates, none of whom will make eye contact, and resume your trip without comment, you'll most likely be exempt from future prods. You're no fun.

If you leap, holler, swear, dance, start speaking in tongues, or otherwise amuse the team, God help you. You are a marked man and will be goosed every day for the rest of your life.

Enter John Unitas, the goosiest man who ever walked the earth.

The Man with the Golden Arm would clear the first class cabin on planes or the front of the bus on a Greyhound, be strolling to the back (sorry) when *goose!* Always the same reaction: involuntary leap, back arched and feet off the floor, and literally the same phrase, every time—*"Geezus Christ! Are you crazy?"* Then he would smile, look around at hysterical teammates, and shake his head. Two more steps, another *goose!* and another *"Geezus Christ! Are you crazy?"* And so on, all the way to his seat (sorry).

Johnny U was nothing if not consistent.

AMONG TEAMMATES, ON-FIELD arguments are common enough, but they usually don't last beyond the shower.

In a 1971 game with the Browns, we were down by six with about three minutes left on the clock. We were at midfield on fourth and three. We all figured John would call a quick out or a hook, something short, to get the first down, but John thought he had the deep ball. He went for the jugular, as he had successfully done so often over the years in such situations, but this time the Browns were ready and intercepted at the goal line.

Since it was fourth down, the correct action for the defensive back would have been to knock the ball to the ground, take over at midfield, and run out the clock. As it happened, the guy looked foolish when we tackled him inside the Cleveland five-yard line. Our only chance to win with the clock ticking away was a turnover. We had a great defense, so that was always a distinct possibility. Hey, it ain't over 'til it's over, right?

On the sideline, the offense stayed on our feet, anxious to go back, counting on the defense. Glenn Ressler leaned over to me and said, "Can you believe that guy intercepted the ball?" I said, "Naw, and I hope he lives to regret it!"

Not this time. The Browns ran out the clock and we trudged in.

Back in our locker room, John must have spent 20 or 30 minutes being hammered by the reporters for his poor decision in the late going. I'm a slowpoke in the locker room, so we ended up walking into the shower at the same time. We were the last two. I could usually tell if he was angry about something, but he this time caught me off guard. He got right up in my face and said, "I heard what you said about me!"

Say what?

He's boiling mad, he looks like he's about to take a shot at me, and I have no idea what he's talking about.

"What the hell are you talking about?"

We were the only guys there and the water was running, so our "exchange" was quite private.

"'I hope he lives to regret it!' That's what I'm talking about! I throw a [bleeping] interception and you say 'I hope he lives to regret it!' I heard you say it to Ressler! That's what I'm [bleeping] talking about!"

I relaxed. I told him what Glenn had said to me, and what I had said to him, and who I was talking about. "So now you know."

"Bullshit, Billy. You shoot your mouth off too much sometimes, and this time I caught you."

"What?" I was truly dumbfounded. "You don't believe me? All these years together and have you ever heard me say anything negative about you? If I have something bad to say about you, I'll say it to your face. I figured you'd have known that by now."

Nothing. Not a word from him. He turned away.

I finished my shower, dried off, wrapped the towel around me, and followed him to the sinks, where we began to shave. All the way through the lathering, scraping, and lathering again for a second go, I implored him to be reasonable, to consider our past relationship, to understand that he'd misunderstood. His response? Hit me with an implacable stare, wipe the vestiges of shaving cream off his face, and march out the door.

Leaders are stubborn—I think they need to be, in order to lead. And they hate losing, especially when they think they're responsible. (As John obviously did.)

By practice on Tuesday, it was clear that he'd either accepted my explanation or decided to forgive me. I longed for verbal vindication, but that wasn't in the cards. In John Unitas' playbook, it wasn't necessary.

This one we just left in the locker room.

CARROLL ROSENBLOOM HAD owned the Baltimore Colts since 1953. Rosenbloom was a player's owner, the kind of guy who, even though the Colts won just three games that first season, awarded each of his players a $500 bonus—serious money back then—in appreciation of their efforts.

By 1958, the Colts had earned their first NFL title in the Greatest Game. Under Rosenbloom's direction, the team signed Weeb Ewbank to coach and acquired the likes of Alan Ameche, Raymond Berry, and Lenny Moore in the NFL draft, and signed John Unitas after he was cut by the Steelers—the core of Baltimore's Glory Years (1958–71).

But the beginning of the 1972 season, Rosenbloom was on the other side of the country as the new owner the Los Angeles Rams. Over the off-season, he had swapped teams with then-Rams owner Robert Irsay.

And our new boss? Until he spirited the Colts away to Indianapolis in the dark of night—literally—in 1984, Bob Irsay earned a richly deserved reputation as a cheap, irascible man who drank too much. As beloved as Rosenbloom had been in Baltimore, that's how vilified Irsay would become by the time he skipped town with the Colts.

Irsay was uneasy at his first meeting with the team that summer, but nobody made much of it. He was the owner, after all; we were just the hired hands. We just went about our business, or tried to. He went about his, whatever that might be.

That would have been fine: you don't rock my boat, I don't rock yours. Fine except for the unfortunate fact that we weren't a very good team. We got off to a 1-4 start—our lone win came against the Buffalo Bills, who would go on to finish 4-9-1—at which point Irsay had GM Joe Thomas fire head coach Don McCafferty.

A pall fell over the team. We were big boys, and we knew that coaches get fired (and players get traded) all the time. It's part of the game. But Mac had been with the club 16 years, and his two previous seasons as head coach hadn't been too shabby: a combined regular season record of 21-6-1. Oh yeah, and McCafferty sported one Super Bowl ring (1970) on his hand.

We were angry. We liked Mac. We thought his firing was premature. And we knew we were responsible.

We immediately began to wonder when the next shoe would drop.

It didn't take long to find out. The morning after Mac's firing became public, there were five or six of us in the locker room. It was Monday, our off day. The phone rang in the coaches' locker room, and since there were no coaches present, I answered it. A voice that sounded like Joe Thomas asked for Unitas. I called John, who walked to the phone, picked it up, listened for maybe 15 seconds, said okay, then walked back into the locker room.

"What was it?" Sully shouted from across the room.

"I'm down," answered John.

"You're what? Down?" Sully pressed. "What does that mean?"

John's face was a frozen mask.

"I said I'm down, benched, sent to the second team, not starting anymore. *Down!*"

A hush descended, and while no one articulated the thought, we knew we were present at a history-making moment. The Greatest Player of the First 50 Years of pro football—look it up; it's on his résumé—had just been sent to the bench, told he was being demoted by a guy who'd been with the organization less than a year, and it had been done in seconds with the aplomb and grace of an assembly line layoff.

By a faceless boss who lacked the guts to do it face to face.

I'm sure Thomas and Irsay felt they made a good football decision. John had turned 39 the previous spring. He wasn't the John Unitas of the glory years. Sitting John down enabled Irsay and Thomas to promote a bright young guy, Marty Domres, who'd been a first-round pick by the Chargers in 1969 and come to the Colts in a trade in 1971.

Maybe none of us would have disagreed with the decision on its merits. But the way it was handled, the intentional humiliation of the man who'd been the heart and soul of the franchise 15 years, was an absolutely unforgivable outrage.

Think about it: we were two years removed from being Super Bowl Champions and one year removed from a 10-4 season and a Division Championship. Suddenly we felt like we'd been taken over by a bunch of thugs who actually enjoyed embarrassing our leader. There is a way to do such things that allows for dignity, respect, and appreciation. You got none of that from the Colt organization of that era.

Today, mention the names "Bob Irsay" or "Joe Thomas" to Colts fans of a certain age and you'll likely get an earful of words that you couldn't repeat here.

PEOPLE OFTEN ASK me about the most exciting moments of my pro football career. After all, I snapped the ball to Bart Starr and John Unitas, I played in Super Bowls, I took orders from Vince Lombardi and Don Shula, and I managed to hang around the NFL for a decade.

I used to struggle with the question, but I have no doubt now. And it's not one moment, but rather a compilation, a highlight video, of the times I was introduced to and ran onto the field before home games as a Baltimore Colt.

Depending on the coin toss, either the offense or the defense was introduced. If it was the offense, the center was the first player to be sent out. As the public address system went through the paces of welcoming the folks the visiting team, and described details of safety procedures, the tension built. During this time I stood at the back of the end zone with the game coordinator holding me by the shoulder pad, waiting for the cue to send me out.

I recall every detail. I got my shoes adjusted on my feet by kicking the dirt with my cleats, first one way and then the other. My body was full of a kind of energy I have felt in no other circumstance. That energy built as the Colts announcer began the chant that signaled the player introductions, near the end of which the roar began. He called my name first, in staccato style. I never got over the thrill, and by the time I reached the 50-yard line and veered to my left to approach the sideline, I was usually teary-eyed.

But what I loved best was not my own introduction. What I loved best was what everybody from that era remembers the most vividly, the introduction of the last player, this one in a decidedly slower voice:

> *"And at quarterback ...*
> *From the University of Louisville ...*
> *Number 19 ... "*

You could never hear the name following the number, as the roar from the stands swept across the field like a tidal wave. Imagine standing next to a jet engine at takeoff and saying the words " ... *Johnny Unitas.*"

To this day, I can close my eyes and see the stoop-shouldered, spindly, bow-legged guy with the shuffling gait make his way to the 50-yard line.

Then, just before the kickoff, I can also see myself and nine other teammates bunched together on the sideline in front of our bench, waiting for that face and those eyes to pop in the huddle, for him to reach out and join hands with us, to *show the way.*

And we followed.

IT WAS THE most tumultuous 24 hours in my 10 seasons in professional football:

- Head coach Don McCafferty, whom all the players admired, was summarily fired.
- Defensive line coach John Sandusky, Mac's best friend, was named interim head coach.
- John Unitas was benched.

I felt bad for Spanky Sandusky, who got his nickname because he reminded us of the character in the old *Our Gang* comedies. (Stumped? That's what Google was invented for.)

Widely acclaimed as one of the best assistant coaches in the National Football League, he now had the top job, but the word "interim" was a kiss of death. The deal with interims was strictly, "Help us out here, big guy, but only until we can find somebody else."

The first sign of where Spanky fit in top management's long-term plans was that they benched his quarterback—the standard bearer for the NFL, a fixture for 17 years, the undisputed and beloved leader of the team—without even giving him advance notice, much less "consulting" him.

Not surprisingly, John Sandusky considered resigning on the spot rather than take over under the circumstances, but we begged him to stay. And he did, out of loyalty to us, not out of any illusion that he could persuade Irsay-Thomas to consider him for the full-time job at the end of the season. We hadn't let him quit, but he didn't see how he could continue.

Big John was caught, classically, between a rock and a hard place.

Black days in Baltimore? You bet, but we had a secret weapon to brighten us up a little bit: Danny Sullivan.

EVERY TEAM HAS ONE. A guy who keeps the locker room loose. A guy with an irreverent sense of humor (but without a mean streak). A guy who's a good enough ballplayer to be respected, but usually not a star. A lineman, usually—most often an offensive lineman.

For us, it was Irish Danny Sullivan—Boston native, Boston College grad, solid player, and relentless wit. A starter at both guard positions and at right tackle over the years (1972 was his 11th and final season in the NFL), Sully had the playing credentials to command our respect and the judgment to know how often (and how far) to insert his ever-handy needle.

Sully possessed a genuinely imaginative sense of humor. And so, we discovered to our glee, did his wife, Lorraine.

Friday afternoons during the regular season, Colts offensive linemen followed a solemn ritual that involved congregating at Johnny Unitas' Golden Arm bar and attempting to break the NFL record for pitchers of beer consumed. The idea behind his team effort was to compare notes on the week's accomplishments, build community spirit, and promote the general welfare.

On one such Friday, though, Sully forgot that Lorraine had planned a dinner party for some special, non-football friends. She reminded him of that oversight upon his return home in the wee hours of Saturday morning in a most creative fashion.

Sully was the proud owner of a box of Cuban cigars that he had purchased at great cost on a Caribbean cruise a bunch of us had taken with our wives several months earlier. Upon finally arriving home long, long past dessert and coffee, he discovered his prized smokes neatly scissored into a thousand pieces and scattered on his front porch.

At least the rest of us thought that was funny.

Over the years, Sully kept us smiling with his good-hearted jibes, frequently at out peerless leader. My personal favorite was delivered in Barnum & Bailey center ring style from the back of the locker room during a team meeting.

Ladeees and gen-tle-men! Gather round! See
the famous body of John Constantine Unitas!

So beautiful! So symmetrical! So functional in shorts, with legs that resemble a pair of pliers! Wherever we travel, women scream, flock to him, and rend his clothes! That's right, they rip his garments from his body! And, *ladeees and gen-tle-men*, upon viewing his birdlike torso, his slumping shoulders, his spindly legs, and his sagging ass, they immediately re-dress him!"

Not surprisingly, Sully was primed and ready when Sandusky convened his first meeting as *interim* head coach on the Tuesday following the ugliness of the previous 48 hours. From the back of the room, as people were settling in, came a lone voice singing, just loud enough to be heard. The tune was a dirge-like version of the sappy Hollies song, "He Ain't Heavy, He's My Brother."

Only Sully had altered the lyrics slightly. "He ain't hea-vyyy, he's Uni-taaas."

And then, when he had everybody's rapt attention, he went into PA mode. "Now introducing, the quarterback! Yes, the *quarterback*! The only player in professional football history to have his jersey retired ... with him still in it."

Next, after a pregnant pause, there came a familiar, disgusting sound, which Sully proceeded to identify in his nasal Boston accent. "That, my friends, was a *faht*."

Moments later, a second, even louder sound. "And that's the rest of it."

By now, everybody was convulsed with laughter, whatever tensions and anxieties they'd brought into the room at least momentarily dissipated. Even Sandusky got in a good laugh before telling Sully to shut his bleeping mouth.

UNITAS WE STOOD

The one courtesy John Unitas had asked of John Sandusky after the changing of the guard was that Sandusky never ask him to do mop-up duty—that is, to take the last snaps in a blowout. That was a common enough request, one routinely granted to the great ones in professional football. If you're a 10-time Pro Bowler, a 5-time first-team All-Pro, and a surefire first-ballot Hall of Famer, you don't get sent onto the field in the fourth quarter to "preserve" a 35-0 lead—or to give the starter a breather if the score's 0-35.

That's SOP in the NFL, as well it should be. Sometimes, though, you don't have any choice but to violate SOP.

Week 12, at home against the New England Patriots, we were up 24-0 in the fourth quarter when Marty Domres got hurt and had to leave the game. Problem: John was the only other QB we had, and he'd seen very little action since the Baltimore Massacre nearly two months ago. But in he trotted to mop up in a blowout.

What happened next is something of a blur, perhaps because I'd had my bell rung, more likely because I wanted to repress my role in it. But thanks to an episode of NFL Films, I must report that my man escaped me and drilled John just as he was throwing. A wounded duck fluttered unto the air. Fortunately, wide receiver Eddie Hinton grabbed it and made a career broken-field run for a TD.

[continued on following page]

Final score: Colts 31, Patriots 0.

Nice mopping up, John.

But that wasn't the No. 1 highlight on TV sports shows across the country that night. (Thank goodness. I wasn't looking for a larger audience to witness my failure to protect John on the play.) Just as the extra point was kicked, a small plane passed over the end zone trailing a huge banner with a simple, three-word message:

UNITAS WE STAND

The hometown crowd seconded that emotion with the longest standing O I have ever heard at any sporting event in my life.

NOT LONG AFTER the 1972 season ended, Unitas got an early morning telephone call from Baltimore sportswriter Larry Harris.

"Hi Johnny, how are you?" Larry was always polite, even at the crack of dawn.

"Sleeping Larry, that's how I am! How the hell are you?" John was not always polite if he was abruptly awakened.

"Johnny, what do you think about the deal?"

"Deal?" John was stumped. "What deal?"

Long silence.

"You don't know?"

Larry told me later that he practically strangled choking out the words.

"No, Larry, I don't know about any deal," John was now wide awake. "Tell me what's going on."

Larry stumbled some more, and then, "Irsay and Thomas have sold you to San Diego."

THAT WAS JUST the beginning of a wholesale housecleaning. Not altogether a surprise, I guess, what with us having just finished 5-9. But a lot of names familiar to Baltimore fans were swept aside, and the way it was done was—let me put it as diplomatically as I can—crude.

Over the next several months, Irsay-Thomas got rid of a third of the 1972 roster, including—more or less in the order they were dumped—Tom Matte, Norm Bulaich, Billy Newsome, Jerry Logan, Dan Sullivan, Fred Miller, Tom Nowatzke, Charlie Stukes, and Bubba Smith.

And me.

I was in Dallas to play in the Pro Bowl on January 21. A reporter asked me about Irsay and Thomas and the Unitas thing, and I decided to keep my mouth shut so as not to be a distraction from the game that weekend.

(I was really looking forward to it. It was my second straight Pro Bowl. You don't get a chance to block for O. J. Simpson; it was like making room for a Maserati to streak by. Gene Upshaw played next to me, and it was all very cool.)

Anyway, I said something bland like, "Oh, well, I suppose management did what they had to, but we were just upset by some of the communication things, but it's over and we need to move on." Of course, when the article came out, the headline was something like, "CURRY BLASTS IRSAY AND THOMAS AGAIN."

According to an account later from somebody who was in a position to know, Thomas flew in that day, bought a paper the next morning, and hit the ceiling. I don't know if it's true or not, but it seems plausible.

I do know that the next week, Thomas called me and said, without so much as hello, "Do you know where I just traded you Curry? *Houston*!" And then he laughed out loud for several seconds. It obviously tickled him pink to tell me that he was sending me to a team coming off a 1-13 season. I replied, "Well, Joe, wherever you sent me, I'll go, because I have to."

He jumped all over that, evidently having misunderstood me. "You *what*? You say you won't go?"

"No, Joe," I responded. "I said nothing of the sort. I'll go wherever it is you've traded me. Goodbye."

I guess you could say that my stay with the Colts didn't exactly end on a warm and friendly note.

THE LAST TIME I saw John Unitas was in the summer of 2001, at the home of Maxie and Dianne Baughan, just outside Baltimore.

This get-together included Tom and Judy Matte, Rick and Charlene Volk (Rick logged 12 seasons in the NFL with the Colts, Giants, and Dolphins), and John and Sandy Unitas. The atmosphere was virtually Christmas-like, fun and festive. I told John that he looked better than when he was a player. He blinked, grinned, and said that was easy, since as a player he was always being beaten to a pulp. With that, he looked pointedly at me, one of his prime guardians for five seasons, and laughed out loud.

Huddle humor never dies.

Maxie Baughan captained the defensive units of the Eagles and the Rams. Equipped with a sharp football mind and superb athletic skills, Maxie was a three-time All-Pro who played in nine Pro Bowls. Later, after a brief stint as an assistant at our alma mater, Georgia Tech, he served as a defensive coordinator in Detroit and Baltimore, and as head coach for six seasons at Cornell University.

Maxie and Dianne are among our closest friends. Wherever they go, they create a space that is warm, welcoming, and beautiful. It is one of the joys of our profession that former foes often come together in our "afterlife."

John's barb about offensive linemen letting him get beaten to a pulp reminded me of guard Glenn Ressler's famous response after a 1970 game against the Bears. John had thrown three interceptions in our first four possessions, launching the Bears to a 17-0 lead. We had fought back to win, 21-20, and the taciturn Ressler was interviewed following the cliffhanger. Glenn told reporters, "Today we went back to basics." When pressed for an explanation, he said, "Well, I'm an offensive lineman, and normally all we do is block. Today we got plenty of chances to block *and* tackle."

On this happy occasion at the Baughans, I thought I'd try one more time to penetrate that famous psyche. "John, did you really love all the crap about football as much as you claimed?"

He looked me dead in the eye. "You're a long time dead, Billy!" And that sent me right back to the summer of 1967.

"Do you realize you said that to me the first time you ever walked to practice with me in training camp back in 1967?" I asked.

FLASHBACK

My first training camp with the Colts, I was trying to convert from center to linebacker and I was no sure thing to make the team. Shula's two-a-days were unbelievable—full pads, full-speed hitting, and it was going to be that all six weeks of camp. Early on, I was beat up and demoralized and riddled with insecurity.

Not in a good place.

One afternoon near the end of the second week, I was plodding along toward the practice field when I happened to glance over to see No. 19 waddling along by me. He was wearing a blue rubber sweat jacket in the 90-degree heat. The sleeves were cut off, but the sight of his outfit nearly gave me a heat stroke. He was carrying his shoulder pads and headgear, and whistling a happy tune.

There's got to be something wrong with this guy, I thought to myself.

"Hey, John, how come you sound so happy?" I asked. What's there to be happy about in weather like this?"

In my book, two-a-days in 90-degree heat was a time for fatigue, bitching, and self-pity.

"You're a long time dead, Billy!" he grinned.

> "You're crazy, Old Man," I said to him. "Nobody could like this part of football."
>
> He stopped in his tracks and looked at me, the grin gone. "Listen, Billy, you aren't here but a little while. You better love what you do, or just don't do it. I love football practice. I love every minute of every day we're out here. If you want to last, you better learn to love it, too. Understand?"
>
> I understood that I had been challenged, and my attitude noticeably improved that very day.
>
> Postscript: I made the team, and to this day I believe that John Unitas' little attitude adjustment was a major contributing factor.

"Hell no," he said. "I don't remember saying that or anything to you in training camp that year—you were new to the team and a linebacker, remember? Why would I be taking notice of you? But I wouldn't be surprised if I did say it, because it's true. I mean, you find something you love, you better do it, and do it right, because we're only on this planet a little while."

And then, after a pause, "We're all going to die, Billy. And once you're gone, you're gone."

THIS QUIET, SIMPLE philosophy fueled, stabilized, and propelled the dominant personality in the history of the league. Neither he—nor the philosophy—ever deviated. But I pressed him. "Come on, John, where does that stuff come from?"

He looked off a little and said, "My father died when I was 5, and my mother worked two jobs just to support us. I learned about work from her. Football was in my heart, in my blood, from the time I can remember. So I worked hard, really hard, to get better, because I knew the coal mines were my next stop if I couldn't figure out something else to do with my life. Also, my grandmother helped out one time."

Your grandmother?

"Yeah," he smiled. "She saw me play exactly one time in her whole life, and you won't believe what she said."

Tell me.

"I was playing semi-pro ball," he said, "and I asked her to come watch me play, and she finally showed up. She had emigrated from Lithuania right after World War I, and she hadn't exactly been assimilated into American culture, especially American sports. I was playing for the Bloomfield Rams at the time, making $8 a game. Well, Grandma sat through it, or at least part of it, and was waiting for me when I got home."

(I'm thinking to myself: $8 *a game*?)

John said he asked her, "Do you like football, Grandma?"

Then he leaned forward a little to deliver the punch line, from Grandma's lips.

Well, all you boys laid in a pile on one another, got up, and then split into two groups. Your group got all close together, and then most of them ran up to that ball, lying there on the ground. You walked up behind one of them, looked around, sniffed his butt,

and all of a sudden the damndest fight I ever
saw broke out. That's all I could tell about it.
I don't need to come back to another one of
those things.

"Best I could figure," John laughed, "she was convinced it
was a total waste of my time."

ON SEPTEMBER 11, 2002, Carolyn and I were walking up
the short flight of steps at Peachtree Road United Methodist, our church in Atlanta, when my cell phone rang. We
were there to attend a service in memory of the victims of
the terrorist attack the previous year, and I started to click
off the ringer and let the phone take the call. But I saw that
it was from my broadcast partner, Dave Barnett at ESPN,
so I answered.

"Bill, have you heard?" he asked.

To this day I recall that his voice had a tinny ring. Funny,
the little things you remember long after hearing stunning
news.

"No, what's up?" I replied.

"I am so sorry to say these words," Dave said, "but Johnny
Unitas died of a heart attack today."

The next hours were a jumble of numbness, sponta-
neous surges of emotion, and gentle hugs from Carolyn. I
didn't call old friends or teammates with the news. I don't
remember what I thought or did, as a matter of fact. I do
know that God provided no comfort. And I know that I
grieved as I have seldom grieved in my life, before or since.

In retrospect, I only recall once thinking that he would outlive us all.

But that was foolish.

My friend had been living on borrowed time.

ONE OF THE happy aspects of my stint as head coach at Kentucky from 1990 through 1996 was the fact that Louisville was the site of the Johnny Unitas Golden Arm Award ceremony. This annual award was established in 1987 by John's foundation to honor the college quarterback that year who embodied values Unitas treasured: hard work, honesty, results on the field, and commitment to the community off the field. I was usually asked to participate. John, of course, was always there.

One year in the early 1990s, we both were cutting it close and hadn't had a chance to speak to each other before it was time to go on stage. While we were waiting for our cue, John turned to me and blurted, without so much as a hello-how-are-you, *"Billy, you ain't gonna believe what just happened to me!"*

He had his best puckish grin on, so I figured I was in for one of his terrible jokes.

"Well, I'm glad to see you, too, John," I responded. "So tell me, what just happened to you?"

"Well," he said, "I went to the hospital to have my knee fixed, some kind of cartilage thing. They put me under, and the next thing I know I wake up with my damn chest all bandaged up. I looked at that doctor and said, 'What the hell's going on? Where's my knee doc? Who are you? Why's my chest all bandaged up?' "

He paused to see if he had my full attention. He did.

"The doctor said to me, 'Johnny Unitas, you are the luckiest man I have ever seen. You got on the operating table and had a heart attack right there. If you had been anywhere else, you would be with your Maker right now.'"

Hearing what just happened to him, barely able to believe the words, I hugged him on the spot, right there on the podium in front of a thousand people, which made him distinctly uneasy. I reminded him that he was too mean to die, and that he had to outlive all of us so he could be around to tell us what to do. We may have chuckled a bit, but we knew that a timer had just started ticking in our heads.

Yet somehow he had managed 10 more years, mostly by taking good care of himself. When his timer finally went off, he was 69.

THIS IS WHAT I wrote later that terrible day for ESPN. com:

Johnny Unitas

September 11, 2002

He was, above all, real. According to the dictionary, the word "legend" implies unverifiable statements reported as historical fact. So Johnny Unitas is the antithesis of legend because everything about him is so documented. It is in the record book. What he did was so astounding that we don't even feel the need to embellish. His persona was so unvarnished, so blunt, so sincere, that we would betray him if we invented an image. He was, and is, real. He always will be.

I think the thing that makes him so hard to describe, even for those of us who spent years with him in the trenches, is that despite his natural humility, his stoic mien, and his simplicity, he really was larger than life. I know that is a contradiction, but once in a great while there comes a person whose reality is of a different and richer substance than that of the rest of us. He becomes what we refer to as legend without the slightest need for embellishment.

Maybe that's because he lived out the American Dream before our very eyes. He really was a skinny kid that no one wanted on their team. He really did come from humble beginnings. He really was cut from the then pathetic Pittsburgh Steelers. He really did play football on glass-strewn fields for eight bucks a game in Bloomfield, Pa. And folks, he really did personally transform the National Football League from the sandlot to the Great American Obsession ...

In the huddle there was no hesitation. The plays were his calls. The execution was his expectation. Miss your man and he might look you in the eye and simply call the number of the big guy that had just rearranged his nose. No change of expression or tone of voice. We vowed to get the man next time, and did whatever was necessary to do so. We could not bear to let him down ...

Once we kicked off, he never changed his facial expression. In a 1970 game with the Bears, he threw three interceptions on his first four passes. He trotted off the field just like he did when he threw touchdown passes. The score in the first quarter was 17-0, Bears. He moved up and down the bench, asking each of us if we were okay, if we needed a draw or a screen on the next series. The last pass of the day was an 80-yard touchdown to John Mackey to win, 21-20. Had you focused a camera on his face, you would have detected nothing new. He expected to do his job.

He was just John Unitas, real man, real winner, and real American hero.

God bless you, John.

We will never forget you.

JOHN'S FUNERAL WAS held on September 18, 2002, in Baltimore's Cathedral of Mary Our Queen.

I would be pleased to record that it was an event packed with tears, a lot of laughter, some touching reminiscences, and a sense of belonging anew to our unique Baltimore Colts huddle.

I was hoping for a scene kind of like those marvelous stories of Irish wakes, in which everyone starts out somber and sober, and ends up laughing out loud and crying out loud, saluting and celebrating a life and cocking a snoot at death.

But an unexpected shadow hung over our efforts to celebrate John's life: the appalling condition of a beloved teammate.

The night before, a bunch of us—maybe 20 in all, including our spouses—gathered together at a local restaurant. (Unfortunately, Johnny U's Golden Arm was no longer around, or you can bet we'd have been there.) There was a radio hookup, and Tom Matte brought several of us onto the air so that we could share our grief and Unitas lore with the mourning public.

My ex-roomie, John Mackey, showed up, and we were all badly shaken by his condition. Now suffering from frontal temporal dementia, the best tight end ever to play the game could only offer one response to any question or salutation: "Yeah, man, go deep!"

He knew he had played football, and he would thrust forward his big hands—one with a ring from Super Bowl V, the other from the NFL Hall of Fame—and he would say again, and again, and again ...

"Yeah, man, go deep."

The great wit and charm we had all loved was now hidden somewhere in the netherworld of his collision-induced illness. Research indicates that there is no cure, that the symptoms worsen—meaning less and less cognitive ability—and that, eventually, full-time care is needed.

The cause? A decade in professional football with too many blows to the head, too many concussions, at a time when too little was known about the cumulative effects.

Sylvia Mackey, always a model of propriety and grace, had to steer her husband to our table in the restaurant, to and from the men's room, to and from anywhere he went. She never left his side. I asked her how it was going, and she replied that it was devastating and that she had been required to go back to work as a flight attendant to make ends meet.

She had been a successful model for more than 30 years, but needed the security of a steady income, somewhat regular hours, and benefits. In 1997, at age 56, she had answered an ad in the newspapers for a bilingual flight attendant. She's fluent in French, and she got the job.

Sylvia, now 66, is going strong, one of the most remarkable people I have ever known. Not a shred of self-pity; just devotion to her task of caring for the man she loves. She is utterly devoted to John and has found a way to make their lives work. One of their daughters, Laura, keeps John much of the time, and a caretaker comes in as well.

The next day we all gathered at Donovan's, a restaurant and club famous for its party atmosphere and joyful community events. There were many hugs in the parking lot, where long, black limousines gathered to drive us to the cathedral. We tried to respond as John Unitas would have wanted us to, with strength and grit. But there was just too much sad, emotional baggage dragging us down.

We made a conscious effort to keep the conversation on John's legacy, his inherent goodness, and the amazing memories he had left to us all. But every so often there would be a lull. After one, a member of our little group shook his head and said, "Can you believe what happened to our team? It still seems like a bad dream."

He didn't have to say that he was talking about the despicable way Robert Irsay moved the team to Indianapolis. We knew.

That prompted someone to ask whether "Jim Irsay and any of his front office people will show up for Johnny tomorrow?" Robert Irsay died in 1997; his son, Jim, took over as president of the Colts. Excuse me, the *Indianapolis* team. With almost 3,500 in attendance the next day, we couldn't tell for sure who was and wasn't there. Nobody spotted Irsay, and I don't think any of us went out of our way to look for him.

Sometimes righteously bad feelings can last a long, long time.

AT TIMES LIKE these, human beings tend to embellish, re-invent, even mythologize their "glory days." We were mourning much more than the death of our friend and standard-bearer. We were mourning the loss of innocence, the loss of our youth, the loss of our health in some cases, and the loss of our mental faculties in others.

Most telling of all, we had lost our *team*. This would be it for the Baltimore Colts of the Johnny Unitas Era—no more reunions, no more raucous get-togethers, no more large turnouts for the funeral of one of us, because without John, we were no longer a team.

I asked my live-in professional historian, Dr. Carolyn Curry, to reflect on the meaning of all this. Here's her response.

> What happened in 1984 when the Colts were ripped out of Baltimore was more than just the loss of a football team. The love affair that had existed between the city and the Colts team was summarily terminated. The Colt Corrals, a statewide network of fan clubs that held regular meetings like big college programs, suddenly had no reason for being. The Dundalk dock workers, our blue-collar buddies who loaded the stands seven Sundays every fall, now had to make do with TV. The amateur marching band that performed at games packed away their instruments forever. No more engagement parties, birthday parties, and just plain Colts parties at Johnny Unitas' Golden Arm. The people of Baltimore loved you guys, and you loved them back, and Johnny Unitas was the last connecting link to that love.
>
> And now he's gone.

But John Unitas brought us all together in a huddle this one last time. And the Colts fans were back, lining the streets of Baltimore three and four deep, as if they were honoring a beloved head of state.

Which, of course, they were.

Estimates of the crowd's size varied, but I'm saying it was exactly 62,238, the number that used to squeeze into Memorial Stadium for our games. Only this time they were silent.

Many of the people on the sidewalk were our age and older, but there were also many young people who could have only seen us play in documentaries. I saw grown men weeping without embarrassment. People waved white banners with blue borders emblazoned with the *Baltimore* Colts emblem. There were women with flowers and children who could only have heard about his legend holding homemade signs that read "We Love U Johnny U!" and "Baltimore Will Miss Johnny U. Forever."

One banner expressed the sentiments of many:

> OUR BALTIMORE COLTS. WHERE ARE YOU? WHAT HAPPENED? WE WILL ALWAYS LOVE YOU. WE WILL ALWAYS MISS YOU!

The message was clear: those guys in Indianapolis are just masquerading as Colts. Or, to express the sentiment in another way,

> Where have you gone, Joe DiMaggio?
> A nation turns its lonely eyes to you ...

Substitute Johnny U. for Joe D., that's what it was like.

UPON OUR ARRIVAL inside the church, there were a few whispers of recognition as people saw the familiar faces of their superheroes. "There's Gino Marchetti! Look, John and Sylvia Mackey! Tom Matte! That's Jim Mutscheller! Lenny Moore! Jim Parker!

And "Hey, Artie Donovan! So sorry, Big Man!"

The guys did their best to stay in line, smile, and move on to their seats. I was really glad to see Mike Curtis as we walked up the cathedral steps. He and Unitas had never gotten along, and his presence was a statement about Mike's class and inner dignity.

Once inside the sanctuary, we ascended to the choir loft, just adjacent to and slightly elevated above the altar. John's teammates were his honorary pallbearers. Looking out in front of me, I could see that the entire sanctuary was packed. Johnny U. had drawn one last S.R.O. crowd.

The mass was solemn and dignified. At least one non-Catholic who'd grown up in hard-shell Protestant country reflected, not for the first time, on the structure and symbolism of the ritual that was so different from what he had experienced as a child.

When communion was served, the Catholics in the massive congregation filed quietly to the front of the church, received the Host, and then went back to their seats.

It was at mid-point during this service that John Mackey stood up from his place among us, moved down the row into the aisle, and headed directly toward the altar as the puzzled congregation looked on. He turned right just before reaching the altar, and walked out the side door of the sanctuary.

Sylvia sat frozen. For perhaps the first time in her life, the always-capable caretaker didn't seem to know what to do. She later told me she was confident John was not a danger to himself or anyone else, but that he could become belligerent when challenged. None of us had the vaguest notion what might happen next, but one thing was certain—no one was focused exclusively on the funeral of Johnny Unitas anymore.

Should I get up and get him? I'd been his roommate. Would he even know me? Would we create a scene that would spoil this precious moment? I could only freeze, taking my cue from Sylvia, as Carolyn took my hand and squeezed hard. After a few very long minutes, Mackey re-entered the sanctuary and began to wander up and down the middle aisle, looking into faces, looking, looking ... for what?

John couldn't remember where he'd been sitting.

After what seemed an eternity, Roy Hilton stood up, moved into the aisle, and carefully made his way to John. A defensive end for nine NFL seasons, Roy had been drafted by the Colts in 1965, the year I became a Green Bay Packer. As the two old teammates approached one another, Roy smiled, nodded, and extended his hand. Obviously confused, John moved toward him, haltingly, but did not reach out his hand. When they were close enough, Roy took John's elbow and gently guided the big man back to Sylvia's side. It was a gut-wrenching moment, but also a great relief to us all to see John settled in next to Sylvia.

I couldn't help but flash back to the great human being we all had known. Acclaimed as the greatest tight end in NFL history and the finest of our NFL Players Association presidents, John Mackey—one of the sharpest minds I had ever known and one of my best friends—had been lost, just a few feet from his wife, his team, his brothers.

This was not just one man's funeral.

FIVE OF JOHN Unitas' eight children from two marriages spoke movingly about their father.

All of them touched us with their sincerity and affection, but the most poignant message came from Paige, John's 19-year old daughter.

Paige spoke with poise, dignity, and humor about being a little girl in restaurants with her famous father. She said she was confused at first, then put off as she grew older by the constant interruptions from fans wanting an autograph or a picture or a quick chat about last Sunday's game. She talked of complaining, often bitterly, about the intrusions. She said she often asked her father just to ignore the fans who were stealing time from his private life, to just say "no."

Paige then summarized her father's response to her: "I know all this attention bothers you. It bothers me too. But we help people to be a little happier, maybe smile a little more. Watch when I'm signing my name on a menu for them. They smile every time, right? If we can make a few people smile, just by sharing a little of our time, isn't that a good thing for us to do?"

It's what you do, not what you say.

As the man said, talk is cheap.

Let's go play.

One can only wonder how great a football player Bubba would have become had he not destroyed his knee in the ugliest on-field horror I've ever witnessed. But the NFL's loss was Hollywood's gain.

9
BUBBA SMITH
COACH

Kill, *Bubba, Kill!*

That's the chant that filled Spartan Stadium in East Lansing, Michigan, in 1966 every time the Michigan State defense took the field during MSU's historic 9-0-1 season, which culminated with the Spartans sharing the national championship with Notre Dame.

Thanks, Bubba, Thanks!

That's the chant that filled the William Alexander Curry household following the trade that put me on a nonstop flight from Green Bay to New Orleans to Baltimore before the 1967 season.

The Colts sent QB Gary Cuozzo (a solid backup to Johnny Unitas for four seasons), the rights to an offensive lineman who never played a down in the NFL, and a late-round draft pick to New Orleans. In exchange, the Colts received the Saints' third-round pick, their seventh-round pick, and me.

Oh, and their first-round pick in the 1967 NFL Draft.

To pretty much no one's surprise, the Colts used that first-round choice—the No. 1 overall—to select the most coveted college football player in the country: an All-American DE/DT from Michigan State named Charles Aaron Smith.

Bubba.

Was I shattered to play second fiddle in Don Shula's calculations when he put together the deal?

Not quite.

I thought I'd won the lottery.

FROM THE OUTSET, Bubba and I hit it off. He pulled up at the Colts training camp in Westminster, Maryland, in a very long, very beautiful brown Cadillac convertible. It had a beige leather interior and I was utterly smitten. Not with Bubba, but with the car. When I needled him about squandering so much of his bonus money on an automobile, he laughed.

"Billy, you think I paid for this thing out of *my* pocket? Naw, Duffy made sure we had real wheels, man."

(I *think* Bubba was kidding.)

The Duffy allegedly in the Cadillac business was, of course, Duffy Daugherty, head coach of the Michigan State Spartans from 1954 through 1972. During that stretch, he won a national championship (1965) shared another with Notre Dame (1966), led the Spartans to two undefeated seasons (1965, 1966), and took them to two Rose Bowls (1955, 1965). The man was a rare combination of football smarts, irreverence, and wit. Of the many great observations ascribed to him over the years, my hands-down favorite is his description of the true nature of the game he loved.

Football isn't a contact sport. Football is a collision sport. Dancing is a contact support.

The brightest thing Duffy did during that turbulent era in American society was to go down South to recruit African-American players. Black players weren't welcome in the SEC or the Southwest Conference, so they essentially had to choose between playing college football in the Southwestern Athletic Conference, made up of traditionally black institutions, or heading up north, often to the Big Ten. Thanks to Duffy's eye for talent and eagerness to open doors, Bubba headed north.

At training camp that July, Bubba and I were both assigned to the second-team defensive unit. Fair enough. For all the ballyhoo surrounding his status as the No. 1 draft pick overall, Bubba was still a rookie and I was a third-year player shifting from offensive center to middle linebacker. That meant both of us had to bust our butts to earn the respect of the rest of the defensive unit. (Of course, at a Don Shula training camp, not busting your butt wasn't an option.)

Bubba and I were both from the Deep South—he grew up in Beaumont, Texas—but we were nurtured in diametrically opposite worlds. He had attended a 100 percent black high school; mine was 100 percent white. He'd never played against white guys in high school; I'd never played against black guys.

Yet here we were, teammates in a sport that, more than any other, requires individual players to bond together. You can't be focusing on the color of one another's skin if you're out there on the field trying to stop the other guys from scoring a go-ahead touchdown.

Our back-and-forth chatter about everything under the sun, football and otherwise, helped cement an abiding friendship from which I drew great strength. Not only that, but as Bubba reminded me frequently, he was partly—okay, mainly—responsible for my presence in Baltimore in the first place.

Among the many lessons Bubba tried to teach me were multiple variations of the locker-room vulgarities, profanity, and special lingo of the brothers on the team, so that I could follow their conversations.

That led me to think—naïvely—that I could actually understand something of the black experience in America. Seeing that I was interested, Bubba seemed to enjoy coming up with ways to help me *feel* what it was like to be an African-American man in a culture dominated by Caucasian males.

This wasn't just Race Relations 101, either; it was advanced schooling under the tutelage of Professor Charles Smith.

BUBBA WAS A giant, a colossus.

Bubba was *b-i-i-i-g*: 265 pounds spread over a 6'7" frame.

By today's standards for a defensive end, of course, that was downright skinny. Consider, for instance, the 2007 New England Patriots' bookend DEs, Ty Warren and Jarvis Green. The former weighs 300, the latter 290. And both are several inches shorter than Bubba: Warren is 6'5", Green is 6'3".

By comparison, of course, defensive linemen *and* offensive linemen in Bubba's day (and mine) were shrimp boats. At 6'3", I weighed "just" 235 pounds. Center Dan Koppen of the Patriots is an inch shorter but 60 pounds heavier.

And so it goes, throughout the NFL: bigger, bigger, bigger.

Everybody knows that. But what you may not have considered is what's going to happen to these behemoths when they leave the game.

The first three months after I stowed my headgear for the last time, I put on 15 or 20 pounds. Part of the weight gain resulted from a profound depression that engulfed me and led me drink a lot and sit around feeling sorry for myself. Part of it came from being physically inactive for the first time in nearly two decades.

Funny what two-a-days and grass drills and gassers will do to get you in shape, and what a 14-game NFL season will do to keep you toned. And the offseason? You do what you need to do to stay fit or summer camp will absolutely, positively kill you.

But whatever the mix of reasons, gaining a bunch of weight after giving up an intensely strenuous, physical activity that you've been engaged in year-round since you were a lad is absolutely common among ex-football players.

Case in point no. 1: two fine young men I coached at the University of Alabama, Roger Schultz and Trent Patterson. Roger was an All-SEC center in 1989 and 1990; Trent played next to him at right guard. They anchored an offensive line that helped get us to the Sugar Bowl in 1990, where we lost to Miami 33-25. (But we were driving the fourth quarter ...!)

I couldn't tell you to the pound how much each weighed when they were playing football for me, but as a center and a guard, they probably tipped the scales at a combined 500 pounds, give or take a bag of Double Quarter Pounders with Cheese.

I can tell you that when they first weighed in as a team on that super-popular reality show *The Biggest Loser*, they *really* tipped the scales: 799 pounds.

That's no typo: *799* pounds.

Over the course of the program, Trent plummeted from 419 pounds to 230, a drop of 45 percent from his starting weight. Roger did even better going from 380 pounds to 180 (minus 48 percent), good enough to get him into the finals, where he was edged out by a woman whose percentage loss was a smidgen higher. But in my book, both guys were big winners by virtue of being such big losers. And I was especially proud of them for doing it without me having to run their large hindquarters around and around a football field.

THINGS WENT GREAT for me after I was moved back to offensive center in 1968—and even better for the team. Over the next four seasons, we were 42-12-2. In 1971, we beat the Cowboys 16-13 in Super Bowl V. The agony of Super Bowl III still lingered, but it felt mighty good to win one.

We were the champs and I had my championship ring, but I knew that NFL defensive schemes were catching up with my limited size. (My "program weight" was 235.)

Neither Don McCafferty, who had taken over as head coach in 1970, nor offensive line coach George Young said anything, but it was becoming clear to me that I wouldn't last much longer in the NFL unless I improved my blocking against the "odd defenses" that were coming into vogue.

The word "odd" in that phrase doesn't refer to unusual or weird defenders. (Though some of them most certainly are.) It means a defensive alignment in which there are an uneven number of men on the line of scrimmage, with one of them usually aligned directly over the offensive center. An even defense simply means there are four, six, or even eight defenders on the line of scrimmage, with the center remaining "uncovered." But even in the "even" case, the middle linebacker usually lines up directly in front of the center, though a few steps back of the scrimmage line.

We had a new line coach when we reported to training camp in 1971. His name was Red Miller, and he was instant dynamite. Enthusiastic, detailed, demanding, and positive, Red related perfectly to our veteran line. He understood the subtleties of each offensive line position. He was a master of everything, from little things like stance adjustments to drills that made us better players to the positive psychology necessary for survival in the pit we inhabited.

Early on, Red pulled me aside. "Bill, I've watched all the film we have on you," he told me. "I can help you with the odd defenses. Let me tell you, if you'll gain a little weight and do the extra work I'm going to prescribe for you, I'll make you the best center in the National Football League." It was if as if he'd been reading my mind, only better, since he actually had answers to the questions I'd been asking myself.

What professional football players want most from their coaches is just what Red was selling. We want to improve.

We want to learn from somebody who knows more than we do. We want an encourager.

Red Miller was all of those things, and more.

We started with extra footwork, new sled drills, and sophisticated change of direction drills to improve my conditioning. Tiny details I had never focused on became part of my daily routine. Check to see where the nose guard's free hand is, the one that's not on the ground. What does he do with it on the snap of the ball? Does he drive it into your facemask? Does he slap you on the side of your head? Does he drop his shoulder? Where are his feet? Can we take advantage of his posture and moves?

I had studied before, but never in such meticulous detail as Red prescribed.

Red's pass protection drills were unlike anything we had ever seen. In the routine he called the Mirror Drill, he paired us up and had us assume the position an offensive linemen finds himself in when the defender has beaten him—meaning, the big guy has you by the shirt, has penetrated your hand thrust, and is about to throw you to the ground. He taught us to fight and use the defenders' strength to redirect, maintain balance, and shuffle back in front of him.

It was grueling, and it was great.

Even during two-a-days, I couldn't wait to get to work. Then, when we got into exhibition season, Red asked Bubba Smith to give us a hand. Once he heard what Red wanted, Bubba said he would be happy to "run over Billy all day long!"

That, you see, was a short but fairly accurate description of his new assignment.

We lined up, just the two of us, and I would snap the ball (to a backup quarterback, or to Red on occasion), set up, and take on the fastest big man in the NFL this side of Joe Greene. Over and over we went, until the pace and even his size seemed normal to me. It was that old "speed of the game" thing: the game slowed down for me.

Coach McCafferty saw our little one-on-one drills and began to move Bubba inside, over the centers, on Sundays. He soon found out that no center in the league could block Big Bubba. That "odd"-looking defense became one of our successful changeups.

BUBBA, AS IT turned out, was having his own trial by fire. Assistant coach John Sandusky had been moved over to defense the year before, and he was riding the big man hard. Sandusky insisted on calling Bubba by his given name. "Charles," Sandusky would intone slowly, more suitable to an arch, drawing-room comedy set in upper-crust England than to a football field, before lashing into Bubba for a missed assignment or a lackluster effort. The most frequent refrain on our practice field was, "Charles, could you please run full speed? Charles, are you a very big wuss? Charles, will you please give us some 'Kill, Bubba, Kill' out there?"

The harder John drove Bubba, the harder Bubba manhandled our offense. Privately, I wanted Sandusky to shut his mouth, because every new epithet, every new goad, just drove Bubba to dig deeper into his amazing reservoir of speed, strength, and raw physical talent, and direct it against us.

A man playing a game with boys? That much-abused aphorism perfectly fit Bubba Smith going against the Baltimore Colts offensive line. I honestly believe Bubba could have grabbed any one of us, shaken him like a rag doll, and used his body to cave in the rest. None of us could handle him one-on-one, not even Bob Vogel, our All-Pro offensive tackle.

Try to imagine a human being who towers over everybody around him like a grizzly bear, who is so flexible he can assume a tightly balled stance like a man six inches shorter than himself, and who can explode from that stance like a cheetah. And imagine that with all that physical superiority, this man-beast is also smarter than you at the lightning-fast mind games that precede the demolition derby unleashed by the snap of the ball.

Bubba was a master at getting inside your head. Periodically, he would stand up during a break in practice and issue a blanket challenge: "Hey, everybody listen up! Anybody want some of my money? If you weigh 230 or more, I'll bet you any amount of money—you say how much—that I can beat you in a 40-yard dash! If you weigh under 230, and this includes you corners and safeties, I'll bet you any amount of money I can beat you the first 10 yards! Any takers? C'mon, people, any takers?"

Think Goliath of the Philistines vs. the Children of Israel. Only I never saw David win one of these. Some tried, but nobody ever took Bubba's money. After a few costly tries, our defensive backs and wide receivers would just smile and shake their heads. Too often they'd seen him bolt out and at worst finish a dead heat with our fastest defensive backs and receivers.

The biggest and strongest man on our team was also the quickest.

AT RED MILLER'S request and with my smiling (but inwardly cringing) acquiescence, Bubba started staying after practice so that he could use his 6'7", 265 pounds of muscle and his cornerback quickness to make me into a better center.

For 15 minutes a day, he would head slap me, arm over me, spin off me, and generally torment me with all the standard moves in a nose tackle's repertoire, plus a few he invented just to make me look like an idiot. I endured it because I knew I was benefiting. I also knew when Friday afternoon rolled around that I had already endured the most difficult days of my week.

After a few practices, Bubba told me that I was stiff.

"Stiff?" I was insulted. "Hey, I stretch just like everybody else! Don't tell me I'm stiff."

"Yeah, Billy," he said, "you do stretch just like all the other white boys, and that's the problem. All y'all are stiff. Only you're lucky. You got a chance to be limber, if you'll be my stretching partner."

"No thanks," I said, still piqued at his criticism and not wanting to reveal the fact that I found stretching the most boring activity on the face of the earth. "Go sell that to those other idiots on defense. Teach Billy Ray or Fred Miller all that stuff."

Now it was his turn to be wounded, and he got his very big back up. "You know what, Billy? You just can't deal with the possibility that a black person might be able to teach you something."

That did it; he'd played the guilt card. We both knew it was BS, but he had me where he wanted me.

"All right, big man, when do we start?" Then, after a moment, "And how much is it going to hurt?"

FOR THE NEXT three years, I enjoyed a flexibility that only comes from partnering up in yoga-like drills with a person who is 6'7", twice as strong as you, and has an intuitive feel of how to push, pull, and cajole just the proper amount to elicit maximum muscle elasticity.

We planted ourselves smack in the middle of the locker room, the only inside place with the square feet we required. We would sit face to face on an exercise mat, legs spread wide, with my feet against his ankles (since my legs, though long, are considerably shorter than his). We leaned forward, arms outstretched, each clasping the other's hands. Carefully, we alternated pulling, then being pulled, in a 360-degree circle rotating around an axis at the center of the space between our legs.

As we continued the movement, which quickly became rhythmic and natural, a synergy formed that was more than the obvious physical stretch. Each of us, directed by verbal commands from the other, learned the other's physical limitations for that day. Given the number and location of bumps, bruises, and strains, the extent to which we could push and pull one another differed in degree and intensity. It became a kind of dance that was indispensable to my preparation.

When I started stretching with Bubba, I could barely bend my torso beyond a 90-degree angle. My groin, hamstrings, and lower back were so stiff—yes, Bubba, stiff as hell—that the pain was excruciating when I touched my limit. I'd been raised by my daddy, so I didn't quit on Bubba, even though I can assure you that I wanted to. Within a week, though, I was over the extra soreness—"extra" because the muscles were gently being extended beyond any place they had ever been before. To my everlasting amazement, I began to look forward to the long stretching sessions.

Bubba was a natural-born leader, and right before my eyes, "Bubba Smith" metamorphosed into "Charles Smith."

No joking. No jiving. No living up (or down) to our stereotypes—me the Southern white, him the Southern black. We went into our zone. Bubba's face across from me was first a gauge of his commitment, next a motivation, and then an inspiration as I would watch his eyes glaze over and he would mutter things like "pull harder on my right ham."

I never did become the best center in the league, but I did become the best center I was capable of being.

THE TELEPHONE CALL came shortly after I became offensive line coach of the Green Bay Packers in 1977.

"Billy, I need your help."

In all my years in the NFL, only two men called me "Billy": Bubba Smith and John Unitas. (Maybe the latter was paying me back for calling him John instead of Johnny.)

"How can I help you, Bubba?"

I'd tried his given name, Charles, a few times but it didn't fit, probably because of the way John Sandusky had used it to torture my enormous friend. But, in the end, Sandusky's taunts had worked. Big John took over the defensive line in 1970 and that year Bubba went to the Pro Bowl. The following season he returned to the Pro Bowl *and* was selected a first-team All-Pro. Under Sandusky, Charles "Bubba" Smith was well on his way to becoming one of the finest defensive ends in the NFL.

"Billy, I know you remember what happened to me that night in 1972 in Tampa."

HOW COULD I ever forget?

We were playing the Steelers in an exhibition game. Late in the fourth quarter, Colts safety Rick Volk picked off a Terry Bradshaw pass and headed up the sideline on our side of the field. Bubba was running at full speed trying to block for Rick. I was on the sideline close to the official holding one of the yard markers. As they reached the sideline in front of our bench, some guys went down ahead of him and Bubba had to leap over them, straight at the marker and the man holding it.

In these situations, the sideline officials are instructed to pick up the pole, which is stuck firmly into the ground, and back-pedal out of the way of players whose momentum might bring them out of bounds. In this case, the guy froze, maintaining a death grip on the pole that he'd driven hard into the turf.

In one of the most horrible injuries I have ever seen, Bubba crashed into the implanted pole, his weight and momentum driving his leg against it with such force that his knee counter-hinged, ripping loose every ligament that held the joint together.

Want a better picture? Straighten out your leg. Now bend your knee. Straighten it again. Now bend it the *other* way. Your knee won't do that. Well, Bubba's did.

Had the guy holding the pole lifted it and back-pedaled away from the oncoming action, per standard instructions, there would have been no injury.

Had he just let go of the pole and headed for the hills, there would have been no injury.

But because he stayed in place holding onto the pole, Bubba's knee was destroyed. He missed the entire 1972 season, and he was hobbled for the rest of his abbreviated career.

Was the official manning the chain at fault? Sure he was, but you have to understand that the guys doing that job weren't trained, full-time NFL guys. They were mostly local high school officials looking to pick up a few extra bucks. And they certainly had no experience dealing with a Bubba Smith closing in on them at full speed.

They were told what to do in this kind of situation, but to say they were adequately trained or that they even practiced the evasive maneuver would be a wild exaggeration. Yes, the young guy who panicked and held on to the pole was the immediate cause of Bubba's injury. But the primary responsibility, in my view, rested clearly and squarely on the NFL.

ED COLT OF THE BLOCKS

That's what Ed Block, trainer of the Baltimore Colts from 1954 to 1977, liked to call himself. And to those of us who knew and loved him, and who always turned to him for help when we were hurting, the words "Block" and Colts" were, in fact, inseparable.

But Eddie's reputation went beyond the Colts. He was known around the league as the best in his field.

A small man (5'2") among giants, Block towered over his training room as well as the psyches of our largest players.

My most vivid memory of Eddie's passion for healing us was the time he ripped into Bubba Smith for omitting a step in Eddie's carefully constructed plan for helping Smith recover from an injury. There was little Eddie, pounding the 6'7", 265-pound behemoth with both of his little fists at about chest level, screaming into Bubba's navel, "You skipped treatment! How dare you! I won't allow it!"

We pulled Eddie off, sat him down, and then gasped in fright as he blanched in pain, clutched his chest, and reached into his shirt pocket to retrieve his ever-present nitroglycerin pills. Bubba was so terrified that big tears rolled down his cheeks as he sat next to Eddie, begging forgiveness.

"I almost killed that little man," a still-shaken Bubba confided in me the next day. "Man, I love him so much. I gotta do better."

One day in 1968, I was sitting at Eddie's table as he taped my ankles. I'd resumed playing full time at offensive center, and I was still serving on all the special teams. That added up to a lot of time on the field, and there's a direct correlation between time on a football field and injuries, so it wasn't all that surprising that my shoulder hurt, my nose was broken again, and my fingers had begun to point in odd directions.

I asked Eddie, "What will my body I be like when I'm 60 years old?"

No answer.

Block wore hearing aids in both ears, and he turned them off when he didn't want to be bothered by us, so maybe this was one of those times. I leaned over, tapped him on his head, and asked again, "*Ed Block, listen to me!*" He crinkled his face into a grin, and his stubby fingers mimicked the process of turning up the volume on one of his earpieces. "Bill Curry, you have my undivided attention."

I repeated my question. This time he frowned, looked down a moment, and resumed taping my ankles, acting as if he still hadn't heard me. Then he raised his head and looked up with serious eyes.

"If I tell you, will you quit playing football?"

I shook my head no, not a chance.

"Then," said Eddie Colt of the Blocks, "you don't even want to think about it."

AT THE TIME I rejoined the Packers as coach, Bubba was suing the National Football League and the Tampa Sports Authority for negligence, and he wanted me to testify about what I had witnessed first hand and close up.

I balked.

I carefully explained to Bubba that I had a *history*. I had been the NFLPA president during the strike of 1974, and later I had been party to a formal complaint lodged with the National Labor Relations Board by the NFLPA. I was a lightning rod for anti-union hostility within the NFL.

But the primary reason for my reluctance to testify on Bubba's behalf was that I was a brand-new member of the Packers coaching staff and I was afraid that my involvement in a legal action against the NFL might be more than my boss could justify. I shuddered at the prospect of walking into Bart's office with more labor baggage. I had been labeled a union agitator in my last years as a player, and now I just wanted to get on with coaching. I was looking for an easy way out.

"Hell, Bubba, I'd probably hurt you instead of help you." That was my story, and I was going to stick to it.

"Billy," said Bubba. And then he paused for a moment. "Billy, are you going to do the right thing here?"

Silence at my end.

I had no choice. Not really.

Deep breath.

"Yeah, Bubba, I'll do the right thing. I'll call you back tomorrow."

Panic. Sleepless night. I would have to talk to Bart, who had taken a lot of heat for hiring me. I had been a line coach for exactly one year on a 4-6-1 Georgia Tech team, and the press and former Packers were accustomed to experienced coaches like Bill Austin, Ray Wietecha, and Leon McLaughlin. I was hoping that Bart would take me off the hook by refusing to give time off to testify. That way I could tell Bubba

I'd tried to do the right thing but that my boss had said no. Bubba would understand that and he wouldn't blame me for being a coward.

Just remembering the moment now makes me want to throw up.

Bart's office was spotless, as always, and his greeting was warm. "Morning, Bill. Now tell me something good."

I could hardly breathe.

"Bart, these things seem to seek me out, and I'd rather jump off a cliff than walk in here and say what I'm going to say. But here it is. A friend is in trouble, and he's asked me to help him."

I explained Bubba's dilemma. Bart's good-morning smile faded from his face. He nodded his head, looked out the window for a moment, and then turned back to me.

"You have no choice," he said evenly. "Go stand up for your teammate."

BUBBA WAS ALREADY at the courthouse in Tampa when I arrived.

The man looked like a delegate to the United Nations: perfectly coiffed Afro, horn-rimmed glasses, neatly trimmed goatee, and an $800 suit. Newly retired from the NFL, he was already something of a TV star thanks to the breakout Miller Lite "LESS FILLING! TASTES GREAT!" commercials with Dick Butkus, which led to a substantial Hollywood career.

That day, though, he was playing the role of plaintiff in a $2.5 million lawsuit.

We walked in together. Sitting at a table was his legal team. I looked around the courtroom: packed house, a special section for the media, and the jury. One thing leaped out at me: all the jurors were white.

Maybe I was being paranoid, but I'd grown up in the South and I'd had my fill of what too often happened when whites sat in judgment of blacks. Okay, I was jumping to conclusions unfairly. But this was Tampa, and it was 1977.

I got a queasy feeling in my stomach.

"Bubba ... "

"Yeah?" he said.

"You're going to lose, my friend. You're going to lose."

Bubba laughed and told me to calm down.

I was called as an "expert" witness, my expertise consisting of having played in the NFL for 10 years, having served as president of the NFLPA, and having been there that terrible night.

I described the frozen horror of the official who, with Bubba flying through the air at him, stood immobile with the yard-marker in a death grip while his life passed before his eyes. Nothing had trained him properly for such a moment, and nothing had prepared Bubba's knee to bend as it did.

Then we screened the film, and I described the proper procedure set out clearly in the NFL Rules Manual that the official should have followed.

I thought it was an open and shut case—on its merits.

I thought it was a no-brainer—if the jurors just looked at the facts.

I figured the NFL owed Bubba Smith—big-time. At age 27, he was entering his peak years. Instead, he missed all of

1972 and struggled through four more seasons, a shadow of his former self. I believed—and still believe—it was the league's fault for not having better procedures in place and better training for the personnel charged with carrying them out.

Bubba lost. The case was tried twice, and both times the jury returned a verdict in favor of the defendants.

But Bubba also won: a settlement between plaintiff and defendants was reached before final judgment was rendered, so Bubba walked away with a bag of cash. (My friend never revealed how much he received, of course; to do that would have been in violation of the terms of the settlement. But I can confirm that he continued to dress straight out of the pages of *Esquire*.)

To me—and bear in mind that I'm just an ex-football player, not a lawyer—the fact that the NFL agreed to any kind of settlement tells me that the league knew there was merit to Bubba's case.

Legal commentators also argue that the case was significant despite its verdict just because the judge allowed the case to go to the jury, establishing for the first time that a sports official—and, by extension, his employer—could be found liable for negligence during an athletic event. In other words, it was a step in a continuing march to make the player-owner relationship more equitable for the player.

The case also had a seamy underside, one with strong (though only circumstantial) evidence that the NFL owners acted in collusion to protect themselves.

After a year of rehab, Bubba was traded by the Colts to the Raiders, who signed him to a new contract at triple his pre-injury salary.

Why? Was it because Al Davis thought Bubba was going to be three times better limping off of a devastating injury? Not likely. Al Davis is a lot of things, but he isn't stupid. I believe he knew quite well that Bubba was (severely) damaged goods, that Al, in effect, was taking one for the team—*i.e.,* the other owners in the league.

Try this on for logical size: I think they tripled Bubba's salary (and by "they" I mean the Raiders along with the other owners pitching in via the NFL Management Council) so that, should Bubba ever sue on the grounds that the injury ruined his career, the NFL could point out that his highest salary came *after* the injury. "Negligence? What negligence? The guy made a whole bunch more money after he was hurt, so how bad could it have been?"

But now, all that's blood under the bridge.

We'll never know how great a football player Bubba might have become without that horrible, preventable injury. But at least he went on to fame and fortune as Cadet Moses Hightower in the *Police Academy* movies.

The NFL's done pretty well, too.

And my role? Well, I was initially reluctant, and even after I had made up my mind to help, I had to get a green light and a nudge from a man—Bart Starr—whom I respected as much as anyone I have ever encountered in football. But in the end I did get it together.

Despite myself, I managed to do the right thing.

As an NFL quarterback, an MLB pitcher, and a PGA Tour golfer, he made a great NYC fireworks commissioner. But he was much more: literary lion, dazzling raconteur, movie and TV actor, and ... dear, dear friend.

10

GEORGE PLIMPTON
MUSE

As I explained earlier, the Nutcracker was an aptly named collision drill that always kicked off the morning sessions at training camp each of the six seasons I played for the Baltimore Colts.

The Nutcracker was a showcase for one blocker, one defender, and one ball carrier. The blocker and defender lined up nose to nose between two blocking dummies placed three yards apart. The ball carrier set up five yards behind the blocker. A center and a quarterback were there to set the Nutcracker in motion, but they were just bit players in the explosive, violent main event.

On the snap of the ball, the blocker smashed into the defender with all his might, while the defender forearm-shivered the blocker and tried to maintain his position. The ball carrier took the ball and tried to run between the two dummies.

If the blocker did his job, the runner zipped by the defender. If the defender won the day, the runner ended up on his back.

The most extraordinary Nutcracker I ever witnessed occurred in July 1971, on the first day of my fifth year in Baltimore. We were reigning Super Bowl Champions. Our quarterback, John Unitas, was a household name. Our lineup was packed with Pro Bowlers. Big crowds showed up to see us, even when we practiced—and on this kickoff practice session of the 1971 season, they got a special treat.

The blocker for our first Nutcracker of that summer was the great tight end John Mackey. The defender was crack outside linebacker Ray May. And the ball carrier was ... *George Plimpton?*

A GRADUATE OF Harvard, where he was a member of Hasty Pudding and a writer for the *Harvard Lampoon*, George Plimpton earned a second baccalaureate degree and an M.A. from Cambridge University in Britain after three years of military service. (He was a tank driver.) At an age (26) when a pro football player was almost halfway through his career, he became founding editor of the *Paris Review*, one of the most influential literary periodicals of the second half of the 20th century. He was also an accomplished birdwatcher and an excellent amateur tennis player.

You might say that George Ames Plimpton didn't exactly match the profile of your typical NFL player.

Yet George was already well-known in the football community for his best-selling book, *Paper Lion* (1966), which chronicled his training camp experiences "playing" for the Detroit Lions in 1963. Ostensibly trying out to be the Lions' third-string quarterback, George, then 36, took part in drills and finally a scrimmage. He didn't survive the cut, but did go on to write one of the most popular sports books of all time about his adventures.

Earlier, he had pitched against Major League Baseball players before the second of baseball's two All-Star games in 1960, which gave him fodder for the book *Out of My League* (1961). And he had sparred against Sugar Ray Robinson and Archie Moore on assignment from *Sports Illustrated.*

In 1971, for a TV special called *Plimpton, the Great Quarterback Sneak,* George was to be our QB for four plays against his old team, the Lions, during halftime of an exhibition game.

His first time around in the NFL, with the Lions, George had stayed pretty much on the periphery of the action. This time, to give authenticity to the TV show, he said he wanted to *experience* training camp. So he asked head coach Don McCafferty to let him carry the ball in the Nutcracker drill.

George was intrepid. He was sincere. But he was also tall, gawky, and awkward, and he knew nothing firsthand about the collisions that define football. Nothing he had experienced in the boxing ring or the goalie's net in ice hockey prepared him for the ferocity of an NFL linebacker's *hitting ability.*

He was also inexperienced, of course, on the baseball diamond, the tennis court, and the golf course, much less the bridge table and the circus, where he also went against the world's elite. But in pro football, he was heading into bad trouble, and he had no clue.

GEORGE WAS A man of exquisite refinement and literary distinction slipping into our warrior world, and my teammates' reactions ranged from amusement to toleration to hostility.

Five-year veteran Ray May, a gentle soul off the field, looked to Coach McCafferty and gestured, both palms up, and asked under his breath, "Am I supposed to *hit* this guy?" Mac smiled and nodded, mumbling, "That's what the TV folks want, I guess."

As the cameras rolled, the ball was snapped, Mackey exploded into May—and *training camp had begun in earnest.*

The powerful May was one of the few players in the league who could stand up to John. He stalemated the block, effectively creating a standoff. It was at this moment that an NFL running back would zip by, but George was not an NFL back. He meandered up the line, carrying the ball as if it were a bouquet of roses. In the eternity it took him to cover the five yards, May slipped Mackey, squared up, and rocketed his right shoulder into George's elongated chest.

Crack! May's pads hit George's sternum.

Whuff! The wind left George's lungs.

Thud! George's head, right shoulder, and right hand collided with the ground.

The helmet went one way, the ball the other, and George's right thumb still another.

To his credit, George staggered up quickly, only to look down, gag, and say, "Dear Gawd! Look at that!" His thumb dangled uselessly, fully dislocated. The trainers escorted him to the locker room as the cameras trailed their would-be hero.

Ray felt bad, and we all assumed our little TV experiment was over.

We didn't know George Plimpton.

That afternoon, he was back in pads, right thumb heavily taped, taking snaps with the other quarterbacks. John Unitas, who was wonderful with him, kept asking, "You sure you want to do this? You're crazy as hell!"

George just nodded and stepped back behind me.

Only someone who's taken a snap from an NFL center with his right thumb dislocated can imagine the pain he endured. But he didn't so much as flinch, and even our veteran skeptics began to watch him with interest and respect.

At the end, we capped the day by running the dreaded conditioning gassers, each one of which consisted of four trips back and forth across the field. We normally ran four sets, or 16 50-yard excursions back and forth at a pace between striding and sprinting.

George finished each excruciating gasser in the 90-degree heat. He struggled to run, wobbling along with long, wet hair hanging in his eyes, and injured right hand tightly tucked against his stomach. And he finished dead last every time. But he finished.

Who would have thought a 44-year-old author could match us gut-check for gut-check? Now *everybody* was impressed.

YOU JUST PLAY. There's an unwritten code in the National Football League, and it's a simple one: *You just play.*

Crazy as it sounds, in that first abbreviated practice session with us, George Plimpton seemed to have comprehended and internalized the essence of that code.

You just play.

My rookie season, Jerry Kramer showed up at training camp weighing 225, a good 20 pounds under his normal playing weight, with open wounds from recent stomach surgery still oozing. He played in all 14 games that season, starting in most of them, while gradually regaining his strength

You just play.

Bob Skoronski practiced and played in exhibition games with a huge black, blue, purple, and yellow knee. He could have taken it easy, nursed the knee until games meant something. Uh-uh. And our coaches used him as an example to drive others to play through pain. "Way to go, Ski! You are a real leader! Look everybody, Ski's the toughest guy out here!" He played in every regular season game that season. That kept going a three-year streak that eventually topped out at six when he retired in 1968 with a set of knees you wouldn't wish on your worst enemy.

You just play.

Colts OT Bob Vogel, a five-time Pro Bowler and two-time All-Pro, played against the Vikings in the 1968 playoffs with a broken left wrist. Opponent Jim Marshall knew it and wore Bob out. Bob's take: "Well, I just got raped in front of several million people, but we won so I'm happy!" Typical Vogel, whose bad games occurred about as often as Halley's Comet.

You just play.

Colts DT Billy Ray Smith played the entire 1970 season with a detached left bicep. He would grin, roll up his sleeve, flex that huge muscle of his so that it would roll up like a venetian blind, and watch the horror in our eyes. He'd then inform us, "A real man don't need a bicep to whup pitiful offensive linemen!"

You just play.

And when you don't, you catch hell for it.

In Super Bowl I in Los Angeles, when the Packers ran over the Chiefs 35-10, I had to come off the field because of an ankle. Hurt like the dickens, but nothing major; my departure was prudent and precautionary.

Now let's move ahead to 1968. I'd earned the starting job at center in Baltimore, and we were preparing for the last league game against the Rams in Los Angeles. We'd clinched the division title, and everybody assumed that some of the starters would not be playing the entire game.

During practice I was hit on the shoulder at a bad angle, felt a jolt of pain, and walked away from the drill. As I rotated my shoulder I walked back toward the offensive line, whereupon OL coach John Sandusky asked, "Hey, Curry, you trying to get out of playing Sunday? Wait a minute, I remember something about you. Didn't you get hurt and leave some big game in Green Bay?"

Different team.

Two years later.

You just play.

Reminder to Sandusky: I played every play that Sunday, every play in two playoff games, every play in the Super Bowl—and every play in the following season.

You just play.

Did that make me special? Not by a long shot. DE Jim Marshall of the Vikings started in 282 consecutive games in his 20 seasons in the NFL. Jeff Feagles (Patriots, Eagles,

Cardinals, Seahawks, Giants) has played in 320 games (and counting) since entering the NFL in 1988. (Feagles gets an asterisk, though—he's a punter.) Merlin Olsen didn't miss a single game in his 15-season NFL/HOF career. And so on and so on and ...

You just play.

In fact, with the exception of one game in 1970, and maybe a handful of times when my substitute came in during a blowout, I played every play of every game until the fourth game of the 1973 season, when I was taken off the Astroturf in Houston in an ambulance after shattering the plateau of the tibia and shredding the ligaments in my left knee.

I swore I would never play again, and then found myself, almost as if by reflex, back in the gym rehabbing so I could catch on with the L.A. Rams the next season. The code gets in your blood, and you honestly feel less than a real man unless you are responding with every ounce of energy to get back onto the field.

You just play.

GEORGE DEVELOPED A growing obsession during our scrimmages: he wanted me to be his personal center.

For the first day or two, he had tried to get the snaps from a rookie center, who usually drilled his injured thumb with the point of the ball, stepped backward onto George's tender toes with his rear cleats, or just dropped the ball altogether.

A bad center-QB exchange that results in a loose ball is, in effect, a fumble, and fumbles are anathemas to offensive units.

Georgia Tech's legendary John Heisman, for whom the trophy is named, once made a coaching point on this subject, or so legend has it. He is said to have held up a football and instructed his players, "It is better that you should have died as a small boy than that you drop this object."

A dropped center-quarterback exchange calls for another QB gut check. Since the ball is sacred and must *not* be left vulnerable, the quarterback is expected to pounce on it, head first. Invariably, he arrives about the same time as a Billy Ray Smith or a Bubba Smith, who goes after it like a wild dog in pursuit of a T-bone steak. Others join in the hunt, and pretty soon you have a pileup, with the QB on the bottom.

ZEKE BRATKOWSKI, BART Starr's backup on the Packers and a certifiably free spirit, once regaled Bart and me in a cab ride with a story from his first game in the NFL as a Bears rookie, in which he learned about Pileup Protocol

After a play in the early going, Zeke found himself sprawled at the bottom of a pileup, left arm folded under him and right one protruding from the stack of bodies.

A big pileup in pro football has its own special unwritten rules. The disentangling seems to take forever, with the officials chattering at the players to be patient. They grab and sort bodies, shouting, "Don't kick, take your time, calm down," and so on.

Once you've played for a while, you develop a kind of resignation and you just lie there, daydreaming until it's your turn to get up. Typically, "pileup courtesy" prevails; 95 percent of the guys never make a fuss. Very large people who seconds before were trying to kill each other lie nose-to-nose, facemasks locked, usually with no hostility.

Then there are the other 5 percent, the guys who watch and wait for a chance to hurt somebody. Like all scavengers and parasites, they have great antennae—and an uncanny talent to avoid detection by the officials.

Zeke had the misfortune of encountering one of the ugly five-per centers. As he waited for the pile of bodies to disentangle, two large, black high-tops stopped next to his outstretched hand. Then the heel of the left shoe was deliberately placed on his hand, weight was shifted to pin it against the turf, and the ankle belonging to the shoe was rotated, grinding the rear cleats into Zeke's hand.

After an eternity, Zeke extricated himself and leaped to his feet. Confronting the shoe's owner, he yelled, "You stepped on my hand! On purpose!" The big fellow grinned through his facemask and said, "Sure I did! You'd step on mine, wouldn't you?"

At least Zeke emerged from the encounter with a hand that was only bruised, not ground into hamburger.

Suffice it to say a pileup is not a happy place for a literary QB. Plimpton had learned that much while he was doing his thing with the Lions.

So this go-around as a pro QB, after some early unpleasantness with rookie ball-snappers, George would start onto the field, turn, and issue a tremulous query. "Hey! Where is that, uh, number 50, that Curry fellow? I do not wish to embarrass anyone, but I believe, uh, that I do somewhat better when he accompanies me. Mr. Curry, would you join me please?"

Starters never scrimmaged with the rookies, but I felt so bad for him that I would jog out into the heat, accompanied by a chorus of jibes and taunts from my teammates.

WE WHO HIKE

Let's examine the ritual of one person passing a hard, pumpkin-sized object between his legs to another man, whose hands are located in the most intimate and suggestive location.

Suffice it to say that when someone, anyone, places his hands near the most sensitive and misunderstood of one's most private and esteemed organs; when that is done in anticipation of a dangerous projectile being routed in the direction of those organs; when this often occurs before a national television audience— when all these things occur repeatedly, thousands of times over the course of a career, be assured that the possessor of those vitals, who is also the propeller of said projectile with concussive force, records every detail in his memory bank for posterity.

It looks so easy.

It's so not.

We Who Hike are always the first men on the practice field. We Who Hike are the last to leave. We go there and stay with our exalted brethren, the QBs, so that we can review and practice the center-quarterback exchange. We practice and practice and practice, and then we practice some more, because unless the C-QE is executed perfectly, *perfectly*, only bad things happen. Among them:

The QB suffers a broken finger on his hand, and it's "Wait 'Til Next Year," because his season is over.

[continued on following page]

The C suffers a painful insult in his nether regions.

The spheroid skitters off onto the turf, where it is claimed by an individual wearing the wrong-colored jersey.

If something goes wrong, the fat guy—Cs are always fat—is always to blame.

Always.

Doesn't matter if the QB becomes distracted and forgets the snap; the C gets chewed out.

Doesn't matter if the QB pulls out early, just prior to the snap. It's the C's fault that the rock-hard spheroid connects with a force and a *surprise* in his own most tender of areas, thereby reducing said C to a mass of writhing Jell-O, no matter how tough he is. (Inevitably, an assistant coach will yell, "Hey, looks like somebody got hit in the family jewels ... *Heh! Heh! Heh!"*)

So it is that Cs remember QBs not so much by their names or accomplishments but by their hand placement.

In that as in other areas of the sport, Bart Starr and John Unitas were Hall of Famers.

And George Plimpton was on his way.

AN ALL-AMERICAN quarterback at Ohio State, Tom Matte played 12 seasons in the NFL, all with the Colts—as a running back. That happens when the starting quarterback when you turn up as a rookie is named John Unitas.

Tom was one of the anchors of the great Colts teams of the 1960s. He went to the Pro Bowl twice and holds the record for highest per-carry rushing average in a Super

Bowl game (1969 vs. the Jets: 10.5—116 yards on just 11 carries).

Matte's other principal contribution to the Colts was as team prankster, in which role he always seemed to come up with creative ways to keep training camp bearable.

True, Tom's pranks weren't exactly what you'd call sophisticated. For instance, he loved to insert long blades of grass into the ear hole of a player's helmet. Sounds benign, right? Well, the effect was to make the guy think a wasp or a cicada —they swarmed during summer camp in Westminster, Maryland—had flown into his ear, and he would rip off his headgear and slap at his ear. This always produced a Matte cackle that could be heard all over the field.

Imagine Tom's glee when he discovered that George Plimpton didn't know how to remove his headgear.

Hey, it's trickier than you might think. You have to pull the ear holes outward with the index fingers and thumbs of both hands to widen the helmet so it can be taken off without also removing the ears. George couldn't quite get the hang of it even before he dislocated his thumb. After the injury, he required help to put the thing on, and a couple of trainers to get it off.

Needless to say, Matte was on him like a duck on a June bug—all day, every day.

To his great credit, George was patient with all of us, even Tom Matte. He lasted through the entire training camp, gassers and all. And because of his gumption, we became hooked on his project.

Some of us more than others.

A HUGE CROWD—91,745—gathered at the Big House in Ann Arbor, Michigan in August 1971 to see if "Everyman" could play with the professionals in our exhibition game against the Lions.

On his four plays, George did a reasonable job of handling the ball, executed a quarterback draw as well as possible for a man with feet of concrete, and almost completed a pass on a slant route. The Lions took one cheap shot when a defensive end clubbed George upside the head seconds after a handoff, but the ensuing penalty gave us a first down, so it was worth it.

No, Everyman couldn't play with the pros. But he got a nice standing O for making the effort.

As we walked toward the locker room after the game, George was disconsolate. Thinking he was disappointed in his performance, I tugged at his shoulder pad and said, "Come on George, you did well. Cheer up."

But he wasn't disappointed with his performance.

He was disappointed with us.

As he turned to face me, I met someone I had not previously known in our three weeks together. The horror in his eyes shook me. I asked if he was okay, thinking maybe he had been smashed in the head.

"That was the most disgusting experience of my life!" he raged. "You guys are sick! The hatred out there was palpable! You are all deranged!"

The Lions had perfected Trash Talk long before Deion Sanders came along. Former *Paper Lion* teammates Alex Karras and Wayne Walker had blistered George's sensitive soul with some of their best profanity. He detested vulgarity, and considering the fact that they were his buddies, he couldn't understand and was genuinely horrified.

"That wasn't hatred, George," I responded. I was really taken aback by his anger. "Intensity, yes. Violence, yes. But hatred, no. No! Absolutely not. We're *competitors,* and we get fired up. But we leave all that stuff on the field."

He would hear none of it, and was defensive for the rest of the time we were together that summer. I found myself being grilled, as if by a serious investigative reporter—which George was, of course, in his own way—and often struggling to match wits with such a bright adversary. I stood my ground, and he stood his.

And so began a lifelong dialogue in which my warmhearted, scholarly friend sought to understand the complex cravings of football people. In the process, he was so curious and so honest that he forced me to understand myself better.

We never reached a meeting of minds on the basic issue he brought up that day in Ann Arbor. In his only experience of two rival teams going at each other in the sport of football, all he could recall was the "palpable hatred." No matter how I argued the good stuff about its community, discipline, synergy, entertainment value, and catharsis, he was resolute. "Too violent, Bill. Too much hatred. It cannot be healthy. Really. I don't ever want to do it again."

We agreed to disagree, and to celebrate and enjoy the wonderful friendship that emerged from our crossing paths in that "disgusting" sport.

GOOD THING GEORGE wasn't around in Green Bay in the summer of 1966, or he'd have found a few more entries for his List of Grievances Concerning America's Game.

Somebody once asked Jerry Kramer if Coach Lombardi suffered from ulcers. Not an unreasonable question: the man often had a pained look on his face. "Naw, he doesn't *have* ulcers," Jerry replied. "But he is a carrier."

If Jerry was right, then we were all at risk of peptic insult in July 1966 as we prepared for the College All-Star Game on August 5. That's right—the man practically drove us all crazy prepping for an exhibition game against a bunch of college kids.

The Chicago Charities College All-Star Game—its official title—was played annually from 1934 through 1976 (except for 1974, when a players' strike wiped out the exhibition season). It was a big deal and drew huge crowds to Chicago's Soldier Field. It was, in effect, the first game of a new season.

The pros dominated the game, naturally, but not so much as you might think. Over the years, the college kids won nine times, most recently in 1963, when the All-Stars squeaked out a 20-17 victory over the ... Green Bay Packers.

Yes, the Green Bay Packers, coached by—you guessed it—Vince Lombardi.

Now are you beginning to grasp why July 1966 was so tense in Packerville? Coach knew, we knew, everybody knew that if the unthinkable were to—*God forbid!*—happen again, it would define him forever as The Only NFL Coach to Lose Twice to a Bunch of College Kids.

That summer was pure hell, in terms of the emotional pressure he subjected us to. Every minute, every grass drill, every play, every practice, every meeting, every tape session, even every casual encounter with our coach was some kind of reminder of what must be done.

Football as a game? Surely you jest.

"Positive reinforcement" to bolster team morale? Not our Coach Lombardi.

Yelling, screaming, bullying, sneering, denigrating hostility? Our daily bread for three weeks.

More than ever for that brief period that summer, he coached through threat, intimidation, ridicule, and fear. He scared the hell out of us every day, raging at every dropped pass, missed assignment, or perceived lack of 110 percent effort. And so we stayed as much on edge as he was.

That July, Lombardi made vengeful promises that we all knew would have been impossible to keep. "I will make you scrimmage every day of the year! I will bring you out here in pads every single day! I will run you until you cannot stand up!"

He shouted and screamed and then screamed and shouted some more.

Final Score: Packers 38, College All-Stars 0.

Thank God! Now we could get on with the easy part of the season: going 12-2 to win the NFL West going away, edging the Cowboys 34–27 in the playoffs, and shellacking the Chiefs 35–10 in Super Bowl I.

GEORGE AND I never quite gave up talking about the "cruel" and "disgusting" sport of football. In fact, we decided to write about it.

This is my first book *by myself*, but it isn't my *first* book. That honor goes to *One More July: A Football Dialogue with Bill Curry*, by George Plimpton and Bill Curry (Harper & Row, 1977).

As you've no doubt guessed by now, *One More July* was a collaboration, a team effort in the best sense of the term. Hollywood didn't make a movie of it, the way they'd done with *Paper Lion*. Its protagonist never attained cult status, the way Sidd Finch did after George profiled him in an April Fools spoof in *Sports Illustrated*. And, more's the pity, it never launched a movie career for George's co-author, the way *Paper Lion* did for George. (Alan Alda played George in *Paper Lion*, of course, but George went on to have over two dozen movie and TV roles.).

But the creative process that brought *One More July* to life did something that was, to my mind, much more valuable: it created a special and lasting friendship between George Plimpton and me.

The title came from a conversation in early 1975 with a friend named Larry Mashburn over lunch in Atlanta. He was an estate planner, and I was considering joining his firm. We discussed the pros and cons, until he leaned across the table and said, "Look Bill, I've been watching you awhile now. If you love the life insurance business, you'll do well in it. But if you're looking for just another off-season job while you get ready for one more July, then you might as well start on training camp preparation now."

One more July!

In fact, that was exactly what I was looking for. Bart Starr, who'd just been named head coach of the Packers, wanted me to play one more season as a backup center for him and then join his staff in 1976 as an assistant coach. But first, of course, I had to make the team. I had to survive *One ... more ... July.*

"What did you say?" I grabbed Larry's arm.

He was startled, but laughed and began to repeat his advice about the life insurance business.

"No, no," I interrupted. "I mean the part about July."

"Well," he said, "your main focus from the end of one season is the training camp for the next. All the rest—working at the bank, sportscasting, selling real estate, maybe insurance—they're all just stopgaps. You seem to shoot for one more July every year."

And so I picked up the phone and called George.

Working on the book with him was an exercise in travel, memory, storytelling—and, yes, some pretty heated debate from time to time about the nature of the game that I had come to love and he was repelled by.

George came to our home in Atlanta (twice), I went to his apartment in New York City (twice), and I visited his parents' estate outside the city. Finally, we drove from the Louisville, Kentucky, airport to Green Bay for my last One More July.

The book came out in 1977. Reactions ranged from a wonderful review by Dave Anderson in the *The New York Times* to a highly objective analysis from my oldest and best friend, Ronnie Jackson. "It's great. I love every story!"

One old friend, Mike Slade, told me he was "surprised at all the anger." (Score one for Mr. Plimpton.) Another dear friend, former Lions cornerback Dick LeBeau, was disappointed at our candid (and sometimes judgmental) look behind the scenes. "Bill, what you did to some people in your book is just not right."

(Later on, of course, I came to agree with him.)

The book didn't crack any bestseller lists, but in a decade chock-a-block with "jock books," starting with Jim Bouton's *Ball Four* in 1970, perhaps that shouldn't have been too surprising. And at the end of the day, it didn't matter— leastways not to me.

What did matter to me was that the creative process of writing *One More July* helped me build an enduring and special friendship with George Plimpton. Our little argument, contained in the pages of that little volume, enabled me to get to know and learn to love a great person.

SOME TIME DURING the first year we spent working on the book, as our football debate spiked and settled, flared and subsided, George asked me if I had ever played baseball.

"Yes," I said. "Baseball was my first love."

"Nice," he said, "but are you any good?"

I told him that I'd been a really good pitcher, but I could play a little at most any position.

George was delighted. "Wonderful! I tell you that's simply scrumptious!" (Yes, that's the word he used.)

I was mystified. I'd known him long enough to know you never could predict what might come out of his mouth next. At least I knew I wouldn't have to wait long.

"I want you to be my catcher when I pitch against the Braves."

What? Him *pitch*? Against *who*? Me? His *catcher*?

"As you know Bill," he explained, as if he were delivering a lecture, "I have this crazy compulsion to participate in the essence of life's most intense experiences. I can only do that if I'm able to talk people into allowing me onto the field—literally, in the case of sports. I'm not sure why I do it, but do it I must. Once I talk myself into the middle of the fray, though, I usually doubt my own sanity. And this time, I really don't want to go it alone. I need your help again, and I need it soon."

The more we talked, the more I realized I was being escorted into an enchanted labyrinth. George was willing to risk public embarrassment and physical injury in pursuits well beneath his considerable intellectual abilities and well above his physical skills, but he was human after all. He wanted—needed—a sounding board, a sidekick, a buddy. And so a man who had hung out with Hemingway, the Kennedys, and Sinatra invited me into his inner circle. Amazingly, it never occurred to me to ask him the obvious, "Why me?" But I'm betting that it was simply because he was looking for someone with as much distance as possible from his world.

George then explained what he'd cooked up. "I'm going to take an All-Star team and play three innings against the Atlanta Braves at Atlanta-Fulton County Stadium after their regular game. When we finish, there will be a huge fireworks display, which I will arrange."

(Did I forget to mention that he was also an expert amateur pyrotechnician who was later named Fireworks Commissioner of New York City by Mayor John Lindsay?)

It was as if the youth pastor at a local Methodist Church were matter-of-factly outlining his plans for the summer picnic and softball game. He might as well have said that Mrs. Pritchett was bringing the potato salad and Reverend Purdue would ice the watermelons.

The Plimpton All-Stars would be selected from among local amateur players from the Atlanta area, based on the most convincing letters about why they should be included. Our opponents would be real, live Atlanta Braves—reserves, mostly, who hadn't played in the regular game, but major leaguers nonetheless.

The promotion was being sponsored by WSB-TV, the dominant station in our town for as long as anyone could remember. George and the promotion department at the station would judge the letters.

I asked him, "Do you know where I work?" In those days, NFL players had to work in the off-season to make ends meet, and I was a sportscaster at WSB's rival station, WAGA-TV. I knew the WSB people would croak at the suggestion that I be included.

After all, I would be a "ringer," a pro athlete *and* a rival sportscaster at a rival station. I figured there was no chance. This was before the days of ESPN or any of the other all-day sports cable companies, and local sports news was very big stuff in the ratings game.

George had his mind made up. "If they won't let you play, by Gawd, I shall take my game elsewhere! There, that settles that. Listen Bill, you just write the letter to the promotions guy and be my catcher for those three innings. You know you want to do it!"

Yeah, I *did* want to do it.

We would be at the wrong stadium. I would be in the wrong position, playing for the wrong team, with a good buddy out on the mound where I rightfully belonged. My boyhood dream was of *pitching* for the *Yankees*, remember?

But George was so fired up that I wasn't about to quibble with the details. I wrote the letter, and if I do say so myself, it was a doozy. I explained that for all his sophistication and talent, George was really insecure on the field of battle. I recounted George's need for my presence at the Colts training camp, and intimated that if he were deprived of my talents, he might not be able to function at all.

And what then? How could there be a major Plimpton Promotion without Plimpton? While my participation might be uncomfortable for WSB-TV, the alternative—canceling the whole thing—would be worse.

WSB-TV was not amused. The promotions guy was seething when he called and said in no uncertain terms that it was a "stupid" letter. I politely concurred, but silently disagreed.

As he ranted on, I daydreamed about strapping on shin guards and a chest protector instead of shoulder pads.

I picked George up at the Atlanta airport and drove straight to *my* station, WAGA-TV. General Manager Paul Raymond and News Director Bob Brennan were delighted. We had managed to get the Great Plimpton for a personal appearance while he was in town for a WSB-TV promotion!

We bought some baseball gear, and I thought it would be nice to get some action film of this latest wonder of baseball, the Plimpton-to-Curry battery. I grabbed a cameraman and we all walked outside. George was wearing a long-sleeved dress shirt, rumpled slacks, Docksiders with slick rubber soles, and no socks. I asked if he wanted to change clothes. He shrugged, shook his head no, and began to roll up his sleeves. I remember hoping that he wouldn't hurt himself.

My only recollection of George's athletic ability had been of just how awkward he looked in a football uniform, and how difficult it had been for him to perform the complex maneuvers required by our sport.

When he took the improvised mound outside our building, he moved with the authority of one who'd been playing baseball all his life.

When he toed the imaginary rubber and began his windup, he looked like a real pitcher.

When he rocked to and fro on the mound, he was at ease, even graceful.

And then he cocked his left leg and pivoted, rotated his body, and delivered the ball with authority and velocity.

Strike one!

My hand stung inside the catcher's mitt.

"What the hell!" I shouted.

He grinned. "I pitched a little at Harvard, Bill. You aren't the only athlete in this battery."

Afterwards, we dropped by our home. We'd put George in the guest room in the basement. He called it The Tomb because it had no windows, and loved it because he could sleep several hours longer than usual.

At the time, Carolyn was working on her PhD in history while raising our children. As she settled George into his

quarters, she wondered aloud how such a scholar and gentleman could be engaged in such absurd pursuits. He responded
that if he could figure that out, he might be regarded as sane
by his peers in the arts and letters. She sighed and said, "Well
at least you and Bill have fun, and he loves chasing around
with you."

We took a couple of trips to the stadium between jaunts
to Six Flags with our kids, who adored George because he
actually listened to them. We drew Braves uniforms, spikes,
and were loaned big-league gloves, mitts, and bats. We were
introduced to the great Lew Burdette, star of the 1957 World
Series and now a Braves coach, who would be our opposition
pitcher the night of the game.

The Plimpton All-Stars had just one practice session,
which turned up a couple of surprises. The first was that I
could still throw a baseball with a little zip. After seven years
of banging around the NFL I feared there would be too much
calcium in the shoulders. The second was that our team was
pretty good in the field. We couldn't hit a lick, even in batting
practice, but we had some decent gloves.

ON GAME DAY, we hung around the clubhouse and dugout
while the "real" game dragged on. George kept his arm loose
by throwing to me in the batting cage under the stadium,
just off the dugout. (That would have been thrilling enough
for me under normal circumstances.)

Then, when the other game was over and it was our turn,
both teams were assembled in the Braves' dugout and given
the ground rules. No hard slides, bean balls, or aggressive

behavior. This was to be a fun event, okay? The Braves would be playing mostly reserves, plus longtime Boston and Milwaukee Braves star Lew Burdette on the mound.

Take the field!

I wondered if the stands would be empty by the time we got going, but a very nice crowd, maybe 15,000, remained.

Top of the first. George Plimpton of the Plimpton All-Stars on the mound. Now coming to the plate for the Atlanta Braves Irregulars, Rico Carty ... *Rico Carty*?

Two years before, Carty had batted .366 to lead the National League. He missed 1971 with a knee injury, but he was back with the Braves in 1972 as the righty half of a left-field platoon. He hadn't played in the "first game," *i.e.* the one that counted in the National League standings, because the other team had started a righthander.

Plimpton stared in, got the signal from catcher Bill Curry, nodded, went into his windup, and ... *strike one*!

Yes! A swinging strike on a fastball, high and tight.

The crowd went crazy, George stared in as if in shock—and I lost my mind. I came out of my crouch, gave out a whoop, and shook the ball in Rico's face, as if saying, "Hey, trying to hit this?" It was the bushest of bush-league stunts. Today, after all these years, I am embarrassed to tell the story. To his everlasting credit, Rico just grinned at me, accepting the taunt as a joke, thereby demonstrating way, way more class than yours truly.

If only it were "*one* strike you're out at the old ball game," because on the next pitch ... *ka-POW*!

I felt the percussion of bat against ball, heard the roar of the crowd, and came out of my crouch to look for the ball. I never saw it, but fractions of a second later I heard it explode off the right-field wall.

On the mound, George didn't look the least bit surprised or disappointed. He was having fun.

George also hit a sharp single to right field off Burdette. It was the only time in all our years that I was jealous of him. He received a huge roar from the crowd, cementing that unique bond he had formed with the sporting public.

As for me, once I realized I could catch the ball and get it back to George, I relaxed and returned to my boyhood. The game I loved first, and most, was back to inform my unconscious. It brought back sunlit visions of my boyhood buddy Ronnie Jackson and me and our friends at The Park, playing until it was too dark to play any more.

The final score? Funny, I don't seem to recall. But it didn't matter. Thanks to George Plimpton, I was back with my first love.

P.S.: That fireworks show George orchestrated? Only the biggest, best, most thrilling one I ever witnessed.

WHAT A LONG, strange trip it was. Oh, how I wish it could have been longer. Walking by George Plimpton's side, and learning at his feet, I gained invaluable insights into the game I played and the reasons I played it. He helped me see my world through new eyes, and weigh honestly and fearlessly what I discovered.

My muse died September 25, 2003.

Way too soon, way too soon.

My father stood by my side throughout
his life. He still does.

MY TWELFTH MAN:
WILLIE ALEXANDER CURRY

F ootball chose me, rather than the other way around. At least, that's the way I felt back at the beginning, back in football-crazy Georgia in the 1950s. Little did I comprehend the love-hate relationship that was taking root in my psyche when I first put on shoulder pads in 1955. All I felt at first was the hate. All I felt was the overwhelming desire to quit.

And so, about the third day of fall practice in my first encounter with football, when every muscle in my soft 12-year-old body was screaming with the overload of lactic acid, when both wrists were sprained and both knees swollen, when I was repelled by every aspect of the game, I decided I'd had enough.

I was going to end my ill-fated association with the whole dreaded ordeal. Yep, after practice I would turn my mound of smelly gear in to Coach Badgett, take a long shower, and ride my bike back to sanity, which meant a baseball mound just up the hill from this chamber of tortures.

I was going to quit the team.

There was just one problem with that plan.

If I turned in my College Park Rams jersey, *if I quit the*

team, I couldn't go home.

My father lived there.

BACK IN THE 1950s, and especially in the South, the fathers of sons with any physical size and basic athletic skills wanted to see their boys play football. Just any sport wouldn't do. Baseball and basketball didn't amount to much back then, not in my part of the country. Only football mattered.

Your dad expected you to play football because ... well, just because.

In a football culture, and goodness knows Georgia was that in the mid-1950s, that's what you did, right? Hut-*one*! Hut-*two*!

So naturally you're thinking that Bill Curry's dad must have ...

Stop right there.

Let me make a few things absolutely 100 percent clear: Willie Alexander Curry did *not* make me go out for football; he did *not* push me to go out for football; and he did *not* in any way, shape, or form indicate that he would think any less of me if I chose not to go out for football and instead stuck with baseball, my first love.

What my father *did* do was make absolutely, abundantly, crystal clear that I could not, must not *quit* anything I started.

You start something, you finish it. Period. In the Gospel According to My Dad, there were 11 Commandments, and the 11th was every bit as important to him as the other 10: *Thou shalt not quit.*

My mother, Eleanor Barnes Curry, still has a tiny, framed photograph. It is square, three inches by three inches, and remarkably clear after all these years. It's of a young man in his mid-20s in a bathing suit, on his knees at a beach. His extended arms are slightly bent at the elbows, his index fingers touching to create a miniature high bar. Suspended from his fingers, hanging on for dear life, is a naked six-month-old boy, his firstborn son. Me.

Having seen it all my life, I'd never given it a second thought until one day, years after we'd gotten married, Carolyn picked it up, grimaced, and said, "There it is! Look! Here's the story of your life. Here's where it all started."

MOM AND DAD had each been brought up in difficult circumstances. Mom's father was murdered when she was a teen, and life was a struggle for her mother, who made ends meet by picking cotton and playing the piano at church. Dad was the only child of a father who had been crippled by polio, and who was determined to make the world pay for his misfortune. Each of my parents became loving, vibrant, productive people despite all the odds against that happening.

They met on a blind date, fell in love, got married, and had one of the great marriages ever for 66 years, until my father's death in 2007 at the age of 89.

Mom craved the security and balance of a healthy extended family, and set about creating that. Her love and attention were totally focused on my father, my two younger sisters, and me. I believe much of the emotional foundation for my life is based on that sacred fact. My first memories are of her beautiful smile and a billowing blue dress that I clung to while we ran barefoot through a field, probably near her mother's home in Jenkinsburg, Georgia, while Dad was at various Army bases, training infantry troops. From my first breath, I was made to feel wanted, important, and worthy.

No one has ever had to explain love to me.

My father, who was born in 1917 in Athens, Georgia, had been sickly and frail as a little boy. Accordingly—and not so uncommon in his day—his parents concluded early on that he would never be able to take part in manly pursuits. They forbade their only child to go out for rough sports. As a bookish, lonely kid, he made crystal radios from scratch as a way to touch the outside world. He built tree houses and dreamed of Tarzan-like escapes from his dreary world. Any small success he had as an inventor or reader was disparaged by his father and trumpeted by his hyper-possessive mother.

As a teenager, he developed some solid friendships and began to widen his horizons. At the local YMCA, he came under the tutelage of Coach L. H. Cunningham, a wonderful YMCA instructor who introduced him to strength training with barbells. For the first time, Dad experienced the magic of belief. Cunningham saw something in him, encouraged him, and released a born competitor on the world of Olympic weightlifting.

Within four years, the former 5'11", 142-pound weakling weighed 191 and was the junior national light heavyweight champion in the three Olympic lifts: the military press, the snatch, and the clean and jerk. Simultaneously, he became a college boxer and an ROTC officer at the University of Georgia. He was cited by *Strength and Health* magazine as the Strongest Man in the South. After placing fourth in the Senior Nationals at Madison Square Garden in 1940, he would have been on the U.S. Olympic team had the Games not been cancelled because of the war in Europe.

An infantry captain in the World War II, Dad taught hand-to-hand combat, strength training, and conditioning to the troops at various Southern army bases: Fort Hood (Texas), Fort McClelland (Alabama), Fort Benning (Georgia), and Fort Breckenridge (Kentucky). He was at Fort Hood when I was born in Atlanta in 1942. (He instructed Mom not to name me after him if I happened to be male. She said "fine," and named me William Alexander rather than Willie Alexander.)

After the war, he became a boxing, gymnastics, and weightlifting coach at Georgia Military Academy in College Park, Georgia. Eventually, he took me on as his principal pupil.

My first set of boxing gloves and first round of instruction came when he was still in the service. I was three or four years old. He patiently but firmly taught me to keep my right hand up and jab straight and hard with my left. Any deviation from the mandated techniques brought on sharp punches to the nose, just hard enough to make me understand that this was not play.

Next, in due course, came the gym. On Saturday mornings he would take me there and introduce me to the principle of tenacity, via a series of gymnastic rings and ropes. The rings were strung 10 feet above the mat on the floor. The idea was to swing Tarzan-like from one ring to another to another by using the hands, arms, and shoulder muscles. Dad would get me started and then shout encouragement as I hung on, creating momentum with gyrations of my torso, grasping first one ring and then the next. His imagery was wonderfully vivid. "Pull hard! Hang on! You're swinging over the river! If you fall, the crocodiles are waiting!"

If I had a bad day and was repeatedly reptile food, I could tell it bothered him, but never so much that he cancelled our afternoon Tarzan movies. I learned to expect remarks like, "You have to develop more initiative, be tougher, if you want to excel."

The weight room was the inner sanctum, the special place in which my father took on the frightening visage of the obsessed, driven competitor. And in the weight room, the competition was raw and palpable, because there were a dozen or so of us acolytes hanging on the master's every wish and word.

The rules—*his* rules—were quite precise. Each lifter was required to wear the proper shoes, trunks, tee shirt, and lifting belt for the sacrificial expenditure of energy. Concentration was to be total, even for a six-year-old. Lifting technique, perfect. Breathing, absolutely correct. No deviation or innovation was permitted.

The weights were arranged just so, in order, on their racks. They were to be carefully taken off, used, and just as carefully replaced. The bars, plates, and dumbbells, the manufacture of which he had personally overseen and which he had personally painted, were the implements of worship. They were perfect, of course, both in balance and poundage.

(They may be inspected today—better still, *used*—in the Major Bill Curry Weight Room at what is now called Woodward Academy in College Park, Georgia.)

The weight room drill was grueling and I didn't like it, so I rebelled. It was here, on his sacred ground, that I took my first stand against him, an act of rebellion that deeply disappointed this powerful presence who was my father/God figure.

I laughed. Out loud. Something about the sanctimony of the drill tickled my funny bone, more than once. And so, now and then, I laughed.

Often banished from the workout in disgrace, I was cast into the outer darkness, away from co-worshippers. I had violated one of the cardinal tenets of the faith. "There is nothing funny about being weak!" had been the edict from the beginning. I was six years old and here I was, laughing at the sacred way.

And sacred it was to Dad. "One day all athletes will be lifting weights. They laugh at us now, but every sport can be improved with strength, skill, and flexibility. You don't have to lift, but whatever you decide to do, you *will* do it with all your heart."

To Dad's credit, he didn't beat the hell out of me with the leather belt when I sinned against the solemnity of the holy place. He just threw me out, which was fine with me.

As I grew up, Dad mellowed. He came to my baseball games, even though that wasn't a sport he cared much for. He was kind, supportive, and great fun most of the time. He developed an appreciation for classical music and many nights I went to sleep to the sounds of Mozart or Rimsky-

Korsakov. He loved to read and study. He even became a Presbyterian Sunday School teacher.

But his competitive nature never diminished, and he was a true believer in weight training all his life. And later he was proud to have been proven right—"One day all athletes will be lifting weights"—by Tiger Woods, A-Rod, Lebron James, and just about every other top athlete you can mention.

And yes, I learned that—like it or not—I would have to train with weights to succeed in the world of professional football.

Carolyn has said that I have two sides—my artist side and my warrior side. One side of me loves music, literature, playing with children, and laughter. The darker, more serious side enters the competitive arena focused on *nothing* but victory. I am only now beginning to understand that complex duality.

THE TEXAS A & M AGGIES have a tradition called the Twelfth Man. It's based on an actual occurrence in 1922, when the Aggies looked like they might be running out of reserves in a closely contested big game against Centre College, the top-ranked team in the country. (Yes, Centre College.)

Coach Dana X. Bible remembered a former member of the football team, E. King Gill, who now played only basketball, and had him summoned from the stands. Gill suited up and stood by for the rest of the game, ready to help his team. Gill didn't play, but he came to be known as the Twelfth Man for accepting the call. A statue of Gill now graces the Texas A & M campus, and today the entire student body stands throughout games to signify their willingness to be the Twelfth Man.

My father was my Twelfth Man. He stood by me all through my life, always willing to help me, always there to pick me up when I stumbled. In today's parlance, he always had my back.

The memories of the men I met in the huddle in my first two decades in football will always be with me. I shall be forever grateful to them all.

And yet, I would never have even gotten to know them, much less enjoyed the opportunity to draw strength from their strength, had it not been for Willie Alexander Curry's guiding moral and ethical absolute:

Never quit.

ACKNOWLEDGMENTS

The passion to understand leaders, those who consistently overcome adversity to light the way for the rest of us, began for me in the fourth grade with Miss Mabel Bolton at Newton Estates School in College Park, Georgia.

I was a new student in her class, a hyper kid whom she shaped up in about two days by applying the only thing that worked: no-nonsense discipline. Plus, in what was in retrospect no accident, she seated me in the back of the room adjacent to a bookshelf bursting with biographies of great people. Somehow she had intuited my love of reading.

As a result, Madame Curie, Stephen Douglass, Benjamin Franklin, Lou Gehrig, Abraham Lincoln, Jim Thorpe, and George Washington became my new best friends.

Providentially, also in that fourth-grade class was the best student I had ever encountered, the loveliest girl I had ever seen, and the best leader I have ever known—all in one person. In time, I decided to marry her. (A few sixth-grade decisions you never regret.) Carolyn Newton, now Carolyn Newton Curry, has inspired and amazed me every day of my life for the last 45 years (and counting).

Carolyn and George Plimpton cajoled and harassed and bullied me into writing this book. That odd couple, who became wonderful friends, are the most interesting—and relentless—two folks I have ever known.

My agent, Craig Foster, set up the meeting with ESPN Books editor Chris Raymond back in March 2006. I am deeply grateful to Craig for initiating the process and to Chris for pushing me through several ideas for the format before coming up with our title. I am indebted to him for his confidence in my ability.

Once the idea became a manuscript, ESPN Books executive editor Glen Waggoner quickly learned to read my mind, a disturbing thing for both of us. He did an astounding job of collecting the best of my ramblings, reorganizing them, and making them coherent.

Managing editor John Glenn transformed a stack of manuscript pages into the handsome volume you hold in your hands. Editors William Vourvoulias and Jaime Lowe, copy editor Beth Adelman, photo editor Linda Ng, and researcher Doug Mittler also played key roles along the way. Thanks for everything, folks.

My friend John Walsh at ESPN has encouraged me at every opportunity. I recall one specific moment during an ESPN staff meeting when he took me aside to give me a positive nudge on this book; I have never forgotten it. Thanks, John.

Pete Wellborn, my former player and brilliant attorney, finds more constructive ways to encourage others than anyone else I know. That gift is regularly extended to his old coach. Pete, you are simply amazing.

Profound thanks go to the following inspirational people in my life, each of whom deserves his or her own chapter in some book sometime: Bamidele Ali, Herb Barks, Susan Collins, Harold Dennis, Jessica Jensen Dixon, Scotty Dodson, Karen Gearrald, Karen Greer, Ron Greer, Johnny Gresham, George Harris, Ronnie Jackson, Bevel Jones, Kim King, Rich Lapchick, Sylvia Mackey, George Morris, Joe Pettit, Homer Rice, Martha Segars, Melissa Segars, Richard Segars, Bill Stacy, Andrew Young, and all the wonderful folks at the Baylor School in Chattanooga, Tennessee.

Finally, and most important, I am inspired daily by our Creator's most precious gifts to us. Through our marriage, Carolyn and I have been blessed with incredible children, Kristin and Bill Jr., now outstanding leaders in their own right. In each case as it relates to me, the pupil has indeed become the teacher. I do very little of substance without seeking their counsel.

Kristin, her husband, Bob Hunter, and our granddaughters, Evelyn (5) and Claire (3), make up the Hunter branch of our family. Bill Jr., his wife, Kelly, and our grandsons, Alex (11), Elliot (9), and Brett (who will enter the world roughly a month prior to *Ten Men*'s publication), are the Currys. My love for them all is beyond words.

Needless to say, in a lifetime that's spanned 65 years, there are many others who deserve recognition. You know who you are. And as I remember you, one by one, I'll thank you separately.

—Bill Curry

ABOUT THE AUTHOR

A college football analyst for ESPN from 1997-2008, BILL CURRY is the new head football coach at Georgia State University. He also coached for 17 years at Georgia Tech, Alabama, and Kentucky after completing a 10-year NFL career as a player with the Packers, Colts, Oilers, and Rams. He lives in Atlanta with Carolyn Newton Curry, his wife of 45 years